APOLC
This book may cont
printing errors as it
part of an experime
paperbacks as cheap ossible.

Miraculous!

Keef
Feeley

www.successfeelosophy.com

'Miraculous'

1st Edition 2012

Author : Keith Feeley

ISBN No. : 978-0-9565210-1-9

Published on behalf of the author by
Connoisseur Crafts Ltd

Typesett in Ariel, printed and bound in Great Britain by
Connoisseur Crafts Ltd
Hartlepool Enterprise Centre
Brougham Terrace
Hartlepool
TS24 8EY
Email : hpoolprint@yahoo.co.uk

Thanks

I'd like to thanks the hundreds of schools, colleges and centres for allowing me to study them, and the thousands of students for providing me with such comprehensive research for almost 40 years.

Chapter 1
"Superboy Tragedy"

"He looks badly hurt. I think he's knocked out! They all seem very worried and calling for help. This must be very serious, he's still not moving."
The commentator's tone was increasing in intensity as he realised the seriousness of the injury. His commentary continued his frantic concerns to the millions of TV viewers.
"There's no sign of movement with him and there looks to be blood coming from his skull. Oh dear, this looks very worrying and such a young lad. Surely this miraculous story is not going to end in such tragedy. Ray, can you see what's actually happened here?"
Ray Wilkins, the ex-footballer co-commentator was also very concerned and began his description using a video replay.
"If we look carefully at this replay, and slow it down, we can just see that as the corner is about to be taken from the left, Scott is on the right corner of penalty area. The goalkeeper comes out to try to punch it over that group of players and it skims off his fist. You can see Scott now dives to head the ball as it almost lands just inside the goal area. It's gone off his forehead like a bullet just inside the post, but Scott's hit the wet ground and slid into the goalpost. Oh, that's horrible! Scott's head has hit that post very hard."
By the time Ray had finished his description, the physiotherapist had got to Scott and the paramedics with the stretcher were about to follow. This was an F.A. Cup semi-final and Scott Spicer, was playing in only his fifth match for Spurs first team, whilst still only 16. He had just scored the first goal of the match with only about 5 minutes of normal time left to play and now his large muscular body lay lifeless face down on the wet green grass, with blood oozing out of his wet curly hair onto his young angelic face. The paramedics carefully placed and strapped him into the specially supported stretcher, lifted him carefully and carried him from the pitch, with the physio holding an oxygen mask over his mouth. The Spurs supporters had been ecstatic initially, when Scott scored what could be the winning goal but had become quiet on realising the tragic circumstances that had now unfurled. But the applause was deafening as the unconscious Scott was carried off the field with virtually all the supporters of both teams clapping vigorously. "That's what happened, that's how Scott Spicer was knocked out. He is still unconscious in intensive care and it could mark a really tragic end to a story that appears too miraculous to be true. I want us to ensure that we are first to run his incredible story, and our readers appreciate that this boy's transformation is seen as a truly historical event in the future."
Dave Mackay, the stocky middle aged editor of The Sun newspaper, was addressing a group of four reporters in a meeting/conference room where they had been watching the video of the sad incident that had occurred only a few

hours earlier. His booming voice, perfectly matching his assertive manner, physique and his namesake, the great Spurs midfielder, continued his presentation to the dumbstruck audience..

"I think if he dies his short life will be comparable to James Dean, Bruce Lee or Elvis in significance. Whatever happens to him now, it is essential that the people out there understand his importance and his influence on our society."

The reporters were totally mystified and the look on their faces, sitting around the table, reflected this. They didn't really understand why he felt that this boy's life would have such significance. Only one had heard of Scott and he was a sports reporter, the others focused on politics, business and education, and were completely confused as to why they were present?

Dave could see their bemused expressions and responded.

"This boy is not just a footballer but a protégé of JC Learner. In less than a year he was transformed from an obnoxious delinquent adolescent, barely able to speak or cope with the world into a mature eloquent adult and an outstanding striker. I think you'll find the story of his miraculous change is more amazing than any 'Rocky', 'Scrooge', 'My Fair Lady', or 'Karate Kid' and should inspire a radical change in our society. When the public and politicians discover the details to this story, it will spark a total rethink of learning. I think it will result in huge changes to parenting, schools, universities, education, health and social services, prisons, economics, business, sport and the media. Does that sound important enough to you?"

All four reporters visibly sat up and scribbled furiously on their notepads.

"I want each of you to study his background carefully and have articles that illustrate clearly how his life is likely to have an effect in each of your specialist areas. I think we need to have a front page headline to emphasise his importance, perhaps something like 'Superboy Tragedy."

*

So who is this 'Superboy'? Why is his life so significant? These questions require a very careful study of the last couple of years of Scott's life, starting ironically, with the previous time Scott had been knocked out, less than two years ago. This incident put him on a journey that seems to have elements of magic, superpowers and a Hollywood storyline.

"Come on then, you big f***ing tart, you think you're so f***ing 'ard!"

This shout could only just be heard over the loud thumping music. It came from a six foot, dark skinned, shaven headed 16 year old boy, wearing a white tight fitting, branded T shirt, showing off his well muscled physique, top brand jeans and trainers. His aggressive stance and glaring eyes were trying to intimidate his opponent, but appeared as though they would burn right through him.

His opponent, Scott Spicer, is a year younger, a few inches taller and wider, but looked much less athletic, being several stone overweight. His round 'baby face' and short bleached blonde gelled hair gave the impression he was just a scaled up version of a seven year old. His lack of confidence and development was reflected in him wearing the 'modern designer uniform' of trainers, jeans, T-shirt, all with the most popular labels and almost identical to all the boys surrounding him.

This confrontation was no sporting occasion but an argument in a school hall at a 'do' to celebrate the end of term.

The hall had been blacked out, but the UV and DJ's flashing lights made it bright enough for Scott to see his strutting opponent and the yelling crowd that had gathered around these shouting, posturing boys. Scott attempted to glare back at this gladiator opposing him, but his awareness of the girls in their low cut tops and skirts barely covering their bums, distracted him. This only added to the realisation that there was definitely no backing down for him.

"You'll soon find out how f***ing 'ard!"

Scott replied, displaying his clenched fists in a boxing pose.

"You're just a big fat pisshead, there's nothing 'ard about you"! You're all mouth".

Being called big was fine, he was over six foot and being a pisshead was not a great problem, in fact, Scott was proud of his reputation as a drinker, but not fat! Any reference to him being fat was the 'proverbial red rag to a bull' and guaranteed to cause 'the rage' he'd experienced so many times in his fifteen years to rise up inside him. He had such poor self-awareness and these were words were like a knife into the heart of his low self esteem and guaranteed to get him to lash out. This poor self-awareness meant Scott was convinced everyone in the audience were thinking the same, so it was time for 'fight or flight' and he weren't running away. What was this argument actually about, Scott didn't know, he never knew, he didn't think he just reacts.

Sadly as any good fighter knows, losing your temper or self control, is 'bad news'. Scott, swung his 'left hook', but Mike, his opponent, was ready and leaned back so the hook missed, immediately responding by jabbing his left hand into Scott's chin. Scott, barely felt it, but became more incensed, and swung his right fist furiously, missing easily. Mike replied instantly with another left jab, but Scott 'saw it coming' and he pushed down hard on his right foot to try to move back away from the punch. However, there was some spillage on the floor and Scott's foot found no grip, his right foot shot forward and his head went back, resembling the classic 'banana skin slip'. Unfortunately, unlike the stuntmen, Scott was not ready for this movement and the first thing to hit the floor was the back of his head.

"What a waste, what a shame, so much potential, just too much too young, like so many others"

Scott could hear a man's voice muttering these words; he looked around to see where it was coming from.

"What the f***! He said.

He was lying down, but he wasn't on the floor in the hall, he was in a bed! He quickly realised he was in his own bed and although it was almost black he was in his own bedroom. He pushed himself up to sit up and tried to peer through the darkness, and as usual when he was on his own he spoke to himself.
"How did I get here? What the f*** happened?"
"You hit your head on the floor when you were fighting"
Scott was startled by hearing the voice again, he looked around him through the gloom and although he could just make out the walls of his bedroom, he couldn't see anyone. He began to feel quite spooked but spoke again.
Where'd that voice come from? Who said that? Where are you?"
In front of him, out of the darkness, a shape began appearing, initially like squat black round snowman wearing a bowler hat, then like Mr Mannering out of Dad's Army in his civvies. Finally it became clear it was a short tubby old man, with white hair, clean shaven and wearing an old fashioned black suit with a waistcoat and bowler hat. Scott was now even more spooked at seeing someone appear before his eyes, even if he did look But as usual, when feeling fear or worried, he used an aggressive manner to hide it.
"How did you do that? Who the f*** are you? What the f*** are you? Why the f*** are you here?"
"I didn't think you recognise me," he said calmly.
Scott stared at him;
"Why? Who are you?"
"You could've seen my photograph, on your parents' mantelpiece in their living room or on the wall in your Grandma Sarah's house." he replied.
"A picture of you in my parents' or grandma's house, you're joking ain't you? That ain't the sort of thing I notice and why would there be a photo of you there?
"Because I'm your great granddad, Arthur, your grandmother's father".
Scott, stared at him and his jaw dropped, struggling to believe what he was hearing.
"Piss off. You can't be, he died 'donkey-years' ago".
"That's right" Arthur replied.
The hairs on the back of his neck stood up and the shiver we feel when we're really spooked hit Scott, worse than any he'd felt watching a horror movie.
"So you're dead are you?
Scott didn't really believe him, but he had appeared in his bedroom in a very unusual way, so he carried on.
"So why are you here?"
"Good question! Why do you think I'm here?"
"How the f*** am I supposed to know? I suppose I'm dreaming?
Scott was still quite frightened so his aggression appeared again.
"Perhaps, you are" Arthur replied.
"Why the f*** would I dream about you, I've never met you. The last thing I recall, I was having a fight in the school hall."

Arthur did not reply and just stared at him.
"Are you a ghost or angel like in the films?
Again Arthur said nothing and continued to stare at him.
"Why would my great granddad appear?"
"You're the grandson of my daughter, shouldn't I be helping you?"
Arthur finally replied.
"Helping me! I don't need any f***ing help!"
"Unfortunately you do! You're life is falling apart, you're stumbling from one problem to another. You haven't realised it but you're drowning. I'm here to offer you one last chance."
"Last chance? Drowning? What the f*** you going on about?
Scott was clearly confused and anxious, so as usual, getting angrier as a result.
"I'm getting pissed of with all this, are you going to tell me why you're here or not?"
"Okay. How well do you know your cousin Stacey?"
Immediately the mention of Stacey's name moved Scott's emotion away from anger, like being stung! Stacey was a few years older than him, and until a few years ago, he'd grown up playing with her and being looked after by her. He hadn't seen her for quite while but his fondness had grown into a very strong attraction and hearing her name was like a minor electric shock.
"I haven't seen her for a few years, but when I was little, she and her sister Suzi, used to play with me. Why?"
"She also made a real mess of her life in her teens and I visited her to help her and give her a last chance, like you. Fortunately, she's made good use of the chance."
Scott felt less aggressive now.
"I remember my grandma, saying how she'd seen a remarkable change in Stacey, but I didn't take much notice. What happened, then?"
"Basically, Stacey was struggling so much that she attempted suicide, I helped her identify why she had got into such a mess and how she could learn to succeed."
"Attempted suicide?"
"Yes"
"I had no idea she was in such a bad way, I did know she'd got into lots of trouble, but I had no idea it was as serious as that."
Realising that his cousin had almost died came as a big shock to Scott, especially as he had such a big attraction for her. His anger and frustration had now become concern and curiosity.
"So what is this last chance all about?"
"Like Stacey you first need to develop your self-awareness enough to become motivated to learn to succeed."
"Self-awareness and motivated to learn to succeed, what's that all about?"
Scott's rudeness had decreased as he began to take Arthur seriously.

"Are you saying this last chance depends on me being willing to learn?
"Yes"
"Well that won't be easy. What am I supposed to learn and how? Is this what happened with Stacey?"
Scott was still struggling to come to terms with the news about Stacey.
"Stacey had lived her teenage years as though she was on a rollercoaster ride, continually going from agony to ecstasy, getting into more and more difficulty, until it all became too much to cope. What I did was to provide her with an opportunity to develop her self-awareness, by helping her to look carefully at her life and thinking deeply about why it happened. Like most people, she'd never really reflected on her life and tried to understand why she felt and behaved in that way. She'd been too busy drowning to learn to swim".
"Too busy drowning to learn to swim? What's that supposed to mean?"
Scott asked.
"So many people are rushing around these days, busy doing things and getting stressed over it. They just get more and more stressed, complaining they don't have enough time, energy, or money. Yet, most of their problems would be solved if they took time out to develop their self-awareness to discover how to live their lives in a different way, with different priorities and greater happiness. It's as though they are thrashing around in the deep end of a swimming pool, they keep thrashing harder and drown, rather that just calming down and learning to swim"
"What about Stacey?"
"Stacey had very poor self-awareness and low self-esteem, like you and most teenagers nowadays. She had no idea how to assess herself accurately and I tried to help her to learn to do that."
"Me and most teenagers have poor self-awareness and low self esteem? How come?"
"I think Stacey will help you with that. In fact, Stacey will probably provide much of the help you need. She's learnt so much in the last eighteen months that she will make a great mentor for you."
Another shock swept through Scott's body on hearing this statement. He then felt a strange glow inside him at the possibility of Stacey being his mentor and the prospect of Stacey being prepared to spend some time with him.
Arthur continued.
"Stacey got into so much trouble in her teens that she was prepared to kill herself. She'd already come very close to losing her life several times before her suicide attempt because of her poor success skills and chaotic lifestyle, and you've been much the same. From the age of eleven you've repeatedly been angry and lost your temper with almost anybody for almost anything. You've never stopped to think why this keeps happening and made no attempt to learn to manage your feelings. Like Stacey and many others, you've been too busy drowning to learn to swim."

Arthur raised his left arm as being lifted by a string and pointed to the wall to his left. Suddenly it looked like a movie screen, showing an eleven year old Scott at home shouting at his parents, then it switched to him behaving in a similar way in school with teachers, then with other students, followed by arguments with policemen in the street. The scenes kept continually changing, with Scott gradually getting older. Scott stared at it in complete and utter amazement, his mouth wide open in disbelief.

Arthur spoke again.

"These are scenes from your life in the last few years, showing you continually arguing with your parents, teachers, police and anyone trying to help you. You are repeatedly storming off, out of classrooms or being sent off in football matches."

Scott found seeing his own life being displayed on the wall very uncomfortable at first but the next scenes were increasingly painful to watch.

"Over the last few years, your life deteriorated into fighting, stealing, causing damage, smoking, binge drinking alcohol, taking illegal drugs and doing high risk activities, like these."

As Arthur slowly described Scott's behaviours as a teenager, they were shown on the wall.

Scott began feeling cold and as though the blood was draining from his body, almost as if it was actually his life draining away. Probably for the first time ever, Scott was actually reflecting on his life and realising it had become a complete mess. Possibly he was just beginning to stop thrashing and realise he was drowning.

"Being knocked out is a warning that your chances and time have run out. How long do you think you could continue to behave like that without coming to a serious end?"

Scott couldn't answer.

"Stacey is your last chance. Unless you let her help you to learn and change, you've had it."

Arthur pointed at him as he said this in a very menacing tone, such that Scott felt frightened, especially as a white light began to grow around him, causing Scott to such his eyes and suddenly both Arthur and the light had gone.

Scott became even more frightened in this blackness, he began panicking and started yelling for Arthur to return and help him.

Chapter 2
"Stacey, we are desperate"

"Scott, Scott, wake up, you're having a nightmare."

Scott could hear a voice answering his plea, but it wasn't the deep tone of Arthur, it was a much higher pitch, more like his mother.

"Scott, are you okay?

It was his mother.
Scott was gradually able to open his eyes, it was as though they were stuck, but slowly they opened and he could see right in front of him, about two feet away, his mother's face. Then he could see, standing behind her, his father, both looked very concerned.
"Where was Arthur?" He thought. "Where am I? I'm not in my bedroom anymore, where the hell am I? It looks like a hospital room, it is a hospital room, I'm in hospital! How did I I get here?"
Scott finally collected his thoughts sufficiently to speak.
"Mum, Dad, where am I? How did I get here? What's happened to Arthur?"
Scott's parents were both delighted and confused, and looked at each other and then back at Scott.
"You're in hospital, Scott. You got knocked out in a fight at your school do, can you remember it? Scott's mother, Ann, managed to reply, whilst cupping her hands around his face.
"Yes, yes I do. I swung at that bastard and slipped or something. But where's Arthur?"
"Arthur? Who's Arthur? What you talking about?" His mum was clearly worried.
"Your granddad, mum. Arthur, your granddad."
Scott replied
Ann was now even more confused and slow to respond.
"Well, yes my granddad was named Arthur, but he died years ago, before you were born, Why are asking about him?"
"I've just been talking to him, mum, he says he's going to get Stacey to help me."
"Stacey? Your cousin Stacey? You haven't seen her for years. What you going on about?"
"He's been dreaming or hallucinating, probably because of all those drugs he's been taking. Silly sod, he's lucky to be alive!"
This was Scott's father, George, chipping in, displaying little sympathy for his son. George, an electrician in his fifties, from a typical working class background. Scott was the youngest of his four children and increasingly become a problem for him. For the last few years they had gradually become enemies, with George unable to understand or accept Scott's behaviour, which was so different from his other children.
Scott looked across at his father, a six foot man, still physically fit, in his usual clothes of rugby shirt, track top, trousers and trainers. He used to admire his dad so much when he was little but now viewed him as an opponent with whom he had nothing in common. He tried to absorb what his dad said and thought how typical a comment that was from him now.
"Lucky to be alive, that's what Arthur said. It may have been some sort of dream and probably I am lucky to be alive, perhaps that's why I had the dream."

"What you going on about, Scott? You must be suffering from shock or concussion or something." George was beginning to feel more concern as he struggled to understand Scott's ramblings.
Scott's mother was very aware of this tension between her husband and son, she'd spent several years attempting to act as referee or mediator. She was also in her fifties and like her husband had kept her good looks, but her eyes were very red from crying and her pretty face drawn over worrying about her 'little baby'. However, her concern was shifting more towards confusion at the mention of her grandfather and niece.
"But why Arthur, why Stacey, Scott? Anyway, how are you feeling?"
"I've got a shocking headache and I do feel quite drowsy"
"You' were 'knocked out cold' and been 'out' for a long time. You've got mild concussion".
Scott suddenly realised that there was someone else in the room, a nurse, who looked a bit like Sandra Bullock to him.
"He'll need to spend a few more hours with us to keep a check on him. He should be able to go home later on today. But he needs to be left alone for a while, now."
"Okay. Come on Ann, let's leave him to recover and finish his hallucinations" Scott's father commented.
"We'll be back later, Scott. You get some sleep and we can try to sort out things later on"
Ann gave Scott a kiss on his cheek, held his hand and released it slowly.
"Okay, I'll see you later"
George and Ann left the room with Scott trying to reflect on what had happened.
Scott was now alone and looked around the simple hospital room, whilst propping himself up in the bed. He was very confused and being alone began talking to himself.
"Did I dream I saw Arthur? But why would I dream about someone I've never met or even really heard of? Why would he be talking about helping me? Stacey, why did he mention Stacey, why would she help me, how could she help me?"
Scott was so confused but decided that, whether it was a dream or not, there was nothing he could at the moment, he'd just have to wait a see what happens.

*

"Scott, do you want a cup of tea?"
Scott's mother yelled from the kitchen.
Scott was now home and sitting in one of the armchairs in his parent's front room.
"Yes, mum and some biscuits!"
"I see the blow to his head hasn't knocked any manners into him" George commented to his wife.

"George, please don't have a go at him again. Let's wait and see if we can sort out this mystery with Arthur and Stacey first."

Ann pleaded with her husband whilst making the tea.

"Okay, but I've had enough of him, we've got to do something with him, very quickly!"

Just then the doorbell rang.

"I'll get that. You finish making the tea"

George went to the front door and Ann put the teapot, cups, milk, sugar and biscuits on a tray and carried it into the front room, where Scott was still sitting in the armchair. She placed it on the table next to him and turned to greet her new guests. Standing in the doorway was the stereotypical little old lady, about 5 feet tall, aged at least seventy, with permed grey hair and spectacles, wearing a white blouse, grey cardigan and calf length tartan tweed skirt.

"Hallo Ann, hallo Scott. How are you?" she said.

"Mum, you timed that perfectly, I've just made the tea." Ann went over to her and gave her a big hug and a kiss.

"Of course I did, after all these years of practice, I can smell the tea brewing miles away. How you feeling Scott? How's your head?"

She went over to Scott and kissed him on the cheek.

"Not too bad, Grandma, much better than it was?"

As Scott was replying to his Grandma, he could hear his father talking to someone outside the room.

"I've brought someone to see you, Scott, I wonder if you'll recognise her?"

His Grandma smiled as she turned to face the doorway.

Scott looked up at the doorway and found his head and eyes unable to move. There was a figure in black that perhaps from Scott's point of view, would've been more appropriately dressed in white with wings and a halo. There stood a 20 year old, five foot nine athletic girl wearing a figure hugging black T-shirt, black jeans, and black trainers. Her black curly hair just caressing her shoulders and acting as a frame for her pale stunning face without a scrap of make-up to detract from it, and giving such a contrast for her red lips and dark eyes. Although her face was magnetically attractive, Scott's stare actually flicked repeatedly between it and the superman type logo on her bosom which seemed larger than he remembered or imagined.

"Hallo, Scott, long time, no see. How are you?"

She said.

Scott, felt paralysed by what seemed like a wave hitting him, removing his breath and control of his limbs. Fortunately, he was sitting down, otherwise he probably would've collapsed. His throat felt swollen and although his mouth opened, no words came out. Scott's mum, dad, and grandma all stared at him, and after several seconds of silence his father said. Scott had been virtually unable to communicate with girls for several years and the prettier the girl the more useless he became.

"Well, do you recognise her, do you know who it is, she's changed a lot."
Although Scott didn't use the word 'understatement' it perfectly fitted the phrase, 'she's changed a lot', in fact it helped to shake him back into the real world and resume his normal aggressive manner and reply.
"It's Stacey, of course I recognise her."
Stacey moved towards Scott and held his shoulders, bent down and gave him a peck on the cheek.
Scott was now 'in shock' as Stacey walked towards him, he could feel his heart pounding, as usual with girls he had little control of his eyes and they flipped from her dark brown eyes to her chest and back again as she gave him the kiss on the cheek.
"So how are you feeling?"
Stacey smiled broadly, realising how much he was struggling to manage his feelings, as she straightened up.
The paralysing shock had now changed to a hot flush for Scott and his tongue suddenly dried and seemed too big for his mouth, but he knew he had to speak.
"Er, Okay. A bit of a headache, that's all."
He finally spoke after what seemed an eternity to him.
Scott's mum could see him struggling and spoke to try to ease his pain.
Come everyone, sit down, the tea's brewed. Stacey do you take sugar?"
"No thanks, Auntie Ann."
Stacey and Grandma Sarah sat on the sofa, and George sat on the other armchair, while Ann poured out the tea she spoke again.
"I bet you are surprised to see Grandma and Stacey, aren't you Scott?"
"Very"
Scott was still trying to control his eyes and not stare at Stacey, but failing dreadfully.
"When you woke up in the hospital, you started rambling on about my Granddad Arthur and Stacey, so I phoned your Grandma and she contacted Stacey." Ann continued.
"But when I phoned Stacey, she was not surprised to hear from me or to hear about your problems."
Grandma Sarah commented.
'Not surprised to hear to hear about your problems', this comment caused Scott and his parents to have similar expressions on their faces, 'surprise and confusion'. George spoke first.
"Could you help us out here Gran or Stace, please. I am very confused by all of this. I don't understand the connection between Scott's continual disasters and either of you, could you explain it to me please."
Grandma Sarah and Stacey looked at each other, smiled and Grandma spoke.
"I'll explain it from my view and then Stacey can take over. About 18 months ago, I went to stay at Stacey's parents' house for a few days over the Christmas period, Stacey's other Grandma, Angela, was there also. You may not be

aware, but for several years until that Christmas, Stacey had been an extremely unpleasant girl, very rude, loud, ungrateful and always in trouble."
They all looked at Stacey, who looked a little ashamed. Ann decided to comment.
"I was aware that my sister was having awful trouble with her, she'd been in tears about her on many occasions to me. But Sheila said that Stacey changed completely at Christmas, she became a completely new person, she reckoned it was a 'miracle'. I was delighted for her, of course, but I thought my sister was clearly exaggerating. But when Scott mentioned Stacey's name in hospital, I remembered it and thought I'd ring you."
"I'm pleased you did, Ann" Grandma Sarah continued. "When I went to stay with Stacey's parents that Christmas I could never have guessed what I would observe. In the few days we were there, I'd agree with Sheila, we did witness a miracle. I think God had decided that Stacey was worth saving and sent Arthur to save her."
"Arthur?" George was confused.
"Arthur was my father-in-law, Stan's dad, Ann's Grandad, Scott and Stacey's great granddad".
Sheila explained.
"But he died before I met, Ann." George commented.
"But both Stacey and Scott have met him. Stacey attempted suicide, just before the Christmas 18 months ago and he visited her to help save her, and now it seems he's visited Scott for the same reason." Grandma Sarah continued. "What I saw during those days at Christmas was like being in 'A Christmas Carol' or 'It's A Wonderful Life', I could feel something powerful occurring, it was magnificent."
Grandma Sarah began to struggle to speak as the emotion began to affect her, so Ann spoke.
"I've heard mum talk about this in the 18 months since it occurred and when Scott mentioned both Arthur and Stacey's names together, I thought I'd better contact her as soon as possible."
George was still clearly mystified by what was being said and decided to ask some questions.
"Can I just get some of this clear? Eighteen months ago, Stacey attempted suicide and was 'visited by Arthur, who saved her'. So how did Arthur visit her and how did he manage to save her?"
"Perhaps, I should take over now Gran" Stacey asked. "Arthur visited me in what seemed like a dream, but it was so vivid and I could recall it all, unlike any other dream I've ever had. He visited me several times and on each occasion explained to me why my life had been such a disaster. He showed me how it would've been different if I'd learnt the skills we need to succeed, how I could still learn them and help others to learn them. My sister Suzi and I then began

researching and learning as much as we could about these 8 skills, and shared what we could each day with mum, dad, Grandma and Nan."

"How it would've been different if I'd learnt the skills we need to succeed, what is that supposed to mean?" George asked.

"Until Arthur explained it to me, I had no idea either, Uncle George. Basically, when we are born, we are 'hopeless and helpless', relying upon others to help us to survive. But we are capable of learning and there are 8 essential skills, key actions or activities that we really need to learn well to overcome the difficulties we meet in modern life."

"What are these 8 skills we need to succeed then?" George asked.

Stacey was clearly ready for this question and replied immediately.

"I'll try to be as brief and clear as I can. The first and most essential skill is Effective Learning. Life in the 21st century is very complex and continually changing, unlike any previous time. Only people able to continually learn to adapt to these new situations are able to cope and succeed, unfortunately many young people don't.

Communication is next, and developing good concentration is essential to learning all the skills. Poor development of listening, speaking, reading, detecting facial expressions and body language has caused many problems for young people.

The third is 'Cognition', and traditionally being good in this skill meant you were called intelligent or clever. Good development in this skill helps us understand our world, solve problems and make good decisions.

Self-awareness is next and good development in this skill means we can accurately assess and understand ourselves. Unfortunately poor development in this skill has resulted in low self-esteem for most young people.

The next one is 'Managing Feelings', and if we don't develop well in this skill we are controlled by our emotions, as we are when young children. Long term success relies on us 'staying in control' and doing what we need rather than what we want.

Motivation is the sixth skill, and learning from setbacks helps us learn to become resilient. Many young people are now unprepared to attempt difficult tasks, fearing failure and avoiding challenges or new situations because they've poor development in this.

Empathy is next, which is the skill of understanding others. This is central to our success because we need to live and work together in groups. Much of the high levels of depression in young people are because their poor development in empathy means they aren't sensitive enough to the different feelings of other people and experience many relationship problems.

The final one is social skills, and key to how effective we are in relationships and teams. Good development in this skill will determine whether we tend to lead or follow others."

Scott, George, Ann and Sarah were clearly impressed and focused on Stacey's explanation, but Grandma Sarah spoke first.
"Thank you Stacey. She's very impressive isn't she, Ann? I first heard about this18 months ago, I was both amazed and confused then, but now it makes so much sense."
"Yes, thanks Stacey." George added. "I think 'amazed and confused' sums up my feelings very accurately, Sarah. I think I am going to need a lot of help in understanding it fully. But, basically, you are saying our chances of being successful in life depend largely on how well we've learnt these 8 skills."
"That's it Uncle George. In recent years there have been many reports emphasising this. 'Preventing Poor Children Becoming Poor Adults' and 'Fair Society, Healthy Lives' are two you may have heard of. There is lots of scientific research to support it." Stacey replied.
Ann had a deep frown on her face and commented next.
"I'm afraid I haven't heard of them and I will need a lot of help in understanding it, Stacey. There were too many terms I didn't really understand, but I can see that there does seem to be something special about these people who overcome such great difficulties. I just put it down to their personality."
Stacey smiled broadly, as she had once thought the same thing herself, and was keen to convey what she'd learnt.
"You're not alone in thinking that way auntie, but research has shown how our personalities can change throughout our lives. Our personalities are basically ways of describing how our skills are displayed or how we behave and can change as we learn."
"But, the reason you are here is for Scott, isn't it? So, Scott, what about you?" George asked.
It had taken Scott a while to recover from Stacey's peck on the cheek and when she started to explain about the skills needed to succeed, he tried hard to listen on what she was saying. However, he repeatedly found himself being distracted in thinking how attractive and sexy Stacey was. When his father asked him the question, he just able to collect his thoughts.
"Er, I'm struggling, Stace. I think I'm going to need much more help with this."
"That's exactly why I'm here, Scott." Stacey responded.
"Right, Stacey. You say you are here to help, what exactly have you got in mind. Do you know how much trouble he's in?" George asked.
"No, I don't, Uncle George."
"Nor do I?" said Grandma Sarah. "Is it bad?"
"Bad! Bad! Since he started secondary school, he's gone from one disaster to the next. We've been up to that bloody school so many times; I reckon the kids think I'm one of the staff!
George was clearly showing signs of anger and carried on.
"We've seen his tutor, his Head of Year, Deputy Head and Head teacher, as well as most of his subject teachers, they have given him so many chances and

do this. So I played the fool, became a rebel, did extremely risky and anti-social activities to try to impress them."

Stacey was now so well developed in the 8 skills that all of them found it hard to imagine her being insecure, and were transfixed by what she was saying.

"As I became older, as a typical girl, I focused more and more on trying to attract boys as being the way of feeling I mattered. I spent most of my time, money and effort on my appearance in an effort to make myself attractive to them and going clubbing to meet them.

Increasingly my time and thoughts concentrated on trying to impress the boys or making my friends jealous, I lost interest in almost everything else. I felt that I needed to be sexy to attract boys and I started to explore different ways to use sex to attract them. I continually changed my hair colour and style, spent hours and a fortune on clothes, shoes, jewellery, make up and perfumes. Whenever I could, I would dressed as sexily as possible, revealing as much skin and cleavage as I could. I even had studs and tattoos to draw more attention to my flesh. My appearance meant that boys and men probably thought that I was keen and available to be groped and snogged. The pressure on me seemed to increase continually 'go to the next stage'.

This did mean I got lots of interest from lots of boys and I thought the girls became more jealous so I continued with it. Of course with so much pressure on me I lost my virginity in my early teens."

Clearly Scott, George and Ann were surprised by what Stacey was saying and the comfortable way she talked about it.

"At the time, I foolishly believed having sex meant I was mature, attractive and important. I thought that my many critics were merely immature, naïve and jealous. So I began to have sex regularly with a variety of boys, I felt 'popular', because they seemed to be very attracted to me but I did not have the skills to maintain a good relationship with them as boyfriends. Of course, a number of girls and some boys called me names, and being unable to manage my feelings I became violent and 'sorted them out'. I became feared by other girls, initially thinking I was important but really I was just a bully.

With such poor self-awareness I was keen to try anything that I thought might cause others to think how 'gutsy' or brave I was, so I tried many high risk activities. I 'got slaughtered' regularly, basically binge drinking, smoking, trying various drugs, doing all sorts of anti-social and criminal behaviour, like nicking stuff in shops or taking and driving away cars."

It was now obvious to Stacey that Scott and his parents were shocked and appalled at what they were hearing, and she had not finished.

"By the time I was Scott's age, I had created such a reputation that there were huge expectations on me from all sorts of people, particularly my mates and boys, so I couldn't back down, otherwise I would 'lose face'. Obviously, I had become known as a 'slut, slag or slapper', but I hadn't the skills to know I was drowning and there was no turning back. Although I had desperately wanted to

feel I belonged and have others admire me, I had actually achieved the complete opposite. The boys only wanted me for sex, the girls hated me and my mates felt they couldn't trust me, My self esteem got even lower and I became increasingly depressed until I decided there were no good things left in my life and no point carrying on, so I decided to end it all."
Scott, George and Ann were clearly shocked and there was an eerie silence. It seemed an eternity before anyone was able to speak and it was George.
"I had absolutely no idea that you found it so difficult being a teenager"
"And you still don't"
Scott commented to everyone's surprise, he never normally spoke in those situations.
"Being a teenager is so difficult now, Dad. You have no idea how hard it is."
George stared at him, but instead of being angry, having heard Stacey's problems, he actually started to feel some sympathy for Scott. Stacey decided she should add to his comment.
"Unfortunately, our world is now so complex and changing so rapidly that growing up in the last few years is actually very different from anything before. Most young people no longer have the learning opportunities to develop the skills they need to succeed and so struggle to cope. I had no idea how widespread and serious the problem was until my suicide attempt."
"So what caused you to change, then Stacey?"
George asked.
"When I was in my coma from my overdose, I was visited by Arthur and he helped me understand why I'd had my difficulties and what I needed to do to overcome them. I suppose he was my first mentor."
"How did he manage to do that, Stacey?" Ann asked.
"I think it was like the ghosts did for Scrooge in 'The Christmas Carol'. He showed me what my life had been like from the moment I began secondary school, explaining how my poor development of the 8 skills continually caused the problems I was having. He also showed me a 'Skilful Stacey', a version of myself who had developed these skills better, when she met the same situations that I had, she dealt with them brilliantly. My self-awareness improved enough for me to realise that if I wanted to have a successful and happy life, I needed to focus on developing these 8 skills."
"So it was my granddad Arthur who saved you, Stacey?" Ann asked.
"Yes, Auntie Ann, he helped realise I was drowning and how I could learn to swim. Now he wants me to try to do the same sort of thing for Scott."
Scott again felt his heart beat harder and faster, at this prospect.
"How, Stacey? How can you help him?"
George was very impressed with what Stacey had said and more importantly how she said it, but was very aware of how difficult this would be.
"How you going to get him motivated to change? How are you going to get him to learn these skills?"

Stacey was prepared for her uncle's response and instantly replied.
"Once Arthur had gained my trust as a mentor, he ensured that I understood the 8 success skills and the importance of the five learning requirements. If Scott is to be helped he needs the same."
Stacey anticipated that she would not be fully and understood and spotted the vacant expressions on their faces, so she continued immediately.
"If people are to be supported and developed effectively by their mentors, parents, teachers or anyone, it is essential they understand and apply effective learning, especially these five learning requirements. The first one, motivation, was achieved by Arthur with me, by creating an opportunity for me to 'stop and think', to reflect, about my life. He provided me with the information to understand why it had happened and how I could change. Scott, like most people in the 21st century, has not yet really had this learning opportunity, he must have it now!"
Stacey really emphasised the 'now', as she knew it was probably Scott's last chance.
"Once Arthur's visits had motivated me to learn, I needed to have the next two learning requirements, an environment to avoid distractions, and concentrate on the learning. Fortunately, these two were possible immediately, with both Grandma and Nan being with us at Christmas, I had over a week with no great distractions The fourth learning requirement was to have tasks that challenged me just enough to keep me progressing and that it provided me repeatedly with the fifth requirement the feeling of success. These were achieved by Suzi and I researching and learning together over that week, at home away from any distractions, where we could concentrate on the information from the internet. Arthur gave me some information to study and each day we would try to learn as much as we could to present and discuss with Mum, Dad, Grandma and Nan, and they provided great positive feedback to us to keep us going."
"It was brilliant!" Grandma Sarah chipped in. "Stacey and Suzi, were like our teachers or presenters, and we had great discussions about the various posters, video clips, and information they prepared. It was so enjoyable and I learnt so much, possibly the best Christmas I've ever had."
"Thanks Grandma, that's so good to hear. Suzi and I both realised then that learning could be great fun. We'd never thought that before, I hated school and although Suzi was only ten at the time, she already thought that 'learning was work' and 'school was boring'."
Scott had gradually become less distracted by Stacey's attractiveness and more focused on what she was saying and listening more intently.
"Arthur suggested I contact a person named J.C.Learner, as he would probably offer me the help I needed."
"J.C. Learner, the ex- footballer and multi-millionaire?" George asked.
Stacey was clearly pleased George had heard of him and answered immediately.

"Yes, but at the time, I'd never heard of him, now I know he is quite famous. Apparently he is in the News frequently, he's been a success in lots of different areas and he now spends his time and money trying to help people, as Bill Gates does. It took me some time and effort to contact him, but eventually I got to meet him, well it was an interview really, though I didn't realise it at the time. After hearing my story, he offered me a chance to train for a role as a Development Mentor at one of his 'Learning For Success Centres'. I'm delighted to say I accepted and it is now my job."

Ann, George and Scott, all had the similar expressions, impressed and bewildered!

"What's a 'Learning For Success Centre' and a 'Development Mentor'?"

George asked what all of them were thinking.

"The 'Learning For Success Centres are absolutely incredible places. I think they are quite magical as they seem to have a power to transform people, like some sort of 'Hogwarts' in the real world."

Scott, George and Ann were ironically spellbound by Stacey's response and bristling enthusiasm.

"These centres bear no resemblance to anything I've ever come across, so not easy to explain, but I'll try. J.C. Learner, like me and Scott, found his teenage years very difficult and secondary school added to his problems. Fortunately, a P.E. teacher supported or mentored him and he finally managed to succeed in the end. In fact, he went to university, and became a teacher before becoming a professional footballer and successful entrepreneur."

"I watched him a lot when he played for Spurs, he was a brilliant." George added enthusiastically.

Stacey's smiled in a way that displayed her huge admiration for JC, and she was keen to continue.

"He is now very concerned about the huge numbers of young people who are struggling to cope with life in the 21st century, like us and has set up these 'Learning For Success Centres' to help them. When JC first met me, he already knew some of my story and was prepared to consider helping me. They are residential centres and I went there first as a student and then became a 'Development Mentor'.

He very much agrees with the famous Friedrich Nietzsche quote, 'That which does not kill us makes us stronger', and recruits people who have learnt to overcome difficulties in their lives. My role is like a personal mentor or trainer for the whole person, to help get people mentally, emotionally and physically healthy by focusing on the effective learning of the 8 skills needed to succeed."

Scott, George and Ann were all desperately keen to hear more, and Ann asked.

"What are these 'Learning For Success Centres' like, Stacey, you mentioned Hogwarts, are they schools?"

"No, nothing like any school I've ever heard of, Auntie Ann. In fact, they are difficult to describe, but I would say they most closely resemble Holiday Camps,

Health Centres, Centre Parcs or places like that. However, as I said before they seem to have the power to transform people."
"What do you mean by the power to transform people, Stacey?" George asked.
"The centres are carefully designed and organised to provide opportunities for very effective learning, causing huge improvement in all 8 skills. JC used his experience at a campus university as the initial idea, where he lived with other students, very close to everything needed to live, learn and enjoy life."
George was clearly fascinated but still very confused and immediately asked.
"But, they are called 'Learning For Success Centres' and you are a Development Mentor. How does this learning occur and what do you do?"
"Students usually want to go to university to learn and also to enjoy themselves at the same time, that's what the centres aim to do. " Stacey replied.
"But the students who go to university, are motivated, have already had success in exams and have to pay to go there." George responded.
"That's why our first priority is to motivate the students and to convince them that they can learn to succeed. Only when that has occurred can they continue to attend the centre. My role is to continually ensure that my students have the five learning requirements so that this learning does not stop."
"They usually go to university for three years, how long do the students spend in the 'Learning For Success Centres', Stacey?"
George asked.
"JC is an expert in the science of learning and this is why the centres are so effective. University students aren't really there for three years, they actually have ten weeks in a term and attend for only about nine terms. But most importantly, they rarely learn effectively in them and are not helped to do so. In the 'Learning For Success Centres', the focus is on the 8 skills, so getting the students to become effective learners who are not dependent on other people having to teach them is essential. This means that learning occurs much more rapidly and thoroughly, and even more importantly, very enjoyably! Usually students are in the centre for six months, by that time they have developed the 8 skills to a much higher level which means they are then capable of learning to succeed in the modern world."
"Does this mean that the students 'live on campus' like the university students?" Ann asked realising that this could mean her son may have to live away from home.
"Yes, they are residential centres. This is very important as they need to have an environment that encourages learning 24/7. The centre has an incredibly positive climate for learning and the aim is use that as much as possible. The learning that occurs in six months is greater than many years in schools, universities or normal life."
The enthusiasm that Stacey was showing was infectious. Scott, George and Ann were clearly becoming convinced that these were very remarkable centres, but Ann picked up on the residential part and asked.

"Stacey, does this mean that if Scott got into one of these centres, he would not be living at home for six months?"
"Yes, Auntie Ann. It is essential that these students are given an opportunity to learn these skills away from their parents. It has been known for many years that this is one of the biggest benefits of going to university."
George realised that his wife was worried about this point and felt he should add his view.
"I think that's a brilliant idea, I've often thought that many of the kids who go to public schools have a huge advantage in studying and exams because they are away from their parents a lot of the time. But those schools are so expensive, as are universities, so too few are able to benefit from them."
Stacey was very aware that Scott had said nothing and his view on this was vital.
"What's your opinion, Scott?"
Although Scott usually struggled to sit and listen carefully he had managed to do so partly because Stacey had such good communication skills and that this was about his future. His response showed he had understood what was being said.
"Are you saying that I could be going to your 'Learning For Success Centre' and I would be living there with you?"
Scott was actually struggling to believe what he was hearing, but seemed excited at this thought.
"With about another 100 students and almost 20 mentors and staff like me."
"If the improvement in Stacey is anything to go by, then you'll come out a different person". Grandma Sarah decided to chip in.
"As I've said before, I think Scott has run out of alternatives and this might be his final and only chance before he's locked up."
George' comment conveyed that he felt that this was a 'golden opportunity' for Scott. However, Scott's mother was still worried about her son 'leaving home'.
"I don't like the idea of Scott having to live away from home, but as his dad says, it's likely that he could be sent away for the other alternatives and this sounds better than those. What happens after the six months, Stace?"
"The intensity and effectiveness of the Learning For Success centres means that I am confident he will probably have developed the 8 success skills so much that he can return here and to school, with a very good chance of being successful."
"And hopefully I won't feel like throttling him everyday! So what happens, now, Stacey? George added.
"I believe one of JC Learner's staff will contact Scott's Head teacher and explain this offer to her and hopefully she will agree to it. If Scott and all of you are in agreement, I will take Scott to my centre as soon as possible."

"We've already been phoned and arranged to have an interview with Scott's Head teacher on Tuesday morning. He's not allowed to go back to school until then. I reckon they'll jump at this chance to get rid of him!"
George glared at Scott as he made this comment.
Stacey was still keen to involve Scott and give him a chance to convey his views.
"But what's your view on this, Scott? The possibility of this happening and success of it depends on whether you want it to happen. Remember, that although I will be with you in the centre most of the time as your development mentor, you will be living away from home in the centre for six months. I'm very confident that like me, you will enjoy it, but it can seem very scary when you are a young teenager."
Scott's thought's and feelings were still dominated by his attraction and view of Stacey, he was still struggling to take his eyes off her. This question basically meant to him at that moment, that he would be spending lots of time with Stacey in what she had described as a 'holiday camp'. Therefore, the thought of having to live away from home for six months did not appear to be unpleasant at all, especially as it would mean he'd be free from the continual battles with his father and the repeated criticism and grief at school.
"Well, it's clear if I stay here, it ain't gonna end well, so I'm up for it." Scott replied.
It was Ann, Scott's mother, who displayed reluctance. Scott was her youngest, calling him and probably often treating him as 'her baby'.
"We will be able to visit him, wont we, Stacey?"
"Of course, auntie, weekly, if you wish and I'll be there when you do to give you an update on his progress."
What about phones? Ann asked
"Mobile phones wont work in the centres, but you'll have a landline number that you'll be able to use to contact him, but only if we consider it necessary. Remember, it is important to provide a new life and environment for him for six months, with few distractions."
"He'll be alright, Ann. It is only six months." Grandma Sarah chipped in. "He needs to have a break from here and you need to stop spoiling him."
Ann glared at her mother, but knew she was probably right.
"I'll phone you to find out if all goes well with your interview at the school on Tuesday, and I'll collect Scott on Wednesday morning at 9am, okay?"
"I certainly hope it is okay, Stace, and we really appreciate what you're trying to do, thanks." George commented
"No problem, Uncle George, I hope it helps him, I'm confident it will".
Stacey got up to leave, but Grandma Sarah was keen to have a final word.
"As you can see by Stacey, it certainly seems to work miracles!"

Chapter 4
"Nothing like a school"

"How many times have we been here, like this, with you?"
George asked whilst sitting outside the Head teacher's office, with Ann and Scott.
"We never had any of this with your older brother and sisters, yet we've been here with you more times than I can remember. Well I reckon, one way or another, this will be the last time."
Alright George, I know how you feel, but perhaps finally, we have a possible solution to his problems." Ann responded.
Scott just sat, sulking and scowling, as he has done so many times before. He knew that whatever he said, his dad would pounce on him, so he learnt a while ago that it was best to keep quiet, if he could!
The waiting area for the Head teacher's room was a small area placed behind the secretary's office, so that it was fairly secluded and quiet. There was just enough room for the three padded chairs in which they sat where they'd been many times before. They were all dressed very smartly, Scott in his school uniform, sipping tea or coffee waiting to discuss Scott's latest problem.
"Mr and Mrs Spicer, Scott, good morning, would come in please?"
Mrs Lucas, the Head teacher, had opened her door and greeted them. She was a slim attractive woman, about five foot tall, looking as though she'd been dressed by a top stylist. She had very light brown shoulder length wavy hair, a white blouse and a knee length dark blue carefully tailored skirt with matching shoes and designer glasses, looking younger than her age of forty plus years. She oozed confidence in her greeting and manner, reflecting her skill and experience with a very wide variety of people, of all ages, backgrounds and positions.
"Bring your drinks, please sit down."
The light beige carpeted room, was a typical Head teacher's office, the size of a large lounge, with a padded swivel chair for Mrs Lucas behind the large modern desk, with three chairs identical to those in the waiting area on the other side.
"Obviously, you know why you're here." Mrs Lucas began.
"Good morning, Mrs Lucas, I'm afraid we do and once again, I want to apologise for our son, you've done so much to help him over the years but he's just got worse." George chipped in immediately.
Mrs Lucas just smiled slightly and replied.
"I've known you both for many years. If I remember correctly, when I came here as deputy head, over 10 years ago, Adam, your eldest, was in year 10."
George was still apologetic mood and commented.
"I suspect until Scott arrived, you barely knew who we were, we never had any trouble like this with Adam or the two girls, Kate and Diane. But we've certainly made up for that with Scott."

"Yes, the other three were very good students and I only seemed to meet them to congratulate them or give them awards."

This comment only prompted Scott to repeat his typical 'sulking and scowling' expression, looking down and trying to avoid making any comments.

"Anyway, I may actually have an offer to put to you that could finally help Scott address his difficulties. I think you may already know some of what I'm going to say, through your niece, Stacey, who I believe is employed in one of JC Learner's centres. I have been contacted by the principal in one of his 'Learning For Success Centres' in East Anglia. They are prepared to offer Scott a place until Christmas. Are you aware this?"

George was already nodding and responded.

"Stacey visited us on Saturday, and gave us an idea of what these centres do and explained how it could help us, but we weren't certain he'd be offered a place."

Mrs Lucas had a very serious expression and shifted her gaze to stare at Scott.

"I should point out that I am a fan of JC Learner and I think what he is trying to do with these 'Learning For Success' centres is brilliant. They appear to have had a lot of success with people like Scott and he is very lucky to be offered this chance, I hope he realises this." Scott had always struggled to maintain eye contact with people, especially attractive females and teachers, so trying to look at Mrs Lucas was a real challenge. He very briefly raised his eyes from the floor to glance at her and look down again before replying.

"I do Mrs Lucas, Stacey has already told me enough to give me an idea of how lucky I am."

Scott had a picture of a holiday camp and university campus in his head and spending six months with Stacey, so he did genuinely feel he was fortunate with this opportunity.

"I have spoken to our Chair of Governors and she agrees with me that this is a great opportunity for you and agreed for you to go. I will be honest; I feared that you would be permanently excluded this time. Hopefully if you do well in the centre we may allow you to return to us in January."

Scott just continued to look down.

"When he'll be a completely new, totally reformed person!" George added sarcastically.

"The centres have only been in operation for a few years, but their success rate is incredible. The radical approach in them has caused a lot of interest and discussion, and I'm hoping to learn from this opportunity as well."

Scott was surprised at what he'd heard; he had not considered that his Head teacher would be so interested in the centres.

Scott's mother had been quiet until then; she was still uncomfortable about Scott having to leave home and was pleased that Mrs Lucas had been so positive.

"I'm so pleased you said that Mrs Lucas. I've been struggling to really understand what these centres are about, but if you say they have been very helpful, I'm much more comfortable with him going."
"I would think that having Scott away from home for six months will not be easy for you"
Mrs Lucas was able to empathise with Ann, as a mother.
"It will be the first time he's been away from home for any length of time so I'm not looking forward to it."
"But I am." George interjected
Both Scott and Ann glared at him.
"I understand, Scott's cousin will be taking him to the centre tomorrow and she will keep me informed of his progress" Mrs Lucas commented.
"Yes, tomorrow morning if all went well today."
Ann replied.
"In which case, if you have no further questions and are happy, we'll leave it there." Mrs Lucas asked.
"No questions that I can think of at the moment, and I'd like to thank you for your incredible tolerance with Scott and agreeing to him having this chance." George responded.
"As I said, I was prepared to give him a permanent exclusino this time, so it is such a relief to have this opportunity, I just hope he makes good use of it."
"So do we, so do we!"
George replied as he stood up and held out his hand for a handshake.
Mrs Lucas immediately stood up and shook his hand, followed by Ann and then Scott, who was last to stand up, clearly uncomfortable at shaking her hand and still unable to look her in the eyes.
"I will try to visit you at the centre if I can, but I hope you really make full use of this wonderful opportunity, Scott."
"Thanks Miss" Scott just about managed to reply with a quick glance up at her eyes.
Mrs Lucas escorted them to the door and waiting area, where the Head's personal assistant met them and lead them to the main door.
"You are so lucky to have such an understanding and pleasant Head teacher, Scott. They weren't like that when we were at school, were they Ann?"
George said as they got into their car.
"Probably not, George, but that was a long time ago and we did what we were told in those days."
Ann replied.
"And they didn't discuss anything with our parents, they just told us what was going to happen and that was the end of it." George added.
Scott was struggling to say anything as he was worried he'd only 'set his Dad off again', so kept quiet.

*

"That'll be Stacey. I'll get it."
Ann said as the doorbell rang the following morning. "Are you ready, Scott?"
"He ain't allowed to take hardly anything with him, so he should be."
George commented as he got up from his seat in the living room.
"Morning Stace, lovely to see you again."
George said as he held out his arms to greet Stacey with a hug.
"Morning Uncle George, yes I'm very pleased everything went well so I could return. Is Scott ready?"
"Yes, I am."
Scott shouted from the stairs as Scott came down with his bag.
Scott's eyes widened and his pulse quickened when he saw Stacey. She had her black curly hair tied back, and was wearing the same tight fitting black T shirt, with what Superman-type logo on it, black leggings and trainers. Scott's immediate thought was how mature and sexy she looked and felt so excited at having to spend the next six months with her.
"I hope you've ensured you've only got the bare essentials, you'll soon realise that anything else is either useless or creates a problem."
"I'm amazed at how little he is expected to take, is he being provided with lots of stuff?"
Ann asked reflecting her concern over her 'baby' leaving home.
"No, but he'll discover that because of the special nature and organisation of the centre he'll be provided with all that he needs, and he won't need that much."
"How long will the journey take, Stacey?"
George asked.
"A couple of hours, Uncle George. Probably just long enough for me to outline and explain some key points to Scott."
"OK, I'm ready."
Scott was keen to get going.
"Give us a kiss and hug goodbye, then."
Ann demanded as she stretched out her arms and kissed and hugged him tightly. She clearly didn't want to let go and her eyes began watering.
"Alright Mum, let me go."
Scott eased himself free.
"I really hope all goes well, Scott, I'm sure you can make a go of it"
George held out his hand and reluctantly Scott did the same and they shook hands.
Stacey gave both Ann and George a peck on the cheek.
"I'll keep in touch and let you know how he's getting on."
Ann and George stayed in the doorway, with their arms around each other and waved as Stacey's car drove away.
"Scott, I want to use this journey as an opportunity to learn more about each other and the 'Learning For Success Centre', okay?"

Scott was still trying to relax as sitting next to Stacey was a little uncomfortable for him. He kept thinking he must not stare either at what he thought was her very attractive face or worse still her boobs, so he decided to just try concentrating on looking straight ahead.
"Any particular questions to begin with, Scott?"
"Lots Stace, in fact, I don't know where to start. You told us the other day how you became a real problem and how Arthur visited you to help. How often has he visited you?"
"About 5 times over the Christmas period, initially, but in the last 18 months since then, only a couple of times. The first time to tell me to contact JC Learner and then last week to tell me about you."
"What did Arthur say about me?"
"Only that you had gone down the same slippery slope as me and you needed to learn the 8 skills."
"So he doesn't visit you often then, will he visit me again, do you think?"
"I think Arthur is like the Angel Clarence in the film 'It's A Wonderful Life', he visits very rarely, and only if it is absolutely necessary, so possibly not."
"I've watch that film several times at Christmas and now you mention it there I s'pose Arthur is a bit like that angel. How did you meet JC Learner and get into the centre?"
"When Arthur mentioned JC Learner, I had never heard of him, but when I did a search on his name I got loads of stuff. I then tried contacting him, which was very difficult, I sent many e-mails and spoke to quite few people on the phone. I contacted the centre we're going to and eventually he actually spoke to me on the phone. I didn't know it was him at the time, I thought it was just one of the leaders there. He gave me an appointment time to visit the centre and it was only when I arrived and met him that I realised it was actually him I spoke to on the phone."
"I've never heard of him, why is he so famous, what's he done?"
"Well, he tries his best to keep 'low key' but he has a fascinating background. He was born in the east end of London in the fifties to a typical working class family, but somehow he passed an exam when he was top juniors that meant he was sent to a secondary school that expected kids to be good at exams, I think they were called grammar schools and the exam was the eleven plus.
Anyway, he struggled in this school and got into lots of trouble, like you and me, but because he was good at sport, his P.E. teacher started to mentor him, and persuaded him to keep out of too much trouble. He eventually managed to get good enough exam results to go into the sixth form and go to university."
"What happened then?"
Scott could see some similarity with himself.
"He was particularly good at football, but played in lots of different school sport teams, reached a high level in many and this will become very significant later on. Nobody either in his family or even where he lived had ever gone to

university, so like when he started secondary school, he struggled initially to cope, but managed to get his degree in chemistry and maths. Because he was still so interested in sport he went to college to study to become a PE teacher."

"Why would he want to become a teacher when, like us, he'd struggled so much in school."

"Excellent point, Scott. But remember the P.E. teacher had been a great help to him, he really loved sport and wanted to be different from the teachers he'd hated at school, who probably didn't like him either. He became a P.E. teacher but because he was good at science and maths, he taught these subjects as well. After a few years he became head of science but was becoming disillusioned with how schools seemed to be stuck in the 19th century, with their priority on exam success and little else. This experience stimulated his study into the 'Science of Learning', which is central to the 'Learning For Success' centres.

However, he was spotted by a scout for Spurs whilst playing for his club side and decided to stop teaching to become a professional footballer."

Scott was already quite interested, partly because it was Stacey talking and also JC Learner seemed to have lots in common with him, Hearing that he had become a professional footballer really interested him.

"For several years he was a top class footballer in the first division, but this is before the premiership and satellite TV, so he didn't earn a fortune like they do now. In his thirties he 'retired' to become employed in the growing industry of computers in the eighties."

"You know a lot about him, Stace?"

Stacey actually felt a huge attraction and admiration for JC and actually felt a little embarrassed so tried to cover it up with a quick response.

"He mentored me in the centre and key to being effective in that role is being open, honest and fair. In fact, the research is clear that this is essential to having any good relationships, so we got to know each other very well. You'll soon discover that this approach is adopted by everyone in the centre."

Scott began to feel uncomfortable as he thought about how he was with his friends and family. Being open, honest or fair is certainly not how he had been with them. Stacey continued her story.

"So in his early thirties he was into his third 'career' really. This is the time when Alan Sugar and Bill Gates are just beginning to establish themselves and make their fortunes. Part of JC's genius was to realise how computers could be used for both entertainment and learning. He has contributed to the development of some of the world's most famous computer games and programmes by providing the initial ideas and concepts. In a similar way to Steve Jobs in Apple."

"I've heard of Apple, but not Steve Jobs. Do you mean early computer games like Super Mario, Sonic, Tomb Raider and stuff like that?"

"Yes, that's the sort of thing and the football games like FIFA and so on."

"I suppose that's how he made his fortune?".
"Yes, he's associated and has shares in lots of big international companies, and when the internet arrived, he was able to apply this creativity and genius to that as well."
"What about these 'Learning For Success Centres'?"
"About 10 years ago, he actually came up with the idea and bought an old primary school that was no longer in use and had it completely transformed, it's actually the one we are going to. There was a TV programme a while ago called 'Jamie's Dream School' where Jamie Oliver was trying to help kids, like me and you. JC attempted to do a similar thing, with phenomenal success. Remember JC was a teacher in his twenties and began thoroughly researching learning to become an expert in 'The Science of Learning'. The centre began about ten years ago applying this research with a radical approach with just a few kids. Since then it has been continually expanding and developing."
"You said it was a primary school, what's it like now?"
"Nothing like a school, for a start. JC only bought this place because he was going to continue to use it for learning, or 'education', as some call it. Also it had rooms about the right sort of size the classrooms, it is fairly remote and the land around it could be easily used for development. It was also important for JC to try to show that it would not be too expensive. All the development mentors are like me, ex-students, who are keen to help people like us. Originally it was basically just JC and a few friends or but the numbers have grown immensely over the years."
Scott was so fascinated by what Stacey was saying that he was able to keep concentrating and very unusually for him, keep asking questions. Stacey was able to provide lots of answers and details on JC, the centres and Stacey's involvement with them.
"You said before that he used his experience of university to help him create the centres, so why a primary school?"
"Good question, Scott and well remembered! You will soon see that it does not now resemble a primary school but he needed rooms that were suitable to have group discussions whilst watching videos and where a student could develop all 8 skills and that means including exercise, dance, and play."
"Play! What do you mean by play?"
"You'll soon see what I mean but remember JC is an expert in the 'Science of Learning', creating computer games and an ex-professional footballer."
"It sounds amazing. What about rooms for sleeping and food and stuff."
"They are very small simple rooms, very much like student accommodation in universities, because they are only used for sleeping and studying."
Since Scott had never seen university student accommodation he had no idea really of what this meant but felt excited at the prospect of 'living away from home' and not far from Stacey.

Stacey continued trying to explain about the centre, and Scott grew more excited as he became more amazed at what she was describing. Scott's very limited experience or knowledge of universities and learning meant each explanation seemed to bring more questions and confusion. However, the journey seemed to pass rapidly and he suddenly heard Stacey exclaim.
"Here we are!"
Stacey's comment surprised him and realised she was slowing down and turned left into a wide tarmac drive, in a gap between two long ten foot high bushes surrounding the grounds of the centre. He just caught sight of a large sign, 'Learning For Success Centre'.

Chapter 5
"it's something magical."

"I can feel it already, I feel different as soon as I pass through those gates, it's something magical."
Stacey exclaimed as they turned into the drive.
Scott could see this huge sign that had SF in a Superman type logo, he realised that it was the same as the one on her T shirt.
"What's the SF stand for then?"
"It stands for Success Feelosophy. It's the approach the centre is based on, trying to help everyone learn to succeed by applying the science of learning and the research on success."
When Scott saw the centre, he was quite confused, as he had just been told that it was once a primary school but could hardly recognise any of the original structure. All around it there was a number of other new buildings, causing it to look more like a small shopping mall. Stacey parked the car in the car park to the left of the buildings and they walked around to the main entrance, above which was the success feelosophy logo. The entrance had large glass doors into a foyer with a large desk opposite making it look like you were entering a modern hotel. There was even a young girl receptionist behind the desk staring at the computer screen on it.
As they entered the foyer, Scott tried to scan it, spotting the large flat television screen on the wall surrounded by posters covering the walls, but was then distracted by the young girl's greeting.
"Morning Stace, how are you, is this Scott?"
The young receptionist said as she stood up and Stacey smiled broadly as she replied.
"Morning Ange, I'm fine, yes he's my cousin, hopefully he'll be with us for the next six months. Scott, this is Angela she's one of our receptionists, she's absolutely brilliant and knows what's going on all the time."
Scott's poor development in the 8 skills, especially self-awareness and managing feelings meant he was really uncomfortable meeting with girls. He

was frightened he might be staring at her and looked at the ground, immediately. He began to feel his usual 'hot flush' that occurred whenever he met girls he thought were attractive. Angela had very blond hair tied back in a ponytail, with large dark earrings. In stark contrast to Stacey's discreet makeup, she wore loads of the stuff, probably reflecting her poor self-awareness and low self-esteem. Angela looked to be in her late teens, but her very smart simple white blouse and A line skirt made her look more mature. She held out her hand to Scott, and he tried to look up at her face but although he didn't realise it, he struggled to stop looking at her chest, where her gaping blouse exposed part of her bra.

"Nice to meet you Scott, I hope you enjoy your stay and find it extremely helpful."

"Er thanks."

Scott's poor communication skills were clearly exposed in this relatively simple situation, he was clearly struggling and Stacey's face illustrated that she had noted this.

Scott then again looked around the foyer and studied the variety of posters, most had simple slogans or sayings on them, but his eyes were drawn to a huge cartoon superhero with the following words written beside him.

"In brightest day, in blackest night,
No evil shall escape my sight
Let those who worship evil's might
Beware my power Green Lantern's light"

"That's Green Lantern! Why is there a poster of him here?" Scott asked.

"Because he was my favourite superhero as a kid, he helped me get through my childhood and hopefully he can help you, Scott."

A deep voice came from the door opening to the left of the foyer and a tall man with broad shoulders and deep chest came through it.

"JC, I didn't know you'd be here, wonderful to see you!" Stacey exclaimed and held out her arms to hug him.

Stacey was almost engulfed by his hug, Stacey kissed him on his cheek and squeezed him a hard as she could, he then kissed her on the cheek and slowly released her grip.

"I think, you'd better introduce me to Scott first, Stacey, don't you?"

"Ah yes, Scott this is JC learner, JC this is Scott."

"Very pleased to meet you, Scott, I do hope you enjoy your time with us and more importantly learn lots."

JC held out his hand and shook Scott's firmly. Scott was more comfortable looking at men, as long as he felt they weren't a threat and his eyes were drawn to this impressive man, who initially looked as if he were a superhero himself. He was about the same height as Scott, about 6 foot 3, but thinner, more muscular, with much broader shoulders and his clean shaven face, short light

brown curly hair meant he looked younger than his fifty plus years. His yellow T-shirt also had a huge Successfeelosophy.com logo on it, Scott kept thinking he recognised JC from somewhere but could not place where.
"I suppose you recognised Green Lantern from the film?" JC asked.
"Yes" Scott replied abruptly unable to look up at JCs eyes.
"To answer your question more fully, the Green Lantern comics helped me learn to read and overcome some of my difficulties as a kid. We didn't have books in my house but my older brother was a big fan of comics in the fifties and I wanted to read them, like him. My great heroes in the comics were Roy Race in Roy of the Rovers in 'The Tiger' and Green Lantern in the Superman DC comics from America. I eventually became a professional footballer, not as good as Roy though, but Green Lantern helped me develop my motivation skill. Do you know what his super power is, Scott?"
Unusually for Scott, he managed to avoid looking away from JC, partly trying to remember where he'd seen him before and also because he was so impressed by his physique.
"Not really, its something to do with his ring, isn't it?"
"He was selected because he had great determination and imagination. His power ring helps him to use his will power to overcome the difficulties he meets. When I was a young kid, I believed if I tried hard enough, really motivated and determined, I could overcome anything that tried to stop me. So I've been using Green Lantern throughout my life to assist people like you, me, Stacey, and many others overcome their difficulties and that's why his picture and oath is up there on the wall."
"You'll see the whole centre is covered with posters, Scott. They are prompts or reminders to inspire us and keep us motivated." Stacey added.
JC then continued.
"When I was a boy in school, I used to spend a lot of time looking at the posters on the walls instead of listening to the teachers and I realised that I often learnt more from them than from some of the teachers. When I went to university, I stuck loads of posters all over my wall and ceiling in my room and I could remember them when I went into exams. It works for lots and lots of students, you'll see loads in your study room, perhaps it'll work for you, Scott."
Scott looked around at the various posters while JC was talking and he spotted this one that reminded him of Arthur's visit.

I'm too busy drowning to learn to swim! –
If we don't take time to learn we won't succeed

Scott pointed at this poster and asked.
"I keep coming across that one."
"This is a saying I've used for many years, Scott. In my early twenties I when I was a teacher, I realised that my students and others were trying hard but doing the wrong things and so were never going to succeed. They reminded me of people who were thrashing around in the deep end of the swimming pool, the harder they thrashed the more they struggled, and they just got exhausted until they gave up. Therefore, I think this saying helps people realise that they must calmly and carefully study to discover what difficulties they really need to overcome if they are to succeed."
Stacey realised that Arthur had used it with both of them and commented.
"It's seems so relevant to so many areas in life and everyone in here."
Scott looked at Stacey realising that Arthur had used it with both of them.
"But that's probably my favourite"
Stacey said pointing at another poster.

We are not born happy, but we can learn the skills we need to achieve happiness!

Until I discovered the 8 skills, I was never really happy, I just went for 'quick fixes and pleasure' all the time, which in reality only made me more depressed."
"Stacey, would you be so kind as to give Scott a quick tour, show him his room and bring him to my office in about an hour, please?"
"Of, course, JC, my pleasure. It's really kind of you to be here to meet him."
"No problem, see you both in a while."
"Okay, Scott, this way."
Scott followed Stacey through the door on the right and Stacey had already turned around in anticipation of the expression on Scott's face.
As Scott came through the door he stood as if frozen apart from his jaw which dropped. His eyes attempted to adjust to the bright light and cope with the shock of what he saw, rather like people would do if they entered Doctor Who's Tardis for the first time. He looked up to the roof which must've been at least as high as a house and appeared to be glass with sun streaming through it, but only a few minutes ago he was outside and it was thick cloud and raining. He thought initially he'd walked into a huge greenhouse and the walkway in front of him should've been in shopping mall as it was lined with trees or vines growing out of pots or planters and rising up to the walkway for the floor above. Stacey burst into laughter.

“I love watching the expressions on people’s faces when they first walk through that door; we all struggle to cope with it at first. No, the sun hasn’t come out, the lighting is very clever, it gives the impression the sun is shining. Behind those walls are our sleeping-study rooms, or if you are posh, the dormitories, you can see the doors, each has a poster and number on it. Yours is number 25, Scott, it’s on the other side of the central atrium.”
"The what?"
“The central atrium, that’s a big central area, like you have in shopping malls, at the end of this walkway, there is more of this the other side of it”
"How many of these rooms are there?"
Scott was clearly amazed and didn’t really know what to ask first.”
“Over a hundred. There’s another set above us, behind that walkway up there with the clear plastic covering it at the front. I think at least twenty in each corridor.”
Scott looked up and they began walking forward with Scott’s head moving around trying to grasp what he was seeing. They reached the central atrium and he became open-mouthed again for a few seconds. Again Stacey had been anticipating this sort of reaction and asked.
“Surprised Scott? It looks a bit like a shopping mall, don’t it?”
They had walked into a wide square area about the size of a tennis court. The very high roof was entirely the greenhouse type structure giving the appearance that the sun was shining through it. There were more of the plants in this area making it look even more like a shopping mall.
“To our right are some toilet and shower cubicles, behind them is the food court, or refectory or eating area or whatever you want call it. In front, there is another walkway like we’ve just come from with more study-sleeping rooms, yours is down there. To our left behind the other toilet and shower cubicles, is the main learning and development area. We’ll go to your room first.”
Scott had been walking through the atrium towards the opposite walkway staring up at the roof and at the posters on the walls, when he saw a large teenage boy walking towards him. As with girls, Scott’s poor success skills meant he struggled with teenage boys, but with them he was very suspicious and felt he needed to be very ‘macho’ with them. His first impression was that he was in his late teens, slightly shorter, with short black hair and looked ‘hard and menacing’. He was wearing a red successfeelosophy.com T shirt, dark blue track trousers and white trainers, Scott could feel his muscles starting to ‘tense up’, preparing to show him he’s not frightened and will ‘take no shit from him’.
“Hi Stacey, how are you? Is this a new student?”
The boy greeted them with a smile and held out his hand to them.
Scott was surprised by the boy’s friendly gesture and Stacey had been studying Scott’s face, shook his hand but Scott just did not know what to do.
“Hallo, Ralph. this is Scott, my cousin, he’s here for six months.”

"I'm almost finished here as a student, but I'm hoping to return soon as a mentor. Sorry, but I must dash, I'm booked for a swim now, good to meet you Scott, all the best."
Scott was unable to respond, he was shocked at how pleasant the boy had been.
"I did try to warn you Scott, that this place is different, not like you are used to. Ralph is typical of everyone in here and he was much like you when he arrived. I told you it's a magical world in here, a 21st Century Hogwarts."
Scott reflected on the various surprises and responded.
"Well it's certainly nothing like I imagined. I suppose it does look more like a shopping mall than a school. I have seen pictures of some of the new schools, academies, I think they're called. They probably look a bit like this, but I didn't expect it to be so different."
They had now gone through the doors into the next walkway when Stacey said.
"Yours is number 25, just here on the right."
Scott looked at the bright yellow door with a number 25 in the top corner and below it was a huge poster that caused him to stop and stare.

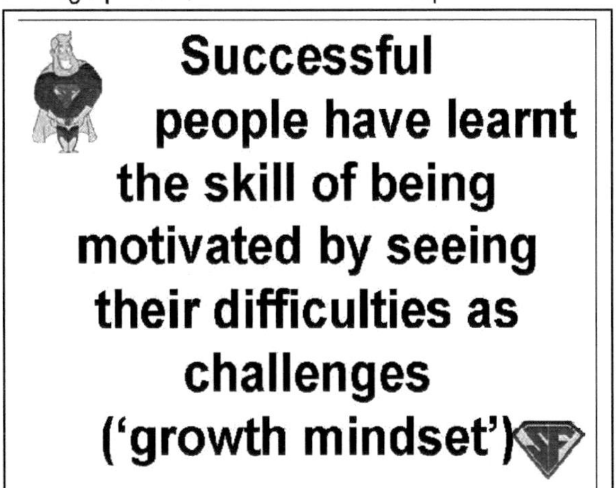

"What's that all about, I don't understand this one and what's a growth mindset?"
Stacey smiled and replied.
"You ain't seen nothing yet, wait 'till you see the posters in the room. This one refers to some more very important research which I'll explain in more detail soon, but basically it points out that to succeed, our motivation skill needs to develop so that we see our difficulties or problems as exciting challenges and learning opportunities instead of using them as excuses."
Scott was slowly getting used to listening to Stacey explaining things, he didn't really understand her this time but managed his feelings and just kept quiet.

Stacey pushed the door and it swung open against the right hand wall revealing a sink with a large mirror on the wall over it. It looked like a typical student dormitory in any modern university but Scott would not know that as he stood in the doorway and carefully scanned the room. His eyes focused initially on the large flat TV screen on a moveable bracket the wall above behind the sink, then down to the table against the wall underneath it, with a keyboard and mouse on it, and a printer under it. The only other furniture, apart from the single bed to his left and against the wall, was an armchair underneath a cupboard on the wall. Apart from the huge TV screen, all the walls and ceiling were covered with posters. Opposite him was a large frosted window and just like the ones in the roof again it seemed as though the sun was shining through it."

"These windows are f***ing amazing, they're so clever how it brightens up th room like sunlight."

Stacey glared at him in a way that made him realise he had made an error and feel embarrassed.

"Sorry Stace, I'll try not swear."

"We all have that difficulty at first in here, It will take time, but as your managing feelings skill develops, I'm sure you'll manage it. You'll see that the good lighting and it always appearing sunny is part of the overall magic effect. This is a very typical student room ideal for it's main purposes of sleeping and studying."

"Where's the toilet?"

"We just passed them in the central atrium".

"Oh yeah, I remember, you called them toilet and shower cubicles. That's a big TV screen, what can you get on it?"

"It's actually for the computer. Don't forget that JC made his fortune from computers and this is a key part of the centre. Although you can only access the successfeelosophy.com, website and the links, you'll soon see that that is more than enough."

"So there's no TV?"

"Well it depends on what you mean by TV, you will watch lots and lots of stuff on it. In fact, you'll see that watching videos as videostudy will become a big part of your learning."

"Videostudy, what's that?"

"Look at that poster, have you ever seen it before, it's the Learning Pyramid?"

Stacey pointed at the wall beside the bed, the walls had a cork like material lining them and several posters pinned onto them. Scott looked across and stared at it, trying to understand it.

"The Learning Pyramid, it's very colourful, what's it about?"

"Arthur showed it to me first and since then I've used it lots. Basically, it simply and clearly shows research into how we learn and it explains why I and probably you as well, struggled to learn in school."

This comment again caused Scott to realise that his difficulties were very similar to those that Stacey had and he tried to increase his concentration as Stacey continued.
"If you look at the top of the pyramid, you'll see that the least effective method of learning is 'Lecturing' and since having teachers talking at you is the most common teaching technique in schools, it helped me understand why I learnt so little from teachers."
Scott was nodding in agreement.

The Learning Pyramid

This diagram shows the average retention rate for different styles of learning. The styles at the top shows the least effective and on average how much is learnt

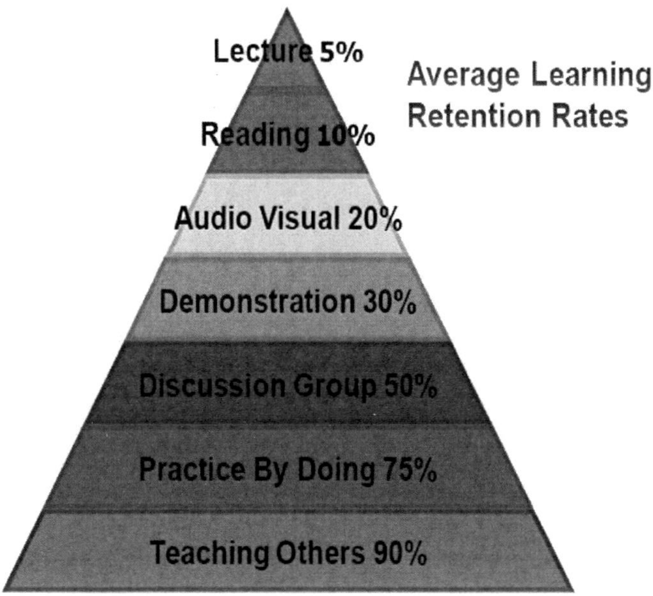

Source: National Training Laboratories, Bethel, Maine

"To make matters worse, just under that is 'Reading' and since my teachers just kept us reading and writing stuff down all the time, I realised why I was learning so little in school."
Scott was now studying the poster much closer as he realised this was so relevant to him.

"That's incredible, but that's all most of my teachers ever use, in most of my lessons I'm expected to sit, listen and copy down stuff. If that's such a poor way of learning, why is used so much in schools?"

"Most teachers probably aren't aware of the Learning Pyramid or the research on effective learning, and there's loads of it, so they tend to teach in a very traditional way."

"So what about these one's at the bottom, the good ones?"

"Since you are so keen on sport, Scott, I reckon these two will be obvious to you. I bet you've become good at sport by doing lots of practice and trying to help others learn, these are 'Practice By Doing and Teaching Others'."

Scott thought about this carefully before replying.

"Yes, of course. But what's this to do with 'videostudy'?"

"Well, quite simply with videostudy, we are given questions to answer before watching a video. We try to answer the questions while watching the video, sometimes stopping and rewinding it if we want. Then when it's finished, we check and discuss our answers, explaining why we think its correct and changing or confirming it as we do."

"You keep saying 'we', is this done in a group?"

"It can be done on your own, or online or best of all in a group. In a short while, you'll get to see the rooms where these videostudy collaborative action inquiries take place."

"Collaborative Action Inquiries', what's that?"

"Oh that's just the scientific term that describes how problems or questions are discussed in groups to try to work out answers or solutions. Basically, this is 'teaching others' in a group situation and a brilliant way to learn, it's very enjoyable, because you are chatting with people but learning as you do so. Videostudy is a great way of providing the questions and information to discuss."

Scott was really trying to concentrate on this as he'd become aware that this could make a huge difference to him.

"Well it sounds much better than what we do at school and this is what we do in lessons, here?"

Stacey laughed.

"Lessons! It's a while since I've heard the sessions called lessons. We don't tend to use the traditional terms like 'lessons' here, since most of us disliked them in school. To answer your question, yes we do a lot videostudy in our group learning sessions, but most of it is done in these rooms."

Scott thought about that for a moment.

"On our own?"

"You are not really on your own in here when you're studying."

"What do you mean by that, Stace?"

"Remember that we are using the centre's internal internet, so you've always got someone you can contact if you want, like a chat line on facebook, or use

the camera and chat. Since everything you do is using the computer, you can always be monitored and supported if needed."
"So, even when you are in this room you are being 'spied on', you mean."
"We wouldn't look at it like that, because we've realised that everyone here is trying to help us, that poster sums it up well."
Stacey pointed at another poster on the wall above the bed.

Remember everyone here is your ally, not your enemy!

"When JC was at school, he felt that virtually all his teachers hated him and were his enemy. Although he knows that it was not true, when he taught he tried to ensure that his students felt he was 'on their side', their ally, and wanted them to succeed. You'll soon see that everyone in this centre is encouraged to have the same approach, again it is part of what makes this place so magical."
"But, what about the other students, they ain't all on your side, lots of them will be your enemy."
"You might think that at the moment, Scott, because you've just arrived, but I bet you change your mind in time, like I did."
Scott's look towards Stacey showed he was finding this hard to believe.
"Anyway, Scott, I've got to show you the rest of the centre, so we'd better get going."
Scott put his bag on the bed and followed Stacey out of the room.
"How do we lock the door, Stace?"
"We don't, well not from the outside, you can lock it from the inside, which can be electronically opened in emergencies, but we have no valuables really, so doors are left unlocked."
"I've never come across that anywhere before, Stace."
"You'll keep saying that, Scott, I did say it was like nothing you've ever been to before, remember."
Scott and Stacey returned to the central atrium and turned left between the toilet and shower cubicles. As they went through some double doors there was a large food hall in front of them.
"This is impressive, Stace. It looks like the sort of food hall you get in shopping malls."
"Yes, it is, but it's actually like a number of school refectories in that it all operates using your thumb print as a credit card."
"What do you mean, Stace?"
"These are becoming quite common in schools and colleges, you stick your thumb in these devices and the food you take is recorded to your account."

To the left and right of the double doors were walls of small transparent cubicles each surrounded by stainless steel, containing different foods and drinks. In the centre of the hall there were about 10 round tables, each with 8 chairs around them.

"Everything is fully automated and available 24/7, so you rarely get many people in here at the same time."

Stacey turned around and went back through the double doors, and after a short delay Scott followed. They walked straight across the atrium and went through the double doors opposite, in between two more sets of toilet and shower cubicles.

Another surprise, this short corridor appeared to be from the original primary school building, with what appeared to be classrooms on the right side and the walls again covered with posters. After a few steps the corridor opened up into a wider walkway as the usual sunny lighting flooded down on them from a very high ceiling. On the left, the wall had no windows, stretched up to the roof, and covered in huge posters. Scott crouched and peered through the small window in the door to his left and his jar dropped.

Stacey laughed and said.

"I think I've seen that reaction before."

"What is it? There's just a kid in there, and he seems to be surrounded by scenes of a football stadium or something. He's got footballs flying at him from somewhere and he keeps heading them into the goal on the wall. He looks quite good and this room looks brilliant."

"I'm glad you said that because I suspect you'll be spending a lot of time in one of the soccer skills rooms."

"Soccer skills rooms, is that what they're called? What are they for?"

"I'll wait until you've seen JC before I say too much. He may want to explain it himself, he's very proud of these rooms. He's combined his three main careers in these rooms, teacher, footballer and computer programmer. He reckons he's created rooms that help people develop sporting skills incredibly quickly."

Scott was clearly excited by this room but Stacey beckoned him to cross the corridor to a similar door opposite and looked through the small window.

"So what's in this room?"

"This is one of the collaborative action inquiry rooms, where the videostudy discussions occur, that we talked about earlier."

"Oh, I can see what you mean now. the classroom has been changed so that you can watch the screen and chat."

The traditional primary school classroom had been modified so that there was a very big TV screen on the wall. In front of it, were 8 typical school tables, about five foot long and three foot wide, but these tables had been placed in a U-shape, with twelve students, in pairs, sitting on the outside.

"What age is that class, Stace? I can't work it out."

Stacey smiled very broadly.

To the left and right of the double doors were walls of small transparent cubicles each surrounded by stainless steel, containing different foods and drinks. In the centre of the hall there were about 10 round tables, each with 8 chairs around them.
"Everything is fully automated and available 24/7, so you rarely get many people in here at the same time."
Stacey turned around and went back through the double doors, and after a short delay Scott followed. They walked straight across the atrium and went through the double doors opposite, in between two more sets of toilet and shower cubicles.
Another surprise, this short corridor appeared to be from the original primary school building, with what appeared to be classrooms on the right side and the walls again covered with posters. After a few steps the corridor opened up into a wider walkway as the usual sunny lighting flooded down on them from a very high ceiling. On the left, the wall had no windows, stretched up to the roof, and covered in huge posters. Scott crouched and peered through the small window in the door to his left and his jar dropped.
Stacey laughed and said.
"I think I've seen that reaction before."
"What is it? There's just a kid in there, and he seems to be surrounded by scenes of a football stadium or something. He's got footballs flying at him from somewhere and he keeps heading them into the goal on the wall. He looks quite good and this room looks brilliant."
"I'm glad you said that because I suspect you'll be spending a lot of time in one of the soccer skills rooms."
"Soccer skills rooms, is that what they're called? What are they for?"
"I'll wait until you've seen JC before I say too much. He may want to explain it himself, he's very proud of these rooms. He's combined his three main careers in these rooms, teacher, footballer and computer programmer. He reckons he's created rooms that help people develop sporting skills incredibly quickly."
Scott was clearly excited by this room but Stacey beckoned him to cross the corridor to a similar door opposite and looked through the small window.
"So what's in this room?"
"This is one of the collaborative action inquiry rooms, where the videostudy discussions occur, that we talked about earlier."
"Oh, I can see what you mean now. the classroom has been changed so that you can watch the screen and chat."
The traditional primary school classroom had been modified so that there was a very big TV screen on the wall. In front of it, were 8 typical school tables, about five foot long and three foot wide, but these tables had been placed in a U-shape, with twelve students, in pairs, sitting on the outside.
"What age is that class, Stace? I can't work it out."
Stacey smiled very broadly.

There were 5 of these rooms, but the next 5 even more remarkable. Instead of a floor there was a swimming lane, created by having the walls extending down to the bottom of a pool, each had someone swimming in them.
"This swimming pool was already here and simply made into swimming rooms instead of having roped off lanes. Again you have no distraction in each room, you can swim up and down without any worries of bumping into anyone. The big screen at the other end is linked to the internal internet so its all part of your personal plan and monitored for you."
"No wonder you said it was more like a holiday camp and health centre than a school."
"You can probably see that the old primary school has been cleverly modified to create these skills and training rooms, with this sports hall built on our right. This is why the centre was relatively cheap, especially compared to the new schools and academies recently built."
At the end of the corridor there were double doors to the left and right. Scott looked through the small window in the double doors to the right and could see a fairly typical sports hall containing about a dozen girls and boys playing a game of basketball. Stacey lead Scott through the double doors on the other side of the walkway into a simple corridor.
"This is where the offices and admin rooms are, this first one on the left is the monitoring room."
It looked as though it was television control for the BBC, with two walls, full of flat screen televisions with two people were sitting in front of them.
"Oh hallo, Stacey, how are you?"
One of these 'observers' a man in his thirties with dark curly hair, spotted them.
"Wotcha Stace! Is this Scott?"
The other one, a woman in her twenties, with short blond hair, now saw them.
"Hallo Dave, hallo Tracey. Yeah this is my cousin Scott."
"Hallo Scott"
They both replied enthusiastically.
"Hallo"
Scott just about managed to reply, after a short delay, barely looking at them, as usual. He stood scanning the room and staring at what must've been almost twenty screens.
"We've been watching you give him the tour, Stace. The expressions on his face were brilliant. I bet he couldn't believe what he was seeing."
Tracey commented
"I think it is fair to say he's been continually amazed. It is a lot to take in when you first see it, particularly as it's so different and difficult to understand at first."
"Does he know about the 24/7 week, Stacey?"
Dave asked.
"No, not yet. We're about to see JC again and we'll explain it to him then"

Scott looked very confused, as he was trying to imagine what they meant about a '24/7 week.

Chapter 6
"I do want to change!"

"Ah, Stacey, Scott, come in!"
They could hear JC's voice from inside the room but couldn't actually see him. The door was already wide open and they walked in. It actually looked more like a living room than an office, with only a table against the wall to their left with a computer keyboard on it giving any clues to that sort of use. The two large TV screens on the wall, sofas and coffee table gave the impression that this was used much more for entertaining and chat.
As they entered the room, JC got up and directed them towards the sofas against the wall in the opposite corner that had a coffee table in front them with a tray of cups, and pots of tea, coffee, milk etc. on it.
"Please, sit down. Would you like a cup of tea or coffee?"
"Tea, milk no sugar for me please, JC"
Stacey replied immediately.
Scott's much poorer social skills meant he was not yet comfortable in these situations and he responded more slowly. Stacey glared at him and he realised she was trying to prompt him.
"Oh er, tea, milk and two sugars."
"Please!"
Stacey said on Scott's behalf, glaring at him again.
"Oh sorry, please."
Scott added, realising he'd upset Stacey.
Stacey and Scott sat on the sofa in front of them and JC moved round the coffee table to sit on the other sofa. He poured out their drinks and passed them across.
"Well, what do you think about the centre, Scott?"
Scott had just sipped his drink and looked up at JC, trying to think of a suitable reply. Scott's opportunities to develop his communication and social skills in these sort of situations had been rare so far and being polite was not really something Scott had been able to master so far. However, he felt a strange sort of sensation, as though a force was almost compelling him to be polite. Perhaps this is more of the magic that Stacey keeps referring to.
"Er, it's incredible, it's nothing like I imagined and nothing like a school."
JC had a huge smile across his face.
"Good, I'd be very disappointed if you thought it was. My aim was to try to create a place that stimulated and encouraged learning, making it enjoyable. Sadly, most people don't seem to feel that way about traditional schools, well not secondary schools anyway. You, me and Stacey are not unusual, in that we

struggled at secondary school, even the ones that do well in exams don't seem to get pleasure from learning and struggle to cope, if not being pushed or supported all the time. Although GCSE results have improved over the years, most struggle immensely at A level and many avoid choosing subjects like Maths, Physics, Chemistry that they find difficult. Even then, many of them can't cope and fail to complete their courses or get good grades. Even those that get good enough grades to go to university, struggle so much that almost 1 in 4 drop out because they can't cope. So I wanted to create centres for learning that would actually prepare the students to be able to overcome the difficulties they may meet in adult life and be able to achieve happiness, rather than seeing learning as just focusing on exam success and qualifications."

JC's outstanding communication skills seemed to be acting like some sort of Stars Wars force on him, and as Scott took another sip of his tea, he thought this was precisely how he felt about secondary school, and 'passing exams' was all that seemed to matter. Then he reflected on how much he disliked school and the teachers in it, so he remarkably he responded.

"So what's different about this centre?"

JC was clearly pleased that Scott had managed to respond and ask this question.

"It is important to be aware that until secondary schools were introduced in the UK in 1902, the only ones had been the very expensive public schools for the rich and upper class. So the Government introduced schools based on these Victorian grammar schools with subjects such as Maths, English, Science, History, Geography, R.E., and Languages with an emphasis on exam qualifications. The timetable, teachers, lessons, discipline, homework, even the holidays all copied these very traditional institutions, and it has remained virtually unchanged ever since then. What we've tried to do here is to avoid just copying this and ensure that we focus on effective learning of the 8 skills needed to succeed."

Scott was actually able to listen comfortably to JC and more importantly also able to reflect on what he was saying. He'd never actually considered why schools did what they did before.

"Has Stacey said anything to you about the 24/7 learning or the unusual lighting?"

Scott shifted his thoughts towards this question and answered after a few seconds..

"Apart from it always appearing that the sun is shining, no."

"When I was at university, many students used to study during the night, but many of the facilities like the library and fitness rooms were shut and I thought they should be open and available all the time. Also I couldn't understand why universities seemed to be virtually shut at weekends and had 22 weeks holiday each year. So with our lighting, we are like shopping malls and sports centres keeping open and available all the time."

Once again Scott thought what JC had said made so much sense and tried to imagine what this might actually mean to him in the centre. While he was thinking deeply, JC and Stacey sipped their drinks and watched him closely struggling with this concept.

"I don't really understand what it means to be open 24/7?"

He finally had to ask. JC had been waiting for this so replied immediately with a huge grin on his face.

"When I was a kid in the fifties and sixties, almost everything had very limited hours of use, shops, pubs, cinemas, television, banks, offices, factories, schools almost everything. But over the years they've virtually all changed except places like schools and colleges."

JC still had Scott's full attention, which was quite unusual for him, and even rarer, he managed to comment.

"Yeah, I suppose you are right. I've never really thought about it."

"Unfortunately, Scott, it seems too few people have really thought about it. So here, all the facilities are available all the time."

Scott was beginning to think on how this could affect him.

"But when do we sleep?"

Stacey was smiling, clearly enjoying watching Scott trying to understand this, and JC continued.

"Learning to organise and plan your time here is a crucial part of your development in the skills of effective learning, cognition, self-awareness and managing feelings. Too few people understand much about sleep and how to manage it effectively, yet it has a huge influence on our well being and success. It is just one of many things I'm sure you'll learn to manage in your stay here."

Stacey decided to intervene here.

"When I came here, I was like you Scott, I struggled to plan or organise myself, I had a very chaotic lifestyle. Fortunately, JC helped me with this a great deal at first and gradually I learnt to do it, I will try to do the same for you."

Again the mention of Stacey helping him sent a shudder of excitement through him, and he asked.

"Chaotic lifestyle?"

"Yes, my life was just a series of spur of the moment decisions, with little preparation or thought of the consequences. I relied continuously on my mobile phone and others to help or put up with me all the time."

"Is that why we don't have mobile phones, here?"

Scott had clearly been waiting for an opportunity to ask that. Stacey seemed to have been expecting that question and replied straightaway.

"To be honest, Scott, I can't see any useful reasons to have mobile phones here. Life is so busy and interesting here, that when I'm here, I have no desire to use it."

Scott looked surprised, struggling to get a picture of what happens in the centre and what he would be so busy doing.

"What do you mean that life is so busy and interesting? What happens here, then?"
JC decided to help out here.
"Scott, that will take time for you to grasp. But with Stacey as your development mentor, I'm confident you'll soon start to slot in"
Again, the thought of Stacey being his mentor caused his pulse to quicken.
"I can see you're attracted to Stacey, Scott."
Scott was surprised at this comment and felt embarrassed. He didn't think he'd done anything to show how he felt about Stacey.
"Your facial expressions and body language clearly communicates your feelings. Your attraction to Stacey is understandable, I am very aware of the research on teenagers and although it was a long time ago, I still remember how I was as a teenage boy. Stacey has developed all her success skills very well, and I'm sure she is able to empathise and help you manage your feelings. She really wants to help you and will be invaluable to you, especially in the first few weeks. It is essential that you develop a very close trusting relationship, your bond to her at the start will be a huge factor in your chances of success."
Once again, Scott was amazed at JC, and his ability to understand him so well. He had been struggling to cope with such a mixture of emotions and felt relieved that JC was able to explain it. Then Stacey spoke.
"I was the same with JC when we first met and I was really lucky to have him as my development mentor. His understanding and support at the start were invaluable and so important to my overall success."
Stacey's look towards JC and voice intonation reflected she still had a very strong attraction to him.
"I think you'd have succeeded with the other mentors Stace, but it is important to develop a good relationship with them and I'm confident that you and Scott will be able to do that."
Scott looked at JC as he said that and across to Stacey, before managing a response.
"If anyone can help me, Stacey can."
"I'm very encouraged to hear that Scott, because the first few weeks will be tough and you'll need that sort of motivation with Stacey's support to get through it."
Scott tried to reflect on what life might be like in the centre and what he was going to find tough. JC and Stacey had both expected and detected Scott's anxiety, but Stacey spoke first.
"When I first arrived here, I just couldn't work out what I would be doing and what I was supposed to achieve, is that how you feel Scott?"
"Yeah, Stace. You and JC speak to me like nobody else has, but I ain't got a clue what I'll be doing or what I'm supposed to learn."
"Everything we do here will focus on trying to help you with your development in the 8 skills needed to succeed. Once I got to really understand what they are

and how they are learnt, I began to really improve, that's why I think I developed more in 6 months here than I had in the previous 19 years.".

"As well as the special lighting, Scott, did you notice the cameras on your walk?" JC asked.

"I saw a few, why?"

"Perhaps I should've pointed them out to you, Scott, there are loads of them, they are a very important part of your learning." Stacey commented.

"What do you mean, Stace?"

"One of the skills we need to succeed is self-awareness, for people like you and me, Scott, who've made a right mess of their lives, its usually the first one to focus on and could be the most important. For us to be motivated to undergo the change and the learning required, we have to become much more aware of ourselves, what we do and why we do it. The centre is full of cameras, so we can use them to study our and others' actions and try to learn from them. It is another example of how we use videostudy here."

"You mean we are being watched all the time?"

"I, like most people, felt a little uncomfortable at first with that thought, but I quickly saw it very positively, as there was so much I learnt from studying myself and discussing it with JC or in a group. I'm sure you'll feel the same."

"What about in our rooms, are there cameras in there?"

"Just one, to look at us when we are studying and we use them for chats, like web chats I suppose. You can switch it off and on whenever you like."

JC had been quiet and studying Scott very closely.

"It is clear that until we develop our skill of self-awareness to identify and understand who and what we are, we cannot really improve and being able to study ourselves closely is invaluable. When I saw the reality programmes like Big Brother, Little Angels, The Family and so on, a few years ago, I realised how useful it is to be able to study ourselves in different situations in this way. The response of everyone in here has shown that this is a very useful learning process."

Stacey was keen to add to this.

"When Arthur visited me about 18 months ago, he actually focused upon developing my self-awareness by illustrating my life like a movie and I began to realise what an idiot I'd been and what I really needed to change. I'm confident that you will also find it incredibly useful to study yourself, and we will start doing that very soon."

This prompted Scott to think about Arthur showing scenes of his life, and the impact they had on him. JC suddenly interrupted these thoughts.

"Before Stacey takes you away, I just want clarify something with you. Why do you think you are here and what do you want to achieve?"

JC looked very closely at Scott as he asked him this question. Scott, as usual in those circumstances, had little idea of what to say and went very silent. Clearly JC had expected this and tried to help him.

"You see Scott, as Stacey has pointed out, for you to succeed you are going to need to be motivated. This place can transform people but only if you are determined to change, and realise that what you need to learn. It is important that you don't view your time here as a punishment and that we are here to help you. Too many students' view school as a punishment and don't enjoy being there, so our aim is to create a place where learning is enjoyable and when you leave here you continue to learn."
Scott continued to be mesmerised by JC and his passion, which remarkably managed to get him to exclaim.
"I do want to change!"
Both JC and Stacey were very pleasantly surprised by Scott's response, prompting JC to respond.
"Well that's good to hear and perhaps a good place to start, Scott. I'll try to see you again in while and Stacey will keep me informed of your progress. All the best."
JC held out his hand and probably for the first time ever, Scott automatically shook it.
"Come on, Scott, let's go, we've got lots of learning to do."
Stacey beckoned Scott and walked towards the door, Scott followed.

Chapter 7
"Why is he called 'Supersocrates'?"

"So what's your opinion of JC, Scott?"
Stacey asked as they walked to Scott's room. Although he was not used to answering these sorts of questions, as it was Stacey he made an effort to answer it.
"Er, I don't know really, Stace. There is something about him that I can't explain, I did feel as though I had to listen to him, he seemed to understand everything and so friendly."
"It seems when almost anyone meets JC for the first time they feel 'strange', some try to explain it as though he some aura or something. He seems to be able to make you feel comfortable with him immediately, as though he can read your thoughts and feelings. He points out that they are communication skills and we can all development them better, but he certainly is an expert in them."
"Yeah, that's it! I felt that he had some sort of amazing influence or power."
"Well you could be right, Scott. He seems to have achieved far more than most normal humans and his 'influence', as you say, certainly seems to have magically helped to transform me and many other people."
"Stace, sometimes you talk about him as though he's a magician like Merlin or Gandalf or Dumbledore."

"Yeah, I suppose I do get carried away at times when I'm talking about him. Anyway, here we are, number 25, your room, Scott."
Scott pushed the door and entered the room, Stacey followed.
"So what happens now, Stace?"
"Self-awareness, Scott! Until people realise they are drowning and that they need to learn to swim, they can't learn to swim."
Stacey smiled and looked carefully at Scott as she said this and saw a knowing smile grow on his face.
"Supporting people effectively requires them to develop their self-awareness skill so that they can assess themselves more effectively, and realise what they need to learn. So we're going to start by focusing on developing your self-awareness with some videostudy."
Scott actually understood what Stacey was saying, and felt excited at the thought of Stacey spending some one-to-one time with him.
"Just before we start, I want to get a drink of water; do you want one, Scott?"
"Yes, but where do we get them from?"
Stacey glared at Scott and focused on the development of his self-awareness.
"The reply should be, 'yes please'. Are you aware that using 'please, thank you and sorry' indicates to people that you probably care and respect them?"
Scott did not like upsetting Stacey, and wanted to explore this further.
"Using key words like these tend to indicate that you are thinking about their welfare, and crucial in improving our communication and social skills."
Scott was used to being reprimanded or 'told off' as he would put it, but usually he didn't care, but this was different it was Stacey. He followed her out of the room and saw the huge water bottle inverted on top of the machine just along the corridor, and couldn't believe he hadn't seen it before.
Stacey poured two cups of water and they both returned to the room, Stacey sat in the armchair and while Scott sat on the swivel chair adjusting it to his own comfort.
"OK, Scott, since if you are to learn to succeed, we should begin with trying to get you to learn more effectively so we'll start with SUPERlearning."
"Superlearning what the f***s that."
Stacey glared at Scott and he realised he'd sworn and felt so ashamed. In fact, he felt more upset than he could remember, almost as though he had done real harm to her and his face showed it.
"I'm so sorry, Stace, I forgot, I just wasn't thinking."
"Perhaps it reflects you're feeling more relaxed and at least it shows your self-awareness is developed enough for you to realise it, but your managing feelings skill is too poor to stop you."
Scott felt a little better with Stacey's response.
"What is superlearning, Stace?"
"That poster shows you what it stands for."

Stacey pointed at this poster on the wall next to the TV screen and Scott stared at it.

S	**START WITH THE END IN MIND**– you must START by knowing clearly what success actually means – being clear what you are actually aiming to achieve (your final destination).
U	**UNDERSTAND HOW TO ACHIEVE SUCCESS** –you must be sure you are clear on the difficulties preventing success and how you can overcome them.
P	**PERSONALISE YOUR LEARNING** – you need to know how you learn most effectively so you can apply it to overcome these difficulties.
E	**EVALUATE YOUR LEARNING** – you must keep checking that you are making progress and 'feel success', so you avoid wasting time and effort and don't give up!
R	**RESOURCES FOR EFFECTIVE LEARNING** – you need to use the most suitable resources for you (including the right environment and tasks) that helps you overcome these difficulties effectively.
l e a r n i n g	

"That's very clever, how the first letter spells out the word SUPER." Scott remarked.

"It's a JC invention. When he was a student at university and then as a teacher, he realised that most students, even when motivated, had no real idea how to learn effectively. He observed how most of them tried hard but had no idea at what they were doing."

"That's me. Although I ain't tried very hard recently, when I did, I found it a waste of time 'cos I didn't learn anything."

"Same with me, Scott. That's why effective learning is the first of the eight success skills. We are born helpless and needing to learn to survive, We start off being brilliant at learning when we are babies but rarely taught how we learn or how to learn effectively and we begin to find it unpleasant and hard work."

"That's definitely true for me!"

"Most schools seem to spend little time on this, yet unless we learn effectively we have little chance of success in the ever changing modern world. Many years ago, JC began providing some of the key parts to the science of learning in a simple to remember and use process called SUPERlearning."

"Well it's a very catchy phrase, but what's it all about?"

"Basically it attempts to show learning as a journey towards success and the steps outline how to get to your destination effectively. The 'S' emphasises that when we start this journey, as with any, we need to be clear on where we aim to go, in this case to be clear on what we need to learn to feel success. For example, when you leave here in six months time, Scott, what would you consider to be a success?"

Scott had his usual blank expression when asked a question of this type. Stacey had expected this response, she had been exactly the same only 18 months previous and so she gave him a few seconds to think.
"Er, I haven't really thought about it, Stacey."
"I was just the same when I came here and when I was in school. This meant that even when I made an effort to improve at school, or at home, or in jobs, or anywhere really, I didn't get very far because I didn't actually know where I was going. I didn't start with the end in mind, and I was like that poster we talked about earlier, I was too busy drowning to learn to swim. I kept flapping away and just kept drowning."
This helped Scott think and he found a reply.
"So what caused you to feel successful when you left here?".
"Good question, Scott. I had developed my eight success skills enough to feel I could understand the difficulties I met and believe I could overcome them. In a way, this is the 'U' in super; I was able to 'Understand How To Achieve Success'. These eight skills need to be learnt, and unless we know how to learn them effectively, we will be wasting our time and effort."
"Stace, I've heard the word skills so many times. I've heard of them in sport, but I'm not sure if I understand what you mean here."
"Another good question. Skills are actions or activities that can be learnt, we can apply it to lots of things that we learn to do, as well as physical skills like in sport."
"Right, so if we can learn to do something it's a skill. I get it now."
"Good. Whatever the skill, we can only learn them with practice, and unfortunately, most of us have not had enough practice to learn the eight skills well enough. The 'P' is about applying this practice to ourselves, we need to 'Personalise our learning', so that we keep doing the right practice for us personally, in the skills we need to succeed."
"You mean we ain't spent enough time practising the skills we need and are rubbish at?"
"Yes, that's it. Practising these skills is not part of our everyday life and it really needs to be, if we are to develop them sufficiently. The 'E' in super is for 'Evaluating Your Learning', because on this journey to success we need to keep checking we are going in the right direction. This means we'll be continually assessing your development of the 8 skills and trying to ensure you are progressing towards your destination."
Scott was pleased that Stacey had used the term 'we', as he was struggling to understand this.
"Finally, the 'R' in super stands for 'Resources for effective learning' and this centre is really special for this one. JC's understanding of the science of learning has meant he has created a place where effective learning resources are available 24/7."
Scott reflected on what had been said for a few seconds before commenting.

"SUPERlearning seems like a good idea, I wish I'd known about before."
"I think you'll say that a lot, I know I did. Everyone in here tries to publicise it and hopefully the incredible success of almost everyone who comes here will encourage others to apply this success feelosophy approach. All the resources are free and available on the success feelosophy website and we try to mention it and SUPERlearning as much as possible. The interest in these centres has grown immensely recently and gradually I think more schools will be using and publicising it."
"My Head teacher was very interested in me coming here; she seemed to know lots about it and about JC also."
"Oh that's good; perhaps she can come here in a few months to see you and the centre. JC, and all of us, would like to see all secondary schools much more like these centres."
Scott felt very uncomfortable at the thought of his Head teacher coming to visit him, but still managed to respond.
"What's this about a website, Stace?"
"We can look at the website now, it's central to your learning."
Stacey sprang athletically from the armchair and sat gently in the chair next to Scott, his pulse accelerated slightly as he swivelled his chair alongside her to face the screen.
"OK Scott, log on."
Scott furtively scanned the machine, found and pressed the 'On/Off button'. Within seconds the huge 'Success Feelosophy' logo covered the screen, with two boxes at the centre, asking for his name and password.
"Do I use my full name, 'Scott Spicer' and what about my password?"
"Yes, Scott Spicer and choose your own password, it doesn't have to be complicated since we don't really have any incentive for hacking or privacy."
Scott completed his logging on, the screen became covered with small logos and Scott's eyes lit up.
"Blimey, there are a few things on here, aren't there?"
"This is the successfeelosophy website; your first task is to discover what's on it. You will be using this for the next six months."
"Er, It may take me six months to discover what's on it!"
Stacey smiled, pleased that Scott was now sufficiently relaxed to be witty.
"I'll give you an outline of the most relevant parts to you and how we'll be using it, and then give you a few hours to experiment or play with it."
Scott was already distracted with the website, but managed to hear what Stacey had just said.
"Okay, budge over and I'll explain."
Scott pushed his chair to one side and Stacey slotted hers into the gap so she could use the computer comfortably.
"If you click on this icon, a photo of you, Scott, you'll enter 'Scott's Journey to Success', where you'll find lots of stuff that relates to you, including the

SUPERlearning we've just been talking about. Here's the eight success skills shown like the poster above your head."
Stacey pointed at the wall above the screen, almost to the ceiling.

Successful people have learnt the skills they need to identify and overcome the difficulties they meet in life to achieve success and improve well being.

- **Effective Learning**
- **Communication**
- **Cognition (thinking)**
- **Self-awareness**
- **Managing Feelings**
- **Motivation**
- **Empathy**
- **Social/Relationship**

Stacey pulled open the top drawer of the desk and took out something that resembled a small version of the cuff used to measure blood pressures.
"Scott, you will find you this very useful. It's a wrist monitor; wear it whenever you leave the room."
"What's a wrist monitor?"
"If we look at the poster, you can see that successful people have developed their cognitive and self-awareness skills. They have learnt to avoid difficulties by planning and organising their lives, needing to be aware of the time and themselves more accurately. This wrist monitor will help you to learn to keep track of time, as well as your pulse and blood pressure and it provides reminders and warnings for you."
Scott suddenly realised that Stacey had been wearing one all the time.
"The Velcro means its easy to put on and take off, they are very robust so you can use them when doing physical activity, even swimming. As well as being a watch, it continually records your pulse and blood pressure, the data will be automatically transferred into your journey to success file. You are responsible for organising your time and this wrist monitor will help you with this, especially with the centre in use 24/7."

Scott enthusiastically put on his wrist monitor.
"It sounds very clever, I'm going to need it if I'm going to get organised. I can feel the cuff swelling, I suppose it's measuring my blood pressure and pulse."
"Yes, it will do this repeatedly and whenever it detects major changes."
"Stace, I've never been any good at keeping and organising my time. In fact, I don't usually wear a watch."
"When I came here I was the same, but this wrist monitor helped immensely. It is brilliant at reminding you of the time, it vibrates at key times and also makes a noise that you'll get used to hearing. You'll find it detects the times planned for you, when you have collaborative inquiry sessions and whatever you've planned."
Scott's eyebrows rose as he looked at Stacey in amazement, and shook his head gently.
"Stace, I don't understand. What about my lessons? When do I get taught?"
Stacey chuckled loudly.
"I've been waiting for this moment, Scott. We all have a similar response. We're so conditioned by the traditional school that we expect it to happen here. This centre does not have a timetable of teachers and classrooms, a structure introduced in Victorian times over a hundred years ago. They used that structure because they did not have access to the technology we now have, the teachers and lessons come to you when you want them, here. That's why this room is your personal study room as well as your bedroom."
Scott's contorted face reflected his confusion and Stacey smiled sympathetically.
"It took me about 3 or 4 days to adjust, but after that, with JC's help, I was able to do it fairly easily. I'll be mentoring you carefully at first, you'll soon get the hang of it and enjoy it as much as I did."
"I'll take your word for it, Stace. But It seems so weird at the moment. When do I sleep?"
"Whenever you like. These rooms can be made as dark as you like, so you can sleep anytime. Everything in the centre is available all the time but you have to book them in advance."
Scott's frown showed his continuing confusion.
"How do you book them in advance?"
"On your computer! Everything can be done through the successfeelosophy website. If you click on this icon that looks like a book, you can see the availability of the rooms."
The screen then showed a list of the various rooms that could be booked, swimming, cardiovascular, soccer, etc. with the word 'booked' written across some of them.
"What about these teachers and lessons that you say will come to me, how does that work?"
"You need to click on the 'Supersocrates' icon for that."

The curser moved on to an icon that had a cartoon of a superhero on it. When he clicked on it, the screen changed to show the same cartoon character but much larger surrounded by various icons labelled Maths, English, Science and a few others.
"I don't recognise that cartoon."
"I'm not surprised. He's 'Supersocrates', JC's own creation. He is your 'Superteacher'; he will help you with the Superlearning of your school subjects."
"Why is he called 'Supersocrates'?"
"Socrates is one of JC's heroes. He was a Greek philosopher who asked brilliant questions that helped people to learn much more effectively as a result. So JC thinks he is a good role model and uses this cartoon version to help everyone learn to succeed. Unfortunately, he upset lots of people and eventually he was put to death."
Scott looked puzzled but managed a smile at that.
"Right Scott, I'm going to leave you now, and I will return at 1700 hours, when we'll go for some food. I want you to put down any questions in this file shown with the question mark icon. We will be planning your journey to success and timetable when I return."
"When is 1700 hours, Stace?"
"If you look at your wrist monitor it only gives the time using the 24 hour clock, it's 14:54 now so I'll be back in about 2 hours, okay?"
"Okay, Stace. Thanks, I'll see you then, bye."
"Bye, Scott, enjoy your play on the website, try not to get too engrossed in any one thing, that's the usual problem, there's so much interesting stuff on it. See you".

Chapter 8
"10,000 hours of their life practising the skills."

"Is it okay for me to come in, Scott?"
Scott was startled by the knock on the door and Stacey's voice.
"Er, yeah Stace, come in."
Stacey walked in and saw Scott sitting at the computer, just where she'd left him.
"Time for some food, Scott."
Scott looked at his wrist monitor.
"Blimey Stace, I can't believe you've been gone two hours."
"That's a good sign, Scott, that's called 'Flow'."
"Flow? What's that?"
"Basically, when our brain focuses on activities that we are enjoying and concentrating deeply, we lose track of time and become more relaxed. In sport it's often called going 'into the zone' and it means they become much more

effective. It can also be achieved with meditation; it shows you are able to concentrate well when you are motivated."

"I've heard of going into the zone in sport but I ain't heard of flow before. There's so much fascinating stuff on here, Stace."

"I'm delighted you think so Scott, because it is central to your journey to success. We'll go for some food first and then come back to it."

Scott sprang up enthusiastically and followed Stacey out of the room towards the food hall.

"So how does this work, Stace?"

He asked as they walked briskly into the food hall.

"You put your thumb here, the screen will show your name when it's registered your account, much like a cash machine would with a credit card. Once that's occurred you choose your items, they're all electronically tagged and as you remove them it registers to your account. It's really simple."

"How much are you allowed to take or spend?"

"That's up to you, Scott. Everything you take is transferred to your personal monitoring system. It shows approximately your daily food and drink intake and allows you to keep measuring it and take responsibility for it. I can also discuss it with you to help identify any difficulties that you may need to overcome."

"So that means you can see my account, Stace?"

"Oh yes, Scott. It is very important that we work together on everything you do in here and this is just an example."

Scott felt uncomfortable for a moment, realising he was being closely watched again, but then he reflected on why he was in the centre and that it was Stacey who was helping him. His emotions then changed and began feeling 'warm inside' at the thought of Stacey being concerned and cared about him.

They chose their food and drink and carefully sat at one of the tables.

"Why are we the only ones here, Stace? You said there were about 100 students and over 20 staff here, and it's tea time, so I thought it would be quite crowded."

"Another thing you'll find very different here. Terms like 'lunchtime or tea time' have little meaning because everything is on a 24 hour timetable. Quite simply we learn to organise our eating and drinking to suit ourselves, along with everything else."

They both began eating and Stacey continued.

I noticed you spent quite a lot of time on the 'inspirational videos' and the 'Supersocrates' sections."

Scott looked up suddenly in surprise at what Stacey said.

"You can see what I do on the computer?"

"Of course, that's automatically stored on hard drives but in my study room, I have a screen for all the students I mentor, since I may discuss any of it with them."

Again Scott's thought about this and as before he reflected on the reasons he was here and felt comforted that Stacey trying to help him.
"I wondered what the inspirational videos might be, I hadn't heard of most of them."
"We use them, as you might expect, for videostudy to develop the eight skills. My favourites are 'It's A Wonderful Life' and 'A Christmas Carol', were there any that appealed to you."
"The Karate Kid has always been one of my favourites and I spotted that immediately."
"I like that and I think there's a lot in it that relates to both of us, we'll use that for some videostudy later."
They continued chatting, finished their food and returned to his room.
"So what's next then, Stace?"
Scott asked keenly as they entered his study room.
"We'll apply SUPERlearning to your journey to success, and start with the end in mind by sorting out clearly what success actually means for you and what you are actually aiming to achieve, your final destination."
Scott's enthusiasm was slightly dampened in trying to understand her reply.
""So what does that actually mean?"
As they both gently sat on the chairs at the table in front of the computer, Stacey pointed at the poster on the wall above the screen.

Successful people have learnt the skills they need to identify and overcome the difficulties they meet in life to achieve success and improve well being.

- **Effective Learning**
- **Communication**
- **Cognition (thinking)**
- **Self-awareness**
- **Managing Feelings**
- **Motivation**
- **Empathy**
- **Social/Relationship**

"Since we know that successful people have developed these 8 skills very well, your aim is the same as mine, to achieve good development in these skills. So we need to assess your starting point on this journey by discovering your development each of the 8 skills so far."

Scott looked at Stacey with a puzzled expression, and she continued.

"Consider if you wanted to become a brilliant footballer, you would need to know how much improvement you've got to make in each of the skills that make a top class footballer, wouldn't you?"

Using football to explain things always helped Scott and his face showed this made sense.

"Oh I see what you mean, now."

Stacey had a contented smile.

"Eighteen months ago, once Arthur had helped me become aware of why I had struggled so much and what I needed to do to succeed, I went through an evaluation of the 8 skills with my sister, Suzi, which was great in helping me assess myself accurately. I think we should do something similar for you, is that okay?"

Scott now had great trust in Stacey, he was confident she knew what she was doing and was able to really help him.

"Yeah, that's fine with me."

"Good. If we click on the 'Evaluation' icon, then it can be completed and stored in your personal file, Scott."

Scott moved the mouse and followed the instructions so that he had 'The Skills We Need To Succeed Evaluation' page on the screen in front of him. He studied it closely for a while before commenting.

"This looks fairly easy, we just have to put numbers in the boxes for each skill, don't we?".

Stacey's smile reflected her awareness that it was not quite that simple.

"Yes, that's the easy bit Scott, but the hard bit is trying to choose a number that accurately reflects your skill level. Each of the eight skills are divided into three parts. I've done a lot now, they've become much easier with practice and you'll soon find the same."

Scott was convinced and even appeared enthusiastic.

"Okay, let's go, I'm ready to start, Stace."

The Skills We Need To Succeed Evaluation

GRADES

10 –	**DEFINITELY/EXCELLENT-**	**IT OCCURS ALL OF THE TIME**
8 –	**VERY GOOD –**	**IT OCCURS MOST OF THE TIME**
6 –	**FAIRLY GOOD –**	**IT OCCURS SOME OF THE TIME**
4 –	**O.K.- -**	**IT OCCURS OCCASIONALLY**
2 –	**VERY WEAK -**	**IT OCCURS RARELY**
0 –	**NO –**	**IT DOES NOT OCCUR AT ALL**

Effective Learning	Grade
Comfortable with change and learning new things.	
Effective independent learner, who does not rely on someone to teach them.	
Readily practices to develop new skills.	

"This is very much about how effectively we learn and the first part, how easy you find learning new things, is how well you cope with new things, such as a new teacher, subject, book, class, classroom or even school. When I went to secondary school, I was very poor in this and just couldn't cope with the changes. I started rebelling straightaway and my problems began to grow immensely. I couldn't cope with having different teachers for each lesson and moving from one room to another."

Scott was nodding in agreement.

"Stace, I was completely the same. I think I was alright in junior school, well not too much trouble, but as soon as I got to secondary school, I kept getting into trouble all the time. I still hate having new teachers and changing classrooms or even moving where I sit in class."

"So what grade do you reckon you should have?"

"Hmmm, I see what you mean, this is trick. Possibly, a two?"

"Yes, 'two' seems about right. The next one is about how well you cope with learning on your own. We're born relying on people helping us to learn, usually our parents or brothers and sisters teaching us. But if we are to learn to succeed we've got manage to learn without people directly showing us or supporting us most of the time. Basically, as with walking, talking, listening, feeding, and so on, we should be able to do it on our own, independently, and use the resources around us."

Scott paused thoughtfully before responding.

"Stace. I've got two older sisters and an older brother; I suppose I've depended on them a lot."

"Of course, I forgot for a moment that you are the youngest of four and that could be a very important factor. Can I just borrow the mouse for a moment, please?"

Stacey clicked the mouse few times and suddenly this slide appeared on the screen.

"Have a look at this, Scott. I think you'll find it very helpful. For over 70 years there has been a lot of research into how our position in the family affects our learning and personality. Basically our 5 learning requirements are different, especially our motivation and environment. I only have a sister, Suzi, who is almost 10 years younger than me and I now know that I've had a huge influence on her learning. For you, your brother and sisters, Adam, Kate and Diane, will have had a big influence on your learning of the eight skills.

The Family Constellation – Birth Order

- Alfred Adler (1870-1937) suggested that birth order can have a large influence on personality.
- Birth order can develop our habitual way of dealing with friendship, love, work and life.
- Firstborns can feel "dethroned" when a second child arrives, having a lasting effect on them.
- Younger and only children may be pampered and spoiled, greatly affecting their personalities.
- These characteristics may not always apply but the relationships that the child forms within the family contribute greatly to his/her learning and personality development.

"This next one shows how you may have been influenced being the youngest child."

The Family Constellation – Birth Order

The Youngest Child may:-

- Become the most discouraged and feel inferior to the others.
- Get more attention from the family
- Get less parental pressure than siblings
- Have things done for them and punished less
- Retain the baby role, feeling like an only child
- Have most decisions made for them by others
- Become the "boss" in the family
- Not be taken seriously.

Scott had already been plunged into deep thought on seeing the first slide. This second one, focusing on the youngest child, seemed to have touched a nerve and his face reflected his feeling that it was describing him.
"I think virtually all that applies to me, Stace. Mum, Kate and Diane have always treated me like a little baby, even though my sisters are only about 5 or 6 years older than me, they wouldn't let me do anything. I've never been allowed to do anything on my own, they think I'm still only little, even though I'm nearly twice their size."
Scott's voice clearly had traces of anger in it.
"I thought you'd find this useful, most people do. So if return to the evaluation, how much do you think you rely on others to teach you?"
"If we are talking about any school work, then I'd say 'completely'. I don't think I do anything if the teacher ain't there."
"Unfortunately, you are very typical in this. The learning in most secondary schools still tends to be very teacher-led and dependent on them. You'll see that it is very different here, virtually all your learning will be not be led by you and only supported by others. As you've already seen, you will have Supersocrates and brilliant teaching resources to support you as well as me as your mentor. I can provide suggestions, advice and support, but I am not a teacher in the traditional sense."
Scott grinned confidently as though he understood.
"I do reckon I do some independent learning in sport, so I shall give myself a two here, Stace?"
"That's sounds fair, so what about this third one, Scott? 'Readily practices to develop new skills', what's your grade for that, do you reckon?"
"Well it probably depends on the skill I'm trying to learn, if it's to do with football, I'm prepared to practice for hours, otherwise I can't think of spending any time on them."
"When we're babies we can't do very much at all, but because we observe others and try to copy them we begin to learn to smile, grasp, walk, talk etc. through many hours of practice. The extensive research in recent years has shown that highly skilled performers in music, dance, sport and others, have usually spent about 10, 000 hours of their life practising the skills."
"10,000 hours of practice, that's hell of a lot!"
"Apparently the soccer skills room is an example of JC's creativity in which greatly reducing that for some soccer skills. I'm sure you'll look at that later. What you going to give yourself on this then Scott?"
"Two, Stace."
"Okay, Scott. I think that gives you a total of 6 out of a possible 30 for the Effective Learning Skill, about the same as me 18 months ago!"
"Stace, I already knew I was rubbish at learning but this has at least helped me understand why."

"And more importantly, Scott, it shows you what you need to improve, and if you are like me, you will be amazed at how much you can improve in this in the next six months."

Scott felt reassured by Stacey's confidence in him and her broad beautiful smile.

"Okay, Scott, I'm suggesting we stop here as I've booked the soccer skills room for you."

This comment really surprised and confused Scott.

"I hope that's alright, I thought you'd like to see what it's like."

Stacey's smile seemed to extend beyond her ears and Scott felt compelled to copy it.

"Very much, thanks Stace, you must've read my mind, I was wondering when I'd get a chance to go in there."

"I thought you might be. It's booked for an hour but if nobody arrives after that you can carry on. Your kit is in here."

Stacey leapt to her feet and prepared to open the door to the cupboard.

"Prepare to be amazed, here's your wardrobe for the next six months."

Stacey stood there for a few seconds to allow the excitement to build and then opened it.

"Voila!"

Scott stared and stared again, struggling to see anything. All he could see were some Success Feelosophy T shirts, track bottoms, shorts, socks, trainers, and towel.

Stacey laughed vigorously, and after a few seconds delay, so did Scott.

"Yes, that's it! I did say you won't need much while you're in here."

"You weren't joking either, were you."

"Anyway, enjoy yourself in the soccer skills room, I'll leave you now. I'm setting our alarms for 0830 and perhaps we'll go for breakfast at 9000, or 8:30 and 9 o'clock if you prefer, okay?"

"Thanks Stace, I really appreciate everything you've done for me, it's been a great day."

Scott showing appreciation or thanking people occurred about as often as Christmas and Stacey was very impressed with it.

"Been a pleasure, Scott, that's why we're here and why we do it, and hopefully one day you'll be mentoring others, goodnight."

Stacey gave Scott a gentle hug and a peck on the cheek and left. Scott fell back on to the bed and felt better than he could ever recall, better than if he'd scored the winning goal at Wembley. Then he realised he needed to get changed and sprung forward to rummage through his extensive wardrobe to put on the few clothes provided for him.

Chapter 9
"we'll call it 'SUPERpractice"

When Scott got to the first of the two soccer skills rooms, he was surprised to see there was an electronic sign next to the door which said 'Scott Spicer'. He stuck his thumb in the small indent under it, just as he had in the food hall and the door swung open as if he'd said 'open sesame'.

"Welcome Scott, please come in, I'm delighted you've chosen to use the soccer skills room."

Scott jumped momentarily in surprise, he recognised the deep voice, but the room had nobody in it.

"Yes Scott, it's me, JC. I'd like to introduce you to the soccer skills room and show you how SUPERlearning can be applied to it. However, before you start, could you take a bottle of water from the machine outside and drink as much as you can, you will need it."

Scott quickly recovered from his shock and did as he was asked. He walked in the room with the bottle and his mouth opened in amazement; it appeared as though he was walking on to the pitch in Wembley stadium.

"When I was a young boy growing up in the east end of London, I used to spend much of my time imagining I was playing in the great stadiums around the world while I was practising my skills. I've tried to create an environment that reflects much of what I was imagining and what I was practising. Many years ago there was a Science Fiction TV programme called 'Star Trek: The Next Generation' and on the spaceship they had a room called the holodeck. It was a virtual reality world in a room and it inspired me to try to create computer programs that could do a similar thing. You'll soon see that the program will interact with you and create environments and activities to help you practise your soccer skills. If you've played with computer games like Wii or Kinect, you will already be aware of some of the technology in use here."

Scott was now in the centre of the room, though he felt he was in the centre circle of Wembley, he just kept turning around on the spot with his mouth still open trying to accept what was going on and where he was. Scott looked up at the sky or actually the ceiling which was the height of a gym, then bent down to touch the artificial turf beneath his feet.

As if he was being watched, JC's voice continued.

"The floor is like a crown green bowling green, in that it has a slight curve towards the corners, this allows the balls to leave the field. At various heights in the walls near the corners there are various holes where the footballs come from at different speeds, directions and trajectories. Behind the walls is a mechanism controlled by the computer program, of course, that will propel these balls towards you, and you will be expected to control, kick, head or shoot as required. The balls will then roll into the corners so you just focus on practising the skill."

Scott stared at the corners and could barely see the holes in the wall through the image of the crowd in the stadium.
"The computer program is voice sensitive but it will be largely based on the most effective and common process in sport called 'Assessment for Learning'. As usual in sport, you are being continually assessed and it will move you on to the next level or activity when it decides you have learnt the previous one. You might realise that this is actually the 'E' in SUPERlearning – evaluate your learning repeatedly, so you don't waste time on things you've already learnt. Place the bottle in one the racks for them on the wall and return to the centre of the room, please."
Scott again did as he was asked then suddenly a ball flew upwards out of the corner to his left and landed almost at his feet. Although Scott was caught by surprise, his very quick reactions helped him to adjust his body and trap the ball instantly.
"Good. Pick the ball up and study it, please."
Scott was again surprised that JC's voice responded to his actions, but bent down as requested, to pick up the ball and thought 'how did he know I trapped it?'
As if he'd read his mind, JC's voice continued.
"No, I'm not actually watching you, but as with the motion sensing video games such as Kinect and Wii, it activates a response, if you had failed to trap it, then my response would've been, 'Hard Luck, have another go', and another ball would've landed near your feet."
Scott had been very impressed immediately, and the more he discovered the more impressed and excited he became. He now realised that he was hearing in a virtual world and basically part of a soccer video game.
"If you are already aware and understand SUPERlearning, you may realise that basically, I've applied SUPERlearning to soccer skills in this room. The extensive scientific research into expertise in various sporting, artistic, musical, craft skills and others usually requires close to 10,000 hours of practice. However, those thousands of hours of practice is usually being carried out in a very ineffective way. By applying SUPERlearning to these skills, we can reduce this time drastically, creating what the psychologist Anders Ericsson calls 'deliberate practice' and others refer to as 'purposeful practice'. In fact, I have found that just hundreds of hours of practice using SUPERlearning, we'll call it 'SUPERpractice', can develop people into experts in these skill areas."
Scott suddenly jumped back in fright as the wall in front of him changed to show this slide across it.

SUPERlearning For Soccer Success

S	**START WITH THE END IN MIND**– you must START by being clear on the skills that need to be learnt to be an expert in soccer (top level)
U	**UNDERSTAND HOW TO ACHIEVE SUCCESS** – you must be sure you understand what the skills are and how they can be learnt EFFECTIVELY
P	**PERSONALISE THE LEARNING** –you need to apply the techniques that ensures YOU learn YOUR weak skills MOST EFFECTIVELY.
E	**EVALUATE THE LEARNING** – you must keep checking that you progress on to the next step as soon as possible, to avoid wasting time.
R	**RESOURCES FOR EFFECTIVE LEARNING** – you only use resources that focus on learning YOUR weak skills MOST EFFECTIVELY

L E A R N I N G

Scott pulse had quickened and as he recovered he began studying the slide.
"The football is smaller than normal to develop skills more effectively, made of a compound that means it is very durable and responds like a normal football. The motion sensors can detect its flight, contact with you and the walls to accurately assess the outcome, so your learning is being continually evaluated. Remember that the program is also voice sensitive so you can ask questions and respond to your needs. It may ignore you or tell you something to explain why it is doing something different. You can also use the computer in your room to sort out difficulties or explain what it wants you to do. Are you ready to start?"
The SUPERlearning slide disappeared and the image of Wembley re-appeared.
"Your first SUPERpractice is ball control. Balls will be delivered to you from the corners from various heights, different angles and force, increasing in difficulty over a period of time depending on how well you control it. As you progress, you will be told what the next step is, what you need to do to progress, and shown what to do."
The wall in front of Scott changed to show a picture of a footballer, that he recognised to be JC learner.
"Throughout the SUPERpractice, an avatar of me will show you what to do and how to do it. The avatar merely represents what I did when I was teaching football in P.E. in school many years ago, which helped to inspire this program.

It will show you what to do in very careful detail, explaining the science behind it, so you understand why it works. Where possible, if the motion sensors can detect a repeated error, the avatar will try to identify it and how to correct it, basically as I tried to do when teaching or coaching soccer skills over the years."

Scott watched the avatar of JC control a ball rolling quickly along the floor and heard his voice explaining what to do, while seeing him do it in slow motion and broken down into steps.

"Okay, that's the demonstration over, now it's your chance. The balls will roll at you in increasing speeds and you've got to try to control it as shown in the demonstration, as quickly as you can."

Suddenly a ball rolled out the corner and Scott did as he was asked, then another from the opposite corner, and so on, over and over again. This process continued with a variety of types of ball control being demonstrated by the avatar and attempted by Scott. Scott, soaked in sweat heard JC's voice say.

"Scott, your time is up."

This really surprised Scott and he instantly looked at his wrist monitor. He'd been in there for almost an hour, yet it had seemed like 10 minutes to him. He was so disappointed that it was over and then thought of Stacey's comment about 'flow' and clearly he'd been enjoying it immensely. JC's voice then interrupted his thoughts.

"There is no booking for the next session, you may continue if you wish, You need to get another drink and place your thumb in the indent as before."

Scott felt elated, punching the air in delight. He immediately did just as he was asked and continued.

"Scott, your time is up."

This was the third time Scott had heard JC's voice say that, but this time it added another line.

"Three consecutive hour sessions is the maximum; you need a break now and a shower."

Scott realised he'd been in the soccer skills room for three hours, though it certainly didn't feel like it, as he'd enjoyed it so much. He left the room buzzing with excitement despite his tiredness, walked to his room, dripping with sweat, collected his towel and went to the toilet and shower cubicles.

Throughout this journey he passed about five young people, all of whom greeted him pleasantly with a 'Hi' or something similar and being so elated he actually managed to respond in a similar way, despite it being so difficult for him. When he returned to his room after his shower, he looked at his wrist monitor again and realised the time was almost 0100 hours or 1am, as he still thought of it. However, there had been nothing to indicate that it was the early hours of the morning. He was now beginning to understand why Stacey and others had emphasised that the centre operated 24/7 and described it as a holiday camp.

Scott lay in his bed thinking about his first day in the centre and felt an emotion he could not recall having had before and so difficult to grasp. He'd experienced many drugs and lots of alcohol on numerous occasions but nothing compared to this, and started wonder why he felt so good, is this magic, spiritual or what?

Chapter 10
"the magic does seem to have begun to work on you"

"What's that?"
Scott had a strange feeling in his wrist, it was a vibration, stopping and starting, getting gradually stronger. He'd actually got into his bed for the first after his shower and slept very soundly. This alarm from his wrist monitor had surprised him as he hadn't actually set it. As he began to regain his senses he looked at his wrist monitor and saw it flashing. He sat up in his bed and saw the time on the large TV screen on the wall.
"Scott, can I come in?"
Stacey was knocking on Scott's door and her melodic voice helped wake him up. He was actually still lying in his bed in almost the same position as he had been when he went to sleep.
"Er yes, Stace, come in."
Stacey entered the room and Scott was sat up briskly in his bed.
"Did you sleep well? You look as though you did." Are you okay to go for breakfast?"
"Er yeah, I think so. I'll need to go to the toilets on the way."
"Yes, of course. Do you want a shower as well? Your towel is still on your bed, it seems quite damp."
"No, I had one just before I went to bed. I'll just have a pee, a quick wash and clean my teeth, okay?"
"Of course, that's fine. I'll meet you in the food hall."
"Okay, Stace."
Stacey promptly left the room and Scott moved to sit on the side of the bed, reflecting on the previous day, and as with the visit of Arthur, contemplating if it was a dream. But this time he had evidence it was real, since he was sitting in the same room as he had been in the day before. He picked up the towel from his bed and opened his little bag, took out his wash bag and set off for the wash room and toilets.
As he walked along the corridor he saw a boy travelling towards him. He looked about 12 years old and as he approached, he stared at Scott, as usual this made him feel uncomfortable and a little threatened despite the relatively small size of the boy. Suddenly the boy spoke.
"Good morning, at least I think it's morning, you're never quite sure in this place."

Scott was still being surprised by the friendliness of everyone and again Scott failed to reply. However, the boy continued to smile as he went by as though he understood Scott's rudeness. Scott felt annoyed that he hadn't replied as he carried on to the toilet and shower cubicles. He tentatively pushed the door to the wet room containing a toilet, wash basin and shower he'd used only a few hours earlier and carefully went in.

When Scott entered the food hall, Stacey was just finishing her breakfast, and chatting to a young girl, who looked about 16 years old, with bright red hair sitting next to her. Scott got some breakfast from the machines and sat down next to them Stacey.

"Scott, this is Beth, Beth this is Scott."

Beth held out her hand.

"Pleased to meet you, Scott. Stacey tells me you've just joined us, I hope you like it, I think it's brilliant and I'm sad I've got to leave soon. What do you think?"

Scott looked at Beth very quickly and looked down towards his food, he immediately felt Stacey touch his hand and glanced at her. Stacey just looked at him, Scott realised she was prompting him and managed to look at her and respond.

"Er, I think it's amazing."

"I just wish all schools were like this, I'm sure I wouldn't have had my problems if any of the schools I was sent to were like it."

Scott had forgotten that all the students in the centre had struggled in the outside world and his eyebrows rose to show his surprise.

"Anyway, I'm pleased to have met you and I hope we meet again before I leave. See you Stace, I've got to go, I've got a swimming room booked."

Beth got up, carefully collecting her utensils and then placed them in the correct container as she left the food hall.

"Scott, are you aware that you rarely look people in the eyes?"

"Er no, Stace. I've not thought about it, don't I?"

"We'll do some videostudy later on to illustrate this, I thought you weren't aware and it makes such an impression people. Making the right amount of eye contact is not easy but is so important to how they view us."

Scott's attraction and respect for Stacey meant any praise or criticism from her had a big effect and he was now very aware that she was very keen to help. He felt a little embarrassed but he had a question for Stacey that he was keen to ask that might deflect from this.

"People seem so friendly here, Stace, why is that? I thought this place was for people like me and you who have had and caused lots of problems, yet everyone seems so pleasant."

"Well done, Scott, excellent observation. Remember that the 'E' in SUPERlearning is for environment and JC was very aware that is crucial to have a positive environment in these centres. The centre aims to be a 'Learning Organisation', with everyone being encouraged to be involved in overcoming any difficulties. We are encouraged to feel we're all helping each other learn, its called 'Team Learning' and we try to act as positive 'role models'. Once we become aware that we all need to try to make the centre a very pleasant place to be, we feel part of a team and learning becomes a pleasure, so we want to be here and feel happy."

Scott looked at Stacey in utter amazement, observing such passion that was almost religious in its nature.

"Trying to develop your self-awareness skill so that you feel this way is a very high priority and I hope that you will reach that level of development within the next two days."

Scott had already begun to experience feelings he'd never had before and commented.

"I've only been here a day, but I have already felt strange, strange in a good way."

"I thought you might. When you've finished your breakfast we'll carry on with your journey to success."

"Good."

"As well as continuing with your evaluation of the eight skills, I need to help you with your organisation and planning."

"Why?"

"As well as having a positive environment, you also have lots of freedom and responsibility in the centre, but it requires you to organise and plan your time carefully. In the first few days, I will try to help you establish your routine and start to develop good habits. Can you remember you first few weeks at secondary school, I can. I just couldn't cope with the timetable and I couldn't get organised at all, I kept forgetting things and was so confused I gave up. It is crucial that your cognitive skills develop so that you become organised as quickly as possible. You'll find your wrist monitor and computer helps with this."

"It already has, Stace, it's very clever."

"There are so many things in here that you could describe like that, Scott."

"Especially, the soccer skills room. I don't even know how to describe that, except that it is absolutely brilliant, such a clever computer game or something."

"I was confident you'd feel that way."

"Well, I'm about finished my breakfast now and ready to start."

"Excellent, keen to start, that's a good sign. Okay, let's go."

They got up together, returned their utensils and continued chatting as they went to Scott's room, where they sat in the same positions as they had the previous day.

Stacey began by pointing to the wall above the top of Scott's bed.

"Look at that poster, Scott, it sums up what I was saying earlier about the importance of organisation and preparation."

Success depends upon previous preparation, and without such preparation there is sure to be failure.

Confucius

Scott stared at the poster and replied.
"Confucius? What's that?"
"It's actually an ancient Chinese philosopher; you'll see lots of quotes from lots of people while you are in here."
"What's strange Stace, is that I actually feel excited about what we are going to do. I thought I'd be scared or worried and not want to do anything."
"That's really good to hear, Scott, perhaps the magic of the centre is already beginning to work on you."
"You may be right, because when I fell asleep last night, I felt really weird, not like I'd ever done before. It was a strange sort of happiness, I suppose."
"Contentment, Scott. Yes, the magic does seem to have begun to work on you. Let's see if we can continue it. We'll start by doing a bit more of the evaluation of the skills needed to succeed."
"Okay, I'll see if I can find it on the computer."
Scott moved and clicked the mouse several times.
"There it is. The next skill is 'Communication."
The computer screen changed to show this skill.

Communication	Grade
Concentrates intently despite distraction.	
Verbal skills (speaking, listening, reading, writing)	
Non-verbal skills (visual gestures, body language, touch)	

Stacey waited patiently for Scott to study it, closely observing his face for signs of understanding and confusion, eventually she spoke.
"I think this can be quite tricky, because each one seems so different. Let's first consider 'concentration', we are born very poor at concentration, but appear to be attracted to people's faces. We can then learn to focus more deeply on various things, for increasing lengths of times, providing we have lots of learning opportunities with people when we are babies. What about you, Scott? When you are in class, or at home, are you able to ignore the distractions of

sounds and people around you, to keep concentrating on the tasks you are doing?"

"Definitely not in class, Stace. I can't really concentrate at all with my class mates around me."

"Unfortunately, lots of kids are like you and me in class, Scott. For teenagers especially, concentrating in class is a huge problem and vast numbers of students like us find it almost impossible to learn in many lessons because there are people around. What about at home, Scott? Are you able to concentrate on things there like homework, television or computers?"

"If I'm watching something I really like, or playing my favourite computer games, I can probably keep concentrating for hours."

"That's important Scott. You've illustrated how important both motivation and the type of activity, are to your ability to concentrate because it shows you can do it sometimes. Since you are capable of doing this in other areas, it will be a question of getting you motivated, but that is the first and most important learning requirement, of course, anyway."

Scott actually had a slight smile.

"I reckon, I can give myself a grade 4 here, Stace. I am able to concentrate despite distraction occasionally, clearly when I'm motivated, but usually in sport. Yesterday, I was in the soccer skills room for three hours, but I concentrated so much that it flew by. That's what you called 'flow', wasn't it, Stace?"

Stacey was smiling and nodded in agreement.

"Yes it is and three hours is impressive. What a good start. The next one is 'verbal skills', and I can introduce you to a bit of videostudy for this, Scott. We've put together a few clips of you in the centre yesterday."

Scott looked at Stacey in surprise.

"What do you mean, Stace?"

"As I said earlier, we have video cameras placed throughout the centre, mainly to help us study what we do and why we do it. The reality TV shows using this approach have become very common and that's what we have here."

Suddenly on the screen, there was a clip of Stacey and Scott entering the centre and approaching the reception desk, with Angela the receptionist, sitting at the computer screen. The picture froze.

"Before we watch the next bit Scott, I want you to look at yourself closely and listen carefully, and tell me what you notice, please."

The video continued and Scott could hear the greeting between Stacey and Angela, then heard Angela speak to him.

"Nice to meet you Scott, I hope you enjoy your stay and find it extremely helpful"

"Er, thanks." Scott replied.

The video was then paused and Stacey looked blankly at Scott waiting for him to respond.

"I don't think I actually looked at Angela, and I couldn't hear what I said to her very well."

"Well spotted, Scott. Using videostudy in this way is so helpful, we can actually study what we do and learn from it. I've found this process absolutely brilliant! I've spent hours studying what I do in lots of situations and it's helped me so much. JC points out that we've been using this technique in sport and drama for decades, yet only recently started using it in other areas. We'll see a few more clips of you and I want you to study where you look when you meet people and how you speak to them."

The video continued for a few minutes, showing Scott meeting various people in the centre on his first day. Scott studied himself closely as requested and replied.

"I almost never look at people's faces; I always seem to be looking down. When I speak, I mumble and I can't hear what I say, but I don't say much."

"Well done, Scott, good observation. What were you actually thinking and feeling when you first saw Angela, Scott?"

Scott looked at Stacey, who was studying his face, and he could feel himself getting hot and his face going red, but he didn't, or perhaps couldn't speak. Stacey observed this and continued.

"When you first saw Angela, you stared at her boobs, in fact, you struggled to look her in the eye as you point out. I was a very young teenager when I first realised that most boys and men would probably look at my boobs a great deal, and I dressed to use them to attract boys as much as possible. However, it was not until I came in here that I learnt to study people's verbal and non-verbal skills, especially their eyes and body language, did I realise how men and boys were actually thinking and feeling."

Scott was clearly fascinated by what Stacey was saying, and she carried on.

"From what I've learnt about you so far, it seems you do not find it easy to talk to people apart from those you know very well. You seem particularly uncomfortable with girls and boys of a similar age to you. I think, when you first saw Angela, you were 'checking her out', and decided she was very attractive and felt uncomfortable. You can see you are 'hot and bothered', with a red face, if you look carefully at the screen, when you met Angela."

Scott did as he was asked, then looked at Stacey, desperately trying to say something, but unable to do so.

"There is now a lot of research evidence to explain that when our ability to detect non-verbal communication has been well developed, we can interpret lots of thoughts and emotions at first sight. I've been very aware that since we first met again a few days ago, you've been kind of embarrassed with me most of the time."

Scott's temperature seemed to soar and glow bright red.

"You are now a 15 year old boy and I am a 21 year old girl. Your body language, facial expressions and eyes tell me that you find me attractive.

Unfortunately because your poor development of several of the 8 success skills you lack are 'shy' with girls."
Scott was really surprised by how perceptive and accurate Stacey had been about him. He was unaware that his thoughts and feelings were being so clearly displayed in this way and began to feel more relaxed with Stacey's analysis and understanding. She waited patiently for him to reply and he finally managed it.
"I'm gob smacked, Stace, you've been 'spot on'. I just don't feel comfortable with girls and the more attractive I find them; the more uncomfortable I seem to get. Even though I've known you for years, when I saw you the other day for the first time in years, I just couldn't speak. Why am I like this?"
"Once you get the hang of thinking about everything in terms of learning of the 8 success skills, you will begin to understand that you just haven't had the learning opportunities to develop these skills, and it has had a huge effect on your confidence, self esteem and social skills."
"I do hope so, Stace. Watching those video clips has shown me how poor I am. Obviously my grade for verbal and non-verbal skills should be very low, one for each?"
"Yeah, I suppose that seems about right."
"So overall, that means my grade for communication skills is 4 + 1 + 1, 6 out 30, not very good is it?"
"Again, almost the same as I had 18 months ago, Scott!"

Chapter 11
"These skills have often been called commonsense"

"So before you came here Stace, your grades on this evaluation were as poor as mine?"
"Yes, Scott."
"That's amazing Stace, you seem so confident and clever now."
"That's very kind of you to say so, Scott, but I was probably worse than you when I came here 18 months ago, and I was 19 at the time."
Scott's glare at Stacey was filled with amazement and admiration, as she moved the computer mouse and the screen changed again to show this table.

Cognitive	Grade
Understands 'cause and effect' and detects the key information or factors needed to make the decisions (Analytical thinking)	
Puts information into context so is able to understand and relate the information to the particular situation. (Conceptual thinking)	
Able to realise the likely outcomes or consequences of decisions.	

"That really is hard to believe. But if you've made so much progress perhaps I can improve, then. Okay, what's this next one, 'Cognitive Skills', what the ..... are they?"

"That's it, well done, Scott, you can stop yourself swearing. There's an improvement. It means you're developing your self-awareness and managing feelings skills."
Scott felt really chuffed, getting praise from Stacey meant so much and it was so well timed. Stacey smiled hugely and answered his earlier question.
"Cognitive skills are the ones we use to solve problems and make decisions. They are still often called 'intelligence', by lots of people. The first intelligence tests introduced over 100 years ago, actually tried to assess these skills, they became known as I.Q. tests. They tended to rely a lot on upon understanding words, numbers and symbols. In this country, all children used to take exams at the end of primary school called the 'eleven plus' which were thought to test these skills. The kids who got a high enough score were said to 'have passed the 11+' and sent to secondary schools called 'Grammar Schools'. These schools were like the traditional private or public schools that mainly concentrated on getting students to pass exams. It was thought at the time that only the kids who passed the 11+ were intelligent and capable of important jobs or doing well in life."
Scott was fascinated listening to Stacey, his confidence in her growing all the time.
"But that's what schools do now! They still only worry about getting kids to pass exams, Stace!"
"Perhaps we should look at a short video on the website, I think it will help."
Stacey moved the mouse to the 'Schools' section on the successfeelosophy.com website and then the videos on classic schools. A video looking at UK schools throughout the 20th century. Scott was fascinated by it and made various comments, when it finished he asked.
"That's amazing, Stace. I had no idea our schools are virtually just like they were a hundred years ago, why is that?"
"Throughout the last century schools gradually began to feel they were judged on their students' exam results. The governments, media and parents seemed to think that good schools were the ones that had the better exam results. Eventually virtually all secondary schools focused mainly on exam success."
"That's partly why I hate school, I'm not very good at exams and that's all that seemed to matter to them."
"Well, Scott, I reckon that by the time you leave here you will be much better at exams. I already know you are better at exams than I was when I came here and I can't believe how much I've improved. SUPERlearning is brilliant at helping you to succeed in exams."
"I certainly hope so, Stace. I don't think I'm going to score very well on this skill either. What's this first bit about?"
Stacey paused for a moment before answering.
"We are born relying on others to solve our problems, usually our parents at first. With lots of learning opportunities to observe, explore, play and

experiment, we can gradually learn to understand our world. Hopefully we can learn to discover what things have the biggest effect and how to make good decisions."

"I certainly don't think I've made many good decisions." Scott observed, but Stacey continued.

"We need to develop scientific or analytical thinking, which is why it was originally referred to as 'intelligence or being clever'. Maths and Science in schools are supposed to help to develop this, but written exams are very limited in assessing these skills."

"But how do I know how good I am at it, Stace? I'm certainly not very good at maths and science tests."

"That is a very good question, Scott, and there has been a lack of assessment of this in real life, everyday situations. When I was a young teenager I began drinking alcohol, but I did not really understand how it would affect me. Sometimes, I got very drunk very quickly, sometimes I was sick, sometimes it hardly seemed to have any effect, sometimes I had a hangover, sometimes I didn't and I never understood why. Basically, if we can understand WHY something has happened then you probably have good analytical skills, but if you are struggling to work out why things keep happening to you, then you probably have quite poor them."

"Mmmm, that helps a lot, Stace. Sometimes I have been able to work out why things have happened and realised that it was because of a particular decision. But most of the time I ain't got a clue, so I suppose I could give myself a score of 4 here."

Scott inserted his score in the grade column.

"Okay Scott, that sounds good and what about this next one, 'conceptual thinking'. This is being able to step back and see the 'big picture', to understand how the various factors join together to cause the final outcome. With my 'binge drinking', I may not have really understood the effects of alcohol very well but I think I realised that I was doing it because I was with my mates, I wanted to be part of the group and couldn't have fun unless I was drunk. Unfortunately, I didn't understand that this was because I had poor self-awareness, causing low self esteem, and this determined much of what I did at the time. Unfortunately, I couldn't see how each of the factors seemed go together to get me into trouble."

Scott's face lit up as if this understanding had hit him like a stone.

"That's me, Stace! Things just seem to happen and then I was in trouble. I start out doing something that is just 'larking about' and then it all seems to have 'gone off' or worse still I've just 'lost it', and doing things that I never intended to. I usually end up involved in fights or committing some violence."

"So what grade for this one then, Scott?"

"I suppose a two would be about right."

"Okay. You've probably realised I had similar difficulties and we may be able to grade the next one more easily. This one says 'Able to realise the likely outcomes or consequences of decisions'. I think we've worked out that neither of us as teenagers were very good at this. I continually thought, 'it won't happen to me'. Unfortunately, if I had understood 'statistics and probabilities' much better I could've been aware that 'it probably will happen to me'. I would've realised that if I kept 'binge drinking' it was likely that some disaster would occur and as I became very sexually active, I was likely to catch STIs and become pregnant."

Scott was very surprised to hear this and his face reflected his astonishment, but helped him again realise that Stacey really empathised with him, strengthening his trust in her.

"I've been 'binge drinking' for years and I can't believe that until now I've never thought that almost certainly I would get into a fight or become violent. Obviously my ability to see outcomes as it says here must be rubbish."

"Mine was also, Scott."

"I reckon, I can give myself 2 at most here then. Stace. This gives me a total of 8 out of 30 in this 'Cognitive Skills' section."

Stacey nodded gently and commented.

"These skills have often been called commonsense or good decision making, and I definitely didn't have that as a teenager. When you were looking at the stuff on the successfeelosophy website, did you see in the inspirational films section 'Good Will Hunting' or 'Homeless To Harvard'?"

"I don't remember seeing them, why?"

"They are a couple of good examples where people have had very good cognitive skills, so they may have been called clever, but because they were weak in some of the other 8 skills, they struggled to cope. I think you'll enjoy them. But now we'll focus on getting you organised, I found this quite difficult when I first came here; it took me a few days to get the hang of it."

"So what have I got to do, Stace?"

"Follow these instructions."

Scott sat up, ready for action.

"Click on your photo icon, this means you enter 'Scott's Journey to Success'. Then you open up your timetable. Now you can see I've put in some of the collaborative action inquiry sessions already, and the rest of the timetable is just waiting to be filled. Those group sessions are when you meet with other people, apart from them, the only other person that you have to organise meeting is me."

"It looks as though I have one or two of those collaborative sessions each day?"

"Certainly, for your first few days, Scott. Once you've got into a routine you'll be able to be more flexible. As I explained these CAI sessions are where you'll have the learning opportunity to develop the 8 skills in a social setting. Most of the them will involve videostudy, where you will be discussing various video clips, sometimes in subjects like English, Maths and Science, but also from films, TV programmes or even from our own CCTV. These are really effective learning sessions, as you have a chance to listen and reflect on things, and share it with others, but also you will be doing some MC Jigsaw puzzles and playing with Quizcards."

"What are MC Jigsaw puzzles and Quizcards?"

Stacey had expected that question and smiled broadly.

"I'll show you later, but like videostudy, I think they are a really brilliant way of learning. But first I need to ensure you know what to do in order to fill up your timetable, so you can continue your journey to success."

"So what do we do first then, Stace?"

"Each of the collaborative inquiry sessions, we call them CAI, nothing like CSI; they're nothing like crime scenes."

Stacey smiled and looked at Scott, who was puzzled at first, then spotted the joke and smiled.

"Anyway, these sessions have a specific focus which you will see on your timetable. You can see your first one is at 1800 today, a videostudy on films, 'Good Will Hunting' and 'Homeless To Harvard: The Liz Murray Story'. This means you will need to have watched them before you go into the session, otherwise you'll probably feel very embarrassed or like a complete idiot. You've already mentioned that you've looked in the 'inspirational films' section and when you click on the film, there will be a few questions to consider when you are watching the films. When you are in the CAI session you will have a chance to look at a few clips from the film together and discuss these questions together, and that's collaborative inquiry."

"So my homework is to watch the films and think about the questions, that don't seem to hard."

"I'm glad you said that, Scott. One of the aims here is to try to get everyone to not think of learning as work. That's why you will see that poster all over the place."

Stacey pointed at the wall above the top of the bed.

WORK is any activity that you NEED to do, but don't WANT to –
If you enjoy the activity it is no longer WORK!

J C Learner

"Mmmm, that's clever; I suppose that's true, that's quite good."
So Scott, you need to watch these films and think about the questions while you do, but I don't think it will be unpleasant and I reckon you'll enjoy it, so it won't be work, will it?"
"No I s'pose not."
"You may recall, I described this place as being 'magical', partly because it changes a school into a holiday camp or a health centre or something like that, and it also seems to transform people."
"I've only been here 24 hours and already I can see what you mean. It does seem at times as though there's some sort of spell in here."
"Now I'd better show you how to book the soccer skills, cardiovascular training, swimming rooms etc."
"Yes please." Scott said enthusiastically.
"At the moment, you can book a one hour session, in two different rooms in a 24 hour period. Once you've been here a few days and shown you are organised, with a balanced routine, and progressing along your journey to success, you can increase your times if they are available. Remember, it is all controlled by a program centrally, so it will keep you informed of you options."
"Sounds amazing, so is that why it won't let me book the soccer skills room until after the Good Will Hunting and Liz Murray Videostudy session?"
"That's it, Scott. The program has built in priorities, so it only allows certain choices at specific times. It aims to help you sort out your priorities, and of course, I'm here to support you in a similar way, when required."
"Right, I can see that, so I can fit the soccer skills in there, and a cardiovascular training session there. It looks as though most of my first day has been filled now."
"Remember, although you can only book a one hour session in the soccer skills room, you can stay in there up to three hours, if it is not booked after you."
"Yes, that happened yesterday."
"I know, Scott. You can choose when you want to sleep, set aside about 8 hours for that, but you can see all the rooms are available 24/7 and the CAI sessions go from 0900 to 2000. I found that because life in the centre is fairly simple, you only have a few things to think about, but also it is essential to plan. What it did for me, and hopefully you, is help me develop my cognitive skills to think ahead, prioritise and organise each day. The wrist monitor automatically downloads your timetable when you are organising it, and reminds you with that vibrating sensation at key times, so you don't forget stuff. When I left here after six months my skills had improved so much that organising and planning had become almost a habit of and it has clearly helped me overcome lots of the difficulties I used to have."

Chapter 12
"I feel as high as a kite, but I've taken nothing."

"So Scott, you know what you are doing for most of today until 2000 hours, or 8pm in 'old money', after that you can book the soccer skills room or the others, they seem to be available."
"So I can book the soccer skills room for 2000 hours, but it's not booked for 2100 hours, so hopefully I'll be able to stay in there."
"I often spend two hours in the cardiovascular and martial arts rooms."
"I can see why you describe it as a holiday camp or health centre, Stace."
"I'm off to see some of the other students that I mentor now, Scott. You've got some videostudying to do. I will also be in the CAI session at 1800 hours, so if you like, we could go for some food before that, at about 1730 hours. Shall I come for you then?"
"Yes please, Stace, thanks."
"You'll also see I've booked for us to meet at 0900 hours tomorrow, so we can continue this assessment, we'll do the same as today and go for some food first. I think you've made some good progress today, Scott. You not only said 'thanks', which you didn't until you came here, but throughout our conversations this morning you've looked me in the eyes most of the time, an important step and you've only been here 24 hours, well done."
Scott felt proud but embarrassed, but did comment.
"Perhaps the magic of the centre is working on me already?"
Stacey chuckled.
"Yeah, you could be right. Okay, see you just after 1700 hours, Scott."
Stacey leapt up athletically and promptly left the room, with Scott feeling a slight lump in his throat in response to the praise from Stacey. He was not used to being praised, and from Stacey it was extra-special.
"Right, let's get this 'show on the road' and begin Scott's Journey To Success."
Scott began talking to himself as usual, as he was now alone.
"Good Will Hunting Videostudy is first."
He adjusted his position in his chair, operated the mouse, the screen showed the following slide, which Scott studied carefully.

Good Will Hunting Videostudy

This superb, Oscar winning film from 1997 is an excellent example of Success Feelosophy, focusing on Will Hunting, who despite a children's home background become a 'Maths Genius'. The film illustrates that:
"Successful people have learnt the 8 skills needed to identify and overcome the difficulties they meet to achieve success and happiness"

While you are watching the film, consider the following questions:
1. Which of the 8 skills do you think Will Hunting had developed very well and which does he need to overcome to succeed?

2. What do you think are the key factors that caused Will to develop the skills to overcome his difficulties and WHO was vital in helping him to do so?

"Right so while I'm watching the film, I've got to keep thinking about the 8 skills, and the main character, Will Hunting, which ones he was good and bad at, how he learnt them and who helped him. Okay, let's go."
Scott moved to the more comfortable chair, clicked the mouse and started watching the film.
The film was broken down into 15 minute sections, and the slide reappeared each time, helping him to keep thinking about the questions. He even made a few notes on the computer, something he would never have done at school.
Towards the end of the film, Scott began crying, which he would never have done this if anyone was with him. The scene that really 'got to him' was when the psychiatrist Sean, who became Will's mentor, like Stacey was to him, kept saying to Will, ''It's not your fault, It's not your fault', repeatedly, until Will cried. Scott was cried almost as much as Will Hunting, he kept thinking how much he was like Will, how they both kept their feelings 'bottled up', and how this anger kept coming out as in such a violent way.
Throughout the film he just kept saying 'That's me', he even felt that the girl in the film, 'Skylar' played by Minnie Driver, looked a lot like Stacey, which made him even more emotional.
Scott had not cried like that for years, possibly ever!
"Brilliant, absolutely brilliant!"
He commented when the film finished.
"Right time for a pee and a drink and then the next one."

When he returned he continued his self-talk.
"Right, what's this next one called? Here it is, Homeless To Harvard: The Liz Murray Story."

Homeless to Harvard: The Liz Murray Story Videostudy

"This film shows the true story of Liz Murray - who managed to develop the 8 skills we need to succeed despite little support from her parents or early schooling. Liz Murray's mother had been addicted to drugs since her early teens. Liz Murray was born to drug-addicted parents in New York. Yet, against all the odds and without a roof over her head, she returned to high school at 17 and went on to win a scholarship to study at Harvard.

"Successful people have learnt the 8 skills needed to identify and overcome the difficulties they meet to achieve success and happiness"

1. Which of the 8 skills do you think Liz Murray had developed very well and which does she need to overcome to succeed?

2. What do you think are the key factors that caused Liz to develop the skills to overcome her difficulties and WHO was vital in helping her to do so?

she did, she made the effort. She didn't even have all the help and support I've got here."
Suddenly there was a knock on the door.
"Scott, can I come in?"
Stacey was knocking on Scott's door and her voice startled him.
"What, Oh yes, Stace, come in."
Stacey entered the room, looked at Scott in his chair and thought he'd been crying, but decided not to comment. Scott sat up and studied Stacey, she was wearing a fairly tight fitting black polo shirt with the Success Feelosophy logo on her left breast and black track bottoms and trainers. He stared at her thinking how sexy she looked and then recalled their previous discussion, shifted his gaze to her eyes and spoke.
"Stace, I've done the two film videostudies."

"I know, Scott, don't forget I have a record of what your computer has been doing. What did you reckon on the films?"
"They are both excellent! There was so much of me in them."
"I'm pleased you realised that, I thought you would."
Scott was still very enthused and added.
"Although Will Hunting was a maths genius and an orphan, most of him was me. What I really liked about Liz Murray was that it was a true story and although she didn't actually start really studying until she was 16, she still managed to go to university, absolutely incredible."
"I was confident you'd like them and there are a lot more videos that I think will help and inspire you. I also think you'll enjoy the CAI session on them."
"That's the bit that worries me, meeting other students. But I am keen to finding out what others think about them."
"You'll be fine, in fact I'm confident you'll be pleasantly surprised. Try to remember the poster, 'Everyone here is your ally' and keep trying to look at their eyes to show you're interested and listening to them."
"Okay, Stace, I'll do me best."
"Let's go for some food first, though."
"Good, I'm starving, lead the way."
Stacey and Scott left the room initially for the food hall, which again was empty. After a quick meal and a visit to the toilets, they made their way to the collaborative action inquiry room. Stacey entered the room first with Scott close behind and clearly apprehensive. The room had a big flat TV screen on the wall and 8 rectangular tables, placed in a U-shape. There were 10 people already sat at the tables, 5 girls, 5 boys, whose ages ranged from about 14 to 20 years. They were all wearing similar clothes to Stacey, either T shirts with the Success Feelosophy logo across the front or a polo shirt with the logo on the left breast in a variety of colours, all had black track bottoms and trainers. As they entered, they were met with a number of enthusiastic greetings. Scott was visibly surprised by the positive attitude and he just managed to recall Stacey's advice of keeping his head up and having eye to eye contact. Stacey was studying Scott, as well as replying to their greetings.
"Hi everyone, this is Scott, my cousin."
"Hi Scott." They all shouted.
Scott was fighting to avoid looking down and did respond.
"Hi."
Stacey smiled proudly, recognising how difficult this was for him and muttered to him.
"Well done Scott, we'll sit here."
She led him to the seats at the front, nearest the TV screen, which had a large plastic box on the table. As they sat down, she took out some paper from the box and placed it on the table.

"Right, according to this list, we should have 12 of us in here. I think I know you all, there's Suzi, Alys, Ben, Sam, Tom, Carol, Claire, Kate, Dave, Andy, Scott and me. Great to see you all here so promptly and looking so keen. Let's just start with some quick feedback, raise your hand if you enjoyed Good Will Hunting."
Everyone raised their hand, Scott was last to raise his.
"Excellent, and raise your hand if you feel you've learnt from it."
Again everyone raised their hand, Scott was not confident but he did likewise."
Stacey scanned around the tables at the students' faces and finished with Scott, and smiled.
"Excellent, now lets have a look at the questions for our inquiry. Most of you are familiar with these sorts of questions now."
Stacey took a remote control from the box and pointed it at the computer in the corner of the room and the slide they had all seen before, appeared on the big TV screen.

Good Will Hunting Videostudy

This superb, Oscar winning film from 1997 is an excellent example of Success Feelosophy, focusing on Will Hunting, who despite a children's home background become a 'Maths Genius'. The film illustrates that:
"Successful people have learnt the 8 skills needed to identify and overcome the difficulties they meet to achieve success and happiness"

While you are watching the film, consider the following questions:
1. Which of the 8 skills do you think Will Hunting had developed very well and which does he need to overcome to succeed?

2. What do you think are the key factors that caused Will to develop the skills to overcome his difficulties and WHO was vital in helping him to do so?

"Okay Alys, you're experienced at this, would you start please. Which of the 8 skills do you think Will Hunting had developed very well?"
Scott looked across the table at Alys, who sat opposite him. She looked slightly older than Scott, had a very attractive face and remarkably at that age, without a trace of make-up. Her straight shoulder length golden hair was parted in the middle. Like Stacey, she wore a red tight fitting Success

Feelosophy T shirt, showing off her very trim figure. As with Stacey earlier, Scott kept thinking, 'look at her eyes, show her you are interested', and Stacey had a quick glance at Scott to see if he was doing just that.
Alys looked at Stacey and around the group, she had been in the centre for several months and had developed her skills so much in that time, that she was now comfortable in this sort of situation.
"Well, I think his most obvious strength is his cognitive skills. Maths is very dependent on this skill and he's brilliant at that."
She paused to allow feedback from the group.
"He also helps out Skylar with her Organic Chemistry, and science also requires good cognitive skills."
Added Suzi enthusiastically, sitting next to Alys.
"He also tries to keep one step ahead of the psychiatrists, and that shows he must be a good analytical and conceptual thinker."
Ben commented immediately.
"But, he struggles to make the decision to leave Boston, to go with Skylar or to take a good job, surely that shows his cognitive skills aren't that good?"
Sam, sitting next to Ben asked, as he scanned the group for a response.
"Isn't that's because his self-awareness skills are poor? He actually doesn't really know or understand himself very well and can't use that information to help him make those decisions. I don't think it shows his cognitive skills are poor, but it shows how his weakness in other skills prevents him succeeding."
This came from Tom, a boy, of similar age to Scott but about half his size.
Carol, a much older girl with bright red hair, was keen to comment on this.
"That's a good point, Tom. I think that's an important part of the film. Despite his excellent cognitive skills and being a maths genius, he's not really very clever in that he's not very able to cope with lots of things in life."
"I agree Carol. It was written by Matt Damon and Ben Affleck, the two stars, and I think that was part of what they wanted to get across. Although Will is an academic genius, because he is poorly developed in too many of the other skills, he did not identify and overcome the difficulties in his life."
This remark came from Claire, a pretty Afro-Caribbean girl with 'big hair' and big earrings.
"Do you think another of Will's strengths is his Effective Learning skills?"
Stacey asked the group.
"I do, because he was able to speed read books and helped Skylar with her chemistry. He also knew lots of information and learnt stuff about the psychiatrists and stuff."
Commented Kate, a very thin girl with dark crinkly hair.
"But he was only good learning from books, he didn't seem to learn much from experience or life, in general. He just kept making the same mistakes and getting into more and more trouble."

Responded Dave, a dark skinned, muscular boy, who looked to be the oldest boy in the group.

"I agree with Dave, completely. I think this is similar to the point Claire made, in that the writers wanted to emphasise that having good academic skills and knowing lots of information is not a great deal of help if you don't have the other skills we need to succeed."

This comment came from Andy, a tall thin boy with very short hair, he continued.

"But I'd be surprised if they have actually heard of the 8 skills we need to succeed."

Throughout this discussion, Scott sat quietly amazed and impressed. He was astonished that it seemed as though they all wanted to take part and were so very interested, he was not used to being in groups or classes like that. As usual, he had not taken part so far, but unusually felt as though he should, but not confident enough to do so.

Alys seized on the point Andy had made.

"I think that's a very important point, Andy. Although there's no mention of skills, the film does seem to highlight how just being good in academic studies is very limiting, I think the Maths professor or lecturer reflects that as well, he also seems only to be confident in his own little group."

"What about Will Hunting's weak skills, what do you think about them?" Stacey asked.

Ben replied immediately.

"I reckon he's quite weak in virtually all of them. I think it is made clear that he has not had the opportunity to learn about his own emotions, and his self-awareness is very poor. He obviously struggles to manage his feelings, he keeps them bottled up with Skylar when he needs to express them, but seems to be aggressive and lose his temper whenever he meets other boys who aren't his mates. I think his motivation skills are dreadful, he seems to have very little resilience, and fears any failure, so avoids stepping out of his comfort zone."

"Spot on Ben, I agree completely."

Said Sam, patting him on the back. "And his empathy is also poor, because he struggles to even understand his best mate's feelings when he is told how they all envy his talent. With Sean the psychiatrist, he doesn't really understand him at all, or Skylar, or how almost anybody else feels."

"That also adds to what Claire said about the point the writers were making. Although Will Hunting was aware of 'Attachment Theory', he mentions it in one of the final scenes with Sean, he couldn't actually really relate to the fact that he struggled with emotions and that he had very poorly developed social and emotional skills. I think they kept emphasising that since Will was an orphan, he had been able to develop his cognitive skills and knowledge through books, but he had not learnt the other 7 skills very well."

Tom added
"What about Will's communication and social skills?" Stacey asked.
Carol couldn't wait to respond to this.
"He appears to be okay with his mates, but has little respect for the authority figures in the court, in jail, in the college. He struggled with Skylar, especially initially in the bar, and he seemed particularly poor with peers who weren't his friends."
Stacey looked at Scott when Carol made this comment, knowing that this applied to him as well.
"What do you think, Scott? Do you think Will has good communication skills?" Alys asked him.
Scott looked in surprise at Alys, unable to speak. This was a very attractive girl speaking to him, and showing him some interest, a recipe for him being 'tongue-tied' and ironically, she was asking about communication skills. All eyes were on him and a hush descended. Scott's pulse was already racing when he felt Stacey's hand touch his in reassurance. Alys realised he was struggling, so spoke again to him.
"Scott, do you think he shows good communication skills with anyone?"
This extra time and Alys' comment distracted the attention enough for Scott to gather his emotions and thoughts. Since he was able to relate very closely to Will, he was determined to try to make a reasonable response.
"Er, he seemed to be okay with his mates and when he was in court and the professors, but he was rubbish with his girl friend. She had to make the first move in the bar; he only met her through his mate, who went to chat them up. He couldn't talk about anything important, he just talked about facts."
"Well said Scott, I agree completely." Alys responded.
Scott felt relieved and proud he spoke, and tried to look at Alys when she said this, but his embarrassment overcame him and he had to look away. He glanced at Stacey who looked really pleased, she knew how big a difficulty this had been for him to overcome, and whispered to him.
"Well done, Scott, excellent."
Scott felt really pleased with himself, comparable to scoring a great goal in an important match, because it was so difficult for him.
Claire then commented.
"I think his poor communication skills are a big factor in his poor social skills. He seemed so restricted in who he was able to be comfortable with. He had a few mates, but otherwise he had no social life."
Andy continued on the same point.
"I think, Sean, the psychiatrist, made a great point when he said Will could rely on his mates who would take a bat to anyone to defend him. Will and his mates are very typical boys in that they are close to their mates because they defend and support each other physically. They all tend to think the same and never discuss their emotions or anything important, so their social circle is

restricted to 'like minded people'. Anyone who is different from them, like the students, girls, professors, businessmen, they struggle with."

When Scott heard this, it 'struck a chord with him', as he realised that this was describing him as well. His mind wandered into occasions when he'd got into trouble either defending his mates or being goaded by them.

Stacey then spoke, which caught his attention.

"So are we agreed that we tend to feel that Will Hunting had poor development of all the 8 skills apart from cognition and effective learning skills in books and academic areas."

"Yes, I agree with that"

Ben replied and the others mumbled agreement.

Stacey then resumed talking.

"So lets carry on the inquiry with the next part, 'what do you think are the key factors that caused Will to develop the skills to overcome his difficulties and who was vital in helping him to do so?"

Many of the students around the table had a big grin on their faces and Claire was first to reply.

"Having been in this centre for a few months, I think the most obvious and important people were his mentors. I think we've all seen the power of effective mentoring and I think Sean the psychiatrist certainly fits into that category. He very patiently and carefully opened himself up to Will to gain his confidence and then kept asking excellent questions to get him to reflect and develop his self-awareness skills."

"Absolutely"

Definitely"

"I agree".

These comments flowed around the room and Scott was very encouraged by so much support for the mentors. He had thought he was lucky to have Stacey as his mentor and not realised that these mentors were key to the success of the centre.

"But Will didn't only have Sean helping him, his girlfriend was important in helping him to reflect. His best mate also helped his self-awareness skills to develop when he explained how he actually wanted Will to make use of his skills and move away."

Ben added.

"I agree with Ben. In this centre, having mentors who we can relate to, makes a big difference but we have so many other people in here supporting us, just like Will's mate." Tom commented.

Claire then added to this point.

"I think that Matt Damon and Ben Affleck wanted to emphasise that point. I think the strength of their friendship is very important as it is with our mentors in here, and when he pointed out that Will should move away to make full use of his opportunities it had a big effect on Will."

Dave then chipped in.
"These CAI sessions are so powerful in that way, we have people in them who provide points of view and advice that I feel are the key factors in causing us to develop the skills to overcome our difficulties."
Everyone in the room voiced their agreement.
Stacey then clicked the remote control and this slide appeared.

Homeless to Harvard: The Liz Murray Story Videostudy

"This film shows the true story of Liz Murray - who managed to develop the 8 skills we need to succeed despite little support from her parents or early schooling. Liz Murray's mother had been addicted to drugs since her early teens. Liz Murray was born to drug-addicted parents in New York. Yet, against all the odds and without a roof over her head, she returned to high school at 17 and went on to win a scholarship to study at Harvard.

"Successful people have learnt the 8 skills needed to identify and overcome the difficulties they meet to achieve success and happiness"

1. Which of the 8 skills do you think Liz Murray had developed very well and which does she need to overcome to succeed?

2. What do you think are the key factors that caused Liz to develop the skills to overcome her difficulties and WHO was vital in helping her to do so?

"This time I've prepared a few clips from the film to try to illustrate some key points."
They sat and watched about 15 minute snippet of the film which emphasised the level of deprivation of Liz Murray's early life and the events that contributed to her developing self-awareness. Then Stacey spoke again.
"Okay, which of the 8 skills do you think Liz Murray had developed very well and which does she need to overcome to succeed?"
The whole group carried out the action inquiry as before, although Scott did not verbally contribute, he listened very carefully and thoroughly enjoyed it.
"Well, I'm afraid we've run out of time, it is almost 2000 hours, and some people have other appointments."

Scott looked at his wrist monitor and was amazed at how quickly the time had passed and how many times had he thought that in his brief time in the centre. He realised that he had booked the soccer skills room and got up to leave.
"Goodbye, Scott" or similar comments suddenly rang out. Scott was shocked and did not know what to do.
He looked blankly into the room, raised his arm and mumbled.
"Er, yeah, thanks, see ya."
Stacey gently held his elbow and gently spoke.
"You've done very well today, Scott. Enjoy yourself in the soccer skills room and I'll see you at 0900 hours, okay?"
Once again Scott felt really good, especially with this praise from Stacey, as he was surprised how well he'd remained involved and how much he'd learnt and enjoyed the session.
"Oh thanks, Stace. That was incredible. I'll see you tomorrow."
He then dashed out the room towards his study bedroom, quickly got changed and went to the soccer skills room. As with the previous day he was able to stay in the room for three hours, after which he had a shower, and returned to his room.
"I really don't understand this feeling, I feel as high as a kite, but I've taken nothing."
Scott was talking to himself, as he sat on his bed, reflecting on the same wonderful feeling he was again having, just like the previous night.
"Perhaps there is some magic in here, to make you feel like this. I can't explain it, any other way."
He shifted his position so he swivelled round and put his head on the pillow and started looking at the posters on the ceiling.

Chapter 13
"If it ain't been difficult, it don't really feel like success."

"Okay, Stace, come in."
Scott was awake and ready this time when Stacey knocked on his door.
"I actually managed to respond to the alarm this morning."
"So I see, well done. Did you sleep well?"
"Brilliant! I fell asleep almost as soon as my head hit the pillow."
"That's a good sign, vast numbers of young people have sleep problems, which the research shows contributes to their struggle."
"I don't sleep like this at home."
"I suspect the routine and constant activity is having a positive effect."
"Whatever it is, I've found the first two days absolutely incredible."
"Good, I hoped you would. Shall we go for some breakfast?"
"Yes."

Scott looked at Stacey's face closely as they walked out of his room and added.
"Please."
A huge smile lit up Stacey's face and she briefly put her right arm around him from the side as they walked along.
"Excellent, Scott, well done. It's amazing how much difference saying please, sorry and thanks makes to how people assess you. Actually, it relates closely to what we are doing this morning."
"What's that, Stace?"
"Focusing on assessing and developing your self-awareness."
Scott's face showed he didn't really understand it.
"Okay."
"So what did you think on your first CAI Videostudy session then, Scott?"
Stacey asked as they entered the food hall, and yet again was empty. They began the process of getting food and drink as Scott replied.
"Excellent! I have never experienced a lesson like that at school. I thought it was brilliant, I can't believe we were in there for almost two hours."
"I thought you had, you looked as though you were enjoying it. What do you think you learnt from it?"
"So much, Stace, I barely know where to start."
Stacey waited for them to both finish getting their food and drink and sit down before following up his comment.
"Alright, what were they?"
"This is a great way of learning. Watching a video with questions in front of you that you can attempt and then discussing them afterwards is brilliant. The time just flew by watching the videos and in the discussion, sorry, the CAI session."
Stacey grinned as Scott said this.
"We all seem to think that the CAI videostudy is a brilliant learning process?"
"But what was really amazing was being in a room with a bunch of teenagers who were so positive and helpful, I never expected anything like that."
"I felt exactly the same in my first one."
"I expected loads of bitching and aggression, or nobody says anything, but in there, everyone spoke and was supportive. How come?"
"All of those students have been here for at least a month and in that time the 'magic' has started to work and they no longer feel any desire to behave in that negative way. We do try to ensure that newcomers go into groups that have a high number of experienced positive students."
"When I was in there, I felt I should be taking part, I never feel like that normally."
"For me that's probably the most magical thing about this centre. Basically, you felt the force of 'positive peer pressure' in there and we've all experienced

that in here. I think it is the biggest factor causing us to be transformed and I felt that you were very different to your previous self."
"I did feel as though there was some sort of force in the room, pushing me to fit in and take part. Normally I'm tempted to disrupt or opt out."
"I know Scott, I was just the same. Even if you had tried to disrupt, they've 'all been there and done that' in their previous lives, so they would've either ignored you or simply discouraged you. We all find that if there is no audience for our antics we just give up. Remember, JC was a behaviour problem when he was a kid and so when he set up these centres, he emphasised that newcomers should have lots of positive influences around them. The third learning requirement, remember is 'Environment that encourages learning'. If that CAI session had someone who wanted to disrupt it, you may have been tempted to play up to them."
"That's good point, I've never thought about that before. Oh, I've said it again."
They both laughed, then Stacey spoke again.
"Is there anything else that you think you may have learnt?"
"I felt the main people in both films succeeded in the end because of the difficulties they had in life."
Stacey looked at Scott with a huge smile on her face and again put her arm around him and hugged him briefly. Scott was pleasantly surprised.
"Outstanding, Scott, well done again. That was one the main reasons for selecting the films but I am very impressed you spotted it. You seem to have analysed the films really well, that's quite a good indicator of your cognitive skills."
"Thanks, Stace,"
Scott was clearly surprised. He was not expecting any praise and still not used to it.
"Let's return to your room, Scott and we'll continue with assessing your skills."

They got up, returned their utensils and went back to Scott's room. As they sat down in their usual positions Stacey spotted a poster and spoke.
"The comment you made about the size of the difficulties being very important in their success reflects the poster over there."
She pointed at the wall next to the TV screen.

Success = Overcoming Difficulties
The Greater The Difficulty
The Greater The Success

Scott stared at it for several seconds and finally spoke.
"Mmmm, I'm not sure if I fully understand it, Stace. Can you explain it?"

Scott looked at Stacey and noticed she was staring at him and keeping quiet. Then he realised why.
"Please."
"That's better, you're getting the hang of it, already. Of course, I'll explain.
"It's an important part of our focus on your self-awareness anyway. I vividly recall JC explaining it to me and I think I can find the inquiry questions he used on the website, let me have a look."
Scott's pulse quickened as Stacey leaned across the desk, she moved the mouse a few times and suddenly the following appeared on the screen.

Analysing Success

Consider each of these questions carefully:-

1) **Suppose you were to run in the London Marathon, which of these times for the 26+ miles do you think you would consider a success?**
   (a) 2 hours (b) 5 hours (c) 24 hours
2) **What do you think would be considered a successful set of exam qualifications?**
3) **What would you consider to be the greatest success in your life so far – why?**
4) **What do you think determines how successful you feel?**

Scott looked at the screen for several minutes, had a deep frown on his face and then responded.
"What's the point of those questions,Stace?"
"They are to try to develop our self-awareness by getting us to think more deeply about what we consider success to be. The first two questions are to help us become aware that we each have a different perception of what success is, there are many other examples we can use. So how would you respond?"
"Well I could walk a marathon in under 24 hours so that is not success, is it?"
"But it would be if you weren't young and sporty."
"Yeah, good point. I reckon five hours would be very difficult for me, I've never run 26 miles before. Two hours is ridiculous, surely that's impossible?"

"Actually the world record for the marathon is almost down to two hours, but your answer was superb."
Scott was pleased but confused by the praise.
"Why is it a superb answer?"
"Cos you are already aware that 26 miles is a very long way to run and not easy for you, but you are also aware that to do this under five hours would be particularly difficult for you and two hours would be almost impossible."
"But why is that such a superb answer?"
"It illustrates that for this example your self-awareness is developed enough to help you judge your success criteria fairly well."
"Success criteria?"
"The measure of feeling success for you. What about question two?"
"Well since I'm doing GCSEs at the moment I'd say five passes of at least grade C."
Stacey looked at him for several seconds waiting for him to say more, but he didn't, and she spoke.
"This time, you answer to this is not so good, in fact, it is quite poor."
Scott was surprised and asked.
"Why?"
"Cos this time you are showing poor self-awareness. You used the term, 'five passes', there has never been any pass or fail in GCSE since they were introduced decades ago, so why did you use it?"
"I thought you could pass or fail, I've heard it used lots of times."
"Yes, incorrectly! It was possible to pass and fail many years ago with the old 'O' level exams. This illustrates your lack of awareness in this area, furthermore, you chose the number 'five', why?"
"I think I got it from teachers, my sisters or possibly other kids, I dunno, really."
"Excellent response, Scott. This illustrates how poor your self-awareness is in this area, yet you are being bombarded with it all the time, especially at school. You are unable to have reasonably accurate success criteria here because your self-awareness is so poor."
"Ah, I see what you're getting at now. Unlike the marathon, I ain't really got a clue of what I could really achieve in exams, so what I think is success is based on some stupid ideas or rubbish information."
"Very well put, Scott. I was just like you and most kids are at your age, their awareness of what they could achieve in exams is extremely poor so we tend to give answers like the one you did."
Scott's expression showed he was thinking deeply about what Stacey had said, but pleased he'd given a good answer. Stacey then continued.
"The next question is a different type, the idea with this one is to be able to show that our greatest success so far will be in an area that we consider to be most important, and it has to be extremely difficult to achieve. I bet that is true for you, Scott?"

Scott had struggled with this question and selected a brilliant goal he scored for the school football team when he was in year 7. He realised that this did apply to his selection, as it is so important to him to be good in football and it really impressed his dad, mates and P.E. teacher, which was also very important to him.
"Yes, it is."
"This means our self-awareness may have developed so much that we can now answer question four. What do you think, Scott?"
Scott thought deeply for a moment and looked at the poster Stacey had pointed out earlier 'Success = Overcoming Difficulties, The Greater The Difficulty, The Greater The Success'. He then saw a poster next to it that he realised answered question four.

Your greatest success will be determined by what you value most and how great the difficulties are that you overcame

He pointed at the poster and his face showed his newly found awareness.
"Got it! If it ain't been difficult, it don't really feel like success."
"That's a good way of putting it, Scott, well done."
Again Scott felt so proud that he'd pleased Stacey, even if it was with just a comment.
"This leads us nicely on to the next skill to evaluate, self-awareness."
Stacey moved the mouse and clicked a few times and the screen showed the next skill.

Self-awareness	Grade
Knows and accepts what they are feeling, and can label their feelings.	
Can identify their strengths and weaknesses, and feel they know themselves well.	
Can reflect on their actions and identify lessons to be learned from them.	

Scott studied the table on the computer screen and Stacey continued.
"Are you aware that since I first came to your house, a week ago, I've asked you how you felt many times and you've never answered me?
Scott suddenly felt and looked very embarrassed. Stacey looked at him and waited patiently for a response.
"Er, no, but I'm not very good at that sort of thing."
"What sort of thing?"

For the second time in a few minutes his faced showed he was struck with a sudden awareness, as he looked at the computer screen.
"Oh right, that's what we are doing. Of course, how good am I at 'knows and accepts what they are feeling and can label their feelings? Well, I think that's obvious, absolute rubbish."
"It's encouraging that you are at least aware that you're poor at this, anyway."
They both smiled at the irony of what she had said and then Stacey continued.
"This is a very common problem in the 21st century, especially with boys. As a teenager, I was like you and had not spent much of my life talking openly and honestly with my family or friends about my emotions, I tended to avoid those sorts of things. Like most children growing up in the last few decades, my life was spent watching television and videos, using the internet, especially social networking, and playing computer games. I had not really spent any time sitting and talking in depth with anyone about how I felt, what worried me and listening to others talk about their emotions. By the time I was 19, I understood very little about my feelings and why I was struggling to cope with life. Unfortunately, your very low score is the same as mine and most teenagers these days."
Stacey was gradually becoming more tearful as she spoke and her voice began to show signs of choking as a 'lump appeared in her throat' and she took out some tissues from her pocket. Scott looked at her and realised again that Stacey's problems as a teenager were very similar to his, and the sight of Stacey crying had a real impact on him. His initial attraction to Stacey a week or so ago, was probably mainly lust, but had now developed into a different type of attraction of 'liking and admiration'. The openness and honesty that Stacey had shown about her own problems and emotions was something he'd never experienced before. Scott could feel himself also 'choking up' and his eyes began to water, when Stacey saw him struggling with his emotions she hugged him.
"Scott, I know exactly how you feel. It's so difficult and painful to become aware of how foolish we've been and what we should've done, but until we do, we can't really begin our journey to success."
Scott found the hug very helpful, especially as his face was no longer visible to Stacey and his crying eyes could not be seen by her. Her words and emotion were incredibly powerful as he had not experienced this before as a teenager. He put his arms around Stacey, partly to ensure she could not see his eyes, but mainly because he wanted to comfort her and demonstrate he could show he cared. The hug lasted for about 20 seconds, until Scott felt he'd stopped crying and could start talking again. He wiped his eyes and moved back to look at Stacey, whose eyes showed she had been crying, she wiped them with her tissues.
"You are absolutely right, Stace. I can't recall ever talking about how I feel about things or even listening to someone tell me how they feel. My life for as long as

I can remember has been muck like yours, watching telly, videos, playing computer games, using the internet and playing football."

"So what grade for the first one, Scott?"

"One, Stace."

"The next one says 'Can identify their strengths and weaknesses, and feel they know themselves well'. It's become clear to me in the last few days that I know little about myself, in fact I can't recall ever really thinking about who I am."

"Again I was the same and so are most teenagers."

"But when we have assessments in school, they only bang on about exam grades, why don't we do stuff like this?"

Stacey looked at him in a way that meant he should know the answer; he saw it and attempted to answer his own question.

"I know, I know, our schools focus on exams, this is not part of the tradition in our country."

"Well done."

"Okay, I'm giving myself another grade of one for this. Right, the next one is 'Can reflect on their actions and identify lessons to be learned from them'. This is simple, I'd be lucky to even get a grade of one for this, I ain't thought about or learnt nothing."

He shook his head and looked at Stacey blankly as he said it, then commented.

"That gives me a total of 3 out of 30 for self-awareness, Stace."

He tapped the numbers into the table on the computer and Stacey spoke as he did so.

"That poster up there shows that the importance of the skill of self-awareness has been known for a long time."

Stacey pointed at the following poster on the ceiling above the bed.

Knowing others is intelligence; knowing yourself is true wisdom.

Lao Tzu

What is necessary to change a person is to change his awareness of himself.

Abraham Maslow

"Lao Tzu is another ancient Chinese philosopher and Abraham Maslow is a psychologist from the last century. When Arthur visited me 18 months ago, he helped me develop this skill enough to start my journey to success."
"Stace, I think you have done the same for me."
Stacey smiled and replied.
"I'm delighted to hear that Scott and I hope you're right."

Chapter 14
"everyone and everything just winds me up"

Once Scott had finished putting in his grades he clicked the mouse and the next table appeared on the computer screen and he studied it.

Managing Feelings	Grade
Expresses their emotions to others and in ways that are clear and appropriate to the situation. (suitable/good behaviour)	
Understands that how they express their feelings may have a big effect on others and how they are treated. (knows how to behave)	
Has strategies to manage their impulses and strong emotions (eg. anger, anxiety, stress, jealousy) to avoid them behaving in ways that has negative consequences for them or for other people.	

Scott stared at it for a long time and he shook his head in disbelief.
"If I was poor on the previous one, then this could be even worse. I think the only emotion I have expressed in a way that is clear is anger!"
"Funny you should say that, Scott, have a look at that poster."

Anyone can become angry
–that is easy.
But to be angry with the right person,
at the right time, for the right
purpose, and the right way
– this is not easy.
Aristotle

"That famous quote by Aristotle, an ancient Greek philosopher, is trying to convey how important and difficult it is to manage our emotions, especially our anger. The poster next to it carries on with this message."

easily. In about five minutes you'll get to see a video that provides all the answers to the questions, and you'll be able to check them when you watch it, before you have it assessed or marked. Is that okay, anyone need further explanation? Good, please start."

All the students immediately began the task set, with Scott being paired with Stacey.

"I think I'm the only one who has done this activity before, Scott, so I'll try to just support you. Is that okay?"

"That's fine, Stace. It don't seem too difficult, I reckon I can work out where these answers go."

Scott started studying the sheet carefully and pencilling in some answers. He then carried on talking.

"Some of these are easy, I've done them already. I'm going guess the rest, I can change them anyway when the video's playing."

Stacey smiled broadly.

"That's just the positive attitude I was hoping for."

"Oh, I don't mind doing fun quizzes like this, it's studying I can't do."

Stacey chuckled quietly, as she knew this was studying, but in a very different way, before commenting.

"But that's the whole point of this process and why it's so effective. There's no real pressure and you feel it's just a quiz. I actually managed to get good GCSE grades by doing the stuff you'll do in this session."

Scott wasn't really listening, as he was so engrossed in the activity.

After a few minutes, Stacey began the video and the pairs whispered to each other, and checked their answers. Scott talked to himself really, mainly congratulating himself on how well he was doing.

When the video finished Stacey spoke again.

"Okay, one of you swaps your sheet with one from the pair next to you, one of you will mark your own sheet and one of you will mark the other pair's attempt."

The sheets were swapped; Scott swapped his with Hannah next to him.

Stacey continued.

"Alys, would you be so kind as to read out what you think are the correct answers, and the rest of you can let her know politely, whether you agree or not. If you disagree, can you explain why you think it is wrong, thanks."

Alys began reading out the answers, and the rest just keep agreeing with her, until she had finished.

"Okay can you give back the sheets to their original owners, please."

Again the students did as they were asked. Scott looked at his score and was amazed that he got full marks.

"Could you please raise your arm if you scored 12 or more."

Everyone raised their arm.

"Of course you can, it's how you evaluate yourself that really matters, I'm only trying to help you be accurate and you sound as though you have understood this one well. I reckon you probably understand the next part as well. You've already said how easily and often you've 'lost it' so it seems managing your impulses has not been good. Before I came here, I just did things without considering the long term effect; my life was the complete opposite of the poster over there."
Stacey was pointing at a poster on the ceiling.

Success in life usually requires short term pain to achieve long term gain.
J C Learner

Scott smiled as he commented.
"It says 'strategies to manage their impulses and strong emotions', no chance! With football particularly, I've been sent off so many times, it's stopped me achieving success. In school, I've got wound up so many times and been thrown out of lessons. I've lost count of the number of fights I've been in because I've lost my temper. It's obvious that this is a real problem for me and I reckon I'm struggling to even give myself a grade of one here."
"Remember JC Learner had a similar problem to you as a young teenager, and he learnt to overcome it to become a professional footballer, so perhaps you can as well, Scott."
"I hope you're right, Stace. My total in this section is 4 out of 30,"
"Scott, I was even worse with only 1 out of 30."
Scott grinned at this comment before clicking the mouse so that the computer screen changed to show the next skill.

Motivation	Grade
Views errors as part of the normal learning process, does not 'fear failure' and bounces back from disappointment or failure (Resilient)	
Uses their and other's experiences, including mistakes and setbacks, to change (improve) their thinking and behaviour.	
Takes responsibility for their lives, believe that they can influence what happens to them and make wise choices. (growth mindset and Internal locus of control)	

"The skill of motivation is the one I've probably learnt most about and I just wish I'd learnt about it when I was younger, I'm sure it would've helped me understand and cope with my life much better. I'll provide you with some suggestions of what to research; the successfeelosophy website has loads on it to help, especially in the 'Self Esteem' section."
Scott was clearly fascinated with what Stacey was saying.

"Stace, I didn't even realise that motivation was a skill. Many people have said 'I lack motivation', even on the football field, so I'd really appreciate some help on this."
"I will explain what I can now, and give you some things to look at on the website. As I keep saying, when we are born we are 'hopeless and helpless', but motivated to learn and if we have the 5 learning requirements in place learning will occur."
Stacey pointed at the poster, above the bed.

THE FIVE LEARNING REQUIREMENTS

MOTIVATION	Unless we are keen to learn, we will lack the determination to overcome the difficulties that will occur.
CONCENTRATION	If we do not focus on the task, our brain cannot receive or store the information needed.
ENVIRONMENT	Distractions can cause concentration to become too difficult to allow us to learn,
ATTAINABLE TASKS	Unless the task to be learnt is broken down into small steps ('bitesize chunks') they are too difficult to grasp ('too large to digest').
FEELING SUCCESS	If we do not feel we are making progress it becomes too difficult to keep motivated.

"I've heard about these five learning requirements several times now, and having a poster of them is really useful."
"As you've seen there are many posters in the centre, and it's fascinating that some suddenly become relevant, useful and inspirational when we are motivated and concentrating on then. Perhaps you are motivated, in a good environment, concentrating so that these posters will be really helpful."
"I think you're probably right."
"If we have these five learning requirements and lots of learning opportunities, we can develop, and may move up levels in Maslow's Hierarchy."
"What?"

Stacey pointed at the Maslow's Hierarchy poster and Scott stared at it while listening to her.
"Maslow's Hierarchy of Needs', that poster shows you it and how 'what motivates us' may change. I suspect for you, like me, Scott, you've mainly been motivated by 'social desire'. We wanted to be part of the gang and liked by our friends, and probably also the next level, 'self esteem', where we are trying to impress our friends and peers all the time."
"What motivates us will probably change as we've grown up, and unfortunately when most of us become teenagers our lives become dominated by wanting to impress our peers. What makes it even worse is that this motivation tends to occur as we 'hit puberty'.

Scott was struggling to understand Stacey, but now he had begun to feel more relaxed with her, so he felt he could show he was struggling and decided to stop her.
"Stace, what do you mean it makes it even worse as it occurs when we hit puberty, why does that matter?"
"Excellent question, Scott."
One of the reasons that Scott now felt so relaxed was that he liked that Stacey almost always commented how good his questions were.
"I think I can direct you to some very useful videos and explanations on this on the successfeelosophy website. I should be able to find have something on the 'Adolescents and Men' section. Yes, here it is, perfect, 'Why do so many children seem to become such unpleasant people when they become teenagers'?"
The computer screen changed and showed this slide.

The Teenage Brain

- The frontal lobe of the brain is responsible for reasoning, controlling emotions and solving problems.
- The hormones produced during puberty act in a similar way to alcohol, in that it reduces (depresses) the effect of this part of the brain.
- So thinking rationally and good decision making becomes difficult.
- This emotionally based behaviour will resemble that of a young child and continue until sufficient learning has occurred to strengthen the neuron pathways to the frontal lobe.
- Therefore this 'adolescent behaviour' can continue for many years, even into old age.

"I think this video will explain this slide more fully."
A brief video clip started to play which illustrated how the brain changed at the start of puberty and how teenagers were very poor at recognising emotions in others and managing their own emotions. Scott watched and listened intently, with his mouth open in amazement on several occasions.

"Wow! I've never heard of this before, but it makes so much sense. Until I was a teenager, I didn't used to get so angry or fight all the time, and I'm sure my concentration got much worse."
"What about the videos on understanding others emotions and their facial expressions, what do you reckon on that?"
"You pointed out earlier that my non-verbal communication skills are poor, which seems to be typical for a boy and a teenager, Since I'm unable to read people's faces, does this mean I don't know when other boys or men are frightened or angry, Stace?"
"Very likely, Scott. It is thought that this is one of the reasons why so many boys in their teens and twenties are so violent. They arc angry or frightened and think others are feeling aggressive towards them all the time, so they attack them, often to show off or to demonstrate how hard they are. I expect once you got a reputation for fighting or being easily 'wound up', the others would deliberately taunt or upset you."
"Definitely. My P.E. teacher always kept telling me that the opposition would try to wind me up in football matches, but I still lost my temper. What about you then, Stace, how did it affect you?"
"Although I'm repeating myself, my concentration in school went to pieces. I became hopeless and easily distracted in class, and seemed to argue with everyone all the time. I spent all my time trying to impress boys particularly, and I couldn't really understand how I was feeling or how others might feel. I spent most of my time and money, trying to attract boys, not realising that they were only really interested in 'sex' and actually didn't care about me. Like most young people, I didn't understand the difference between like, love and lust, so I got frustrated and depressed frequently, eventually attempting suicide."
As before, Stacey's eyes watered, as did Scott's, so he hugged her again to comfort her. After a few seconds, Stacey refocused and quoted from the evaluation.
"So Scott, do you think you view errors as part of normal learning and bounce back from disappointment or failure?"
Scott thought for a moment before replying.
"No, probably the opposite! As a teenager I've tried to avoid anything that I felt I might fail at."
"I was the same Scott, another grade one, then?"
"Yep. But sometimes I've tried to learn from others' experiences, especially their mistakes, so that I avoid doing it."
"But that's more about you 'fearing failure' isn't it Scott, rather than improving your thinking?"
"S'pose so, but it's still learning though, ain't it?"
"Yes it is, so what grade for this then?"
"I reckon four."
"Okay, four it is and what about the last one?"

Scott studied it closely, Stacey could see he was struggling and tried to help.
"This is basically about whether you blame others or luck when things go wrong and decide there's nothing you can do about it."
"I do reckon I'm unlucky, and been 'picked on', all my life."
"Aren't you using it as an excuse, rather than as an explanation? I think this means you don't feel you are responsible, it's other people fault, not yours."
"Well it is!"
Scott reacted abruptly, as he didn't like what Stacey was saying.
Stacey's expression showed she knew she'd 'hit a nerve'.
"So on this one Scott, what do you think you should score?"
"Well, if that's what it's about, I suppose it's another one, then!"
Scott's tone showed he was struggling to accept that perhaps his problems were his fault, and he was looking for excuses much of the time.
"This is a crucial part in developing your self-awareness, Scott. If you are to improve, it is essential you realise that you need to stop blaming others, and decide to take responsibility for what happens to you."
"Humfff"
Scott's grunted, expressing his reluctance to accept this statement, despite appreciating it was probably true.

Chapter 15
"I have never enjoyed a Science lesson so much."

"Okay, we're going to take a break from your evaluation again, now Scott, and start your journey to exam success."
Scott looked at Stacey as if she was joking, but he could see she was being serious.
"My journey to exam success?"
"A crucial part of your journey to success is for you to develop your effective learning skills, and a useful way of doing this is by applying it exams."
"That's going to be tough."
"I was older and much worse than you at exams when I came in here, and I improved tremendously, so I reckon you'll be fine."
Scott bemused look at Stacey, reflected his difficulty in accepting what she had said. However, his respect and confidence for her had grown so much he thought as she'd been so open, honest and fair with him that he showed some faith and responded positively.
"Okay, we'll give it a go, what's it involve?"
"In a short while, we are going to same room CAI room we were in yesterday, and this time we will have a session on 'The Solar System and Earth In Space'."
Scott's face expressed his surprise, Stacey smiled and continued.
"It will give you a chance to see how SUPERlearning is applied to exam success; I think you'll be very impressed."

"We'll see."
Scott replied sceptically, clearly not convinced.
"Okay, if you are ready, Scott, we need to be fairly quick and we can pop to the loo on the way."
When they arrived at the CAI room, there about 10 people already sat around the table chatting, and Scott actually recognised some of them from yesterday's session. Stacey suggested they should sit in the similar positions as they had in that session.
"Morning Scott, morning Stacey."
Was the friendly yell from most people in the room, Stacey responded immediately and following prompting from some strange felt a force, Scott managed to respond
"Morning"
Stacey knew that this one word greeting was not easy for him and she smiled at him, giving him a charge of positive energy as he sat down next to her.
"Well done, Scott"
She said as she touched the back of his hand, and he felt more positive energy flowing into him.
Scott felt so relieved and pleased that Stacey was aware this sort of thing had been so difficult for him in the past, and how important she felt they were in his journey to success. Stacey began to address the group.
"Well you've got me in charge again, I'm afraid. I think you all know me, I'm Stacey and correct me if I'm wrong we have Claire, Alys, Dave, Andy, Kelly, Grace, Aron, Dean, Amy, Hannah, and Scott."
Stacey had begun with the girl opposite, Alys, and identified the people on their right each time going around the table. Scott recognised Claire, Alys, Dave and Andy from his previous CAI session.
"As usual for the traditional school subjects we will be following the 'SUPERlearning For Exam Success' process." Stacey's left hand gestured towards the screen.

SUPERlearning For Exam Success

	PROCEDURE	KEY POINTS
1	**Attempt VIDEOSTUDY Questions - before watching video**	• **Basically this is just multi-choice, you are given ALL the answers but 'not in the right order'** • **The answers can be repeatedly changed**
2	**Change or tick answers to VIDEOSTUDY Questions – whilst watching video**	• **All the answers will be given to you in the video** • **You can stop and rewind it when you want**

3	Change or tick answers to VIDEOSTUDY Questions –	• Ensure you get the 'correct answers' from the videostudy answer sheet
4	Attempt MC JIGSAWS (a 'big picture' with key words removed)	• By studying the information, the missing words are selected from the list and the relevant number written beside the word on the list.Attempt all questions – this is also multi-choice with ALL the answers provided
5	Change or tick answers to MC JIGSAWS Questions using MC Jigsaw answers	• Ensure you get the 'correct answers' from the MC Jigsaw answer sheet
6	Use QUIZCARDS to quiz yourself - or get someone to quiz you!	• Each sheet needs to be printed out, folded and glued together so that the answers back on to the questions. • Cut out each square to make quizcards
7	Attempt VIDEOSTUDY questions WITHOUT using the answers	• This means you can assess how much you've learnt
8	Use Exam papers and Mark Schemes to attempt exam questions on this topic and then mark them using the mark scheme.	• This means you can assess how much you've learnt and what you still need to learn.

"The topic today is 'The Solar System and Earth In Space'. We begin as usual with a videostudy and I have sheets printed off here for that, could you take one and pass them to your right, please Scott."
The sheets with the title, 'The Solar System and Earth In Space Videostudy, were passed around and then shown on the screen.

The Solar System and Earth In Space Videostudy

Select the answers from this table below and write them in the box you think it matches.

MERCURY	**24**	**SATELLITE**	**EAST**
MERCURY	**6**	**WINTER**	**VENUS**
PLUTO	**365**	**SUMMER**	
MOON	**POLE**	**SUN**	

Tick or alter when you watch 'The Solar System and Earth In Space' video

	QUESTION	ANSWER
1	How many hours does the Earth take to do one complete rotation?	
2	In which season is the North Pole tilted AWAY from the Sun?	
3	In which season will the North Pole have sunlight at midnight?	
4	To the nearest day, how many days does the Earth take to do a complete orbit around the Sun?	
5	Does the Sun appear to rise in the east or the west?	
6	What is the name of the star that does not appear to move?	
7	What is the planet that is closest to the Sun?	
8	What is the planet that is just closer to the Sun than the Earth?	
9	What is the planet that is furthest from the Sun?	
10	What is the name of the star that is closest to the Earth?	
11	How many planets take more time to orbit the Sun than the Earth?	
12	Which planet orbits the Sun quickest?	
13 (a)	What S is the name given to smaller objects that orbit around a much larger object?	(a)
(b)	And which is the nearest natural one to the Earth?	(b)

"I know most of you are familiar with the procedure but I'll explain it, anyway. You will be attempting these questions in pair, but you both need to put down the answers on your sheet in pencil, so you can rub them out and change them

easily. In about five minutes you'll get to see a video that provides all the answers to the questions, and you'll be able to check them when you watch it, before you have it assessed or marked. Is that okay, anyone need further explanation? Good, please start."
All the students immediately began the task set, with Scott being paired with Stacey.
"I think I'm the only one who has done this activity before, Scott, so I'll try to just support you. Is that okay?"
"That's fine, Stace. It don't seem too difficult, I reckon I can work out where these answers go."
Scott started studying the sheet carefully and pencilling in some answers. He then carried on talking.
"Some of these are easy, I've done them already. I'm going guess the rest, I can change them anyway when the video's playing."
Stacey smiled broadly.
"That's just the positive attitude I was hoping for."
"Oh, I don't mind doing fun quizzes like this, it's studying I can't do."
Stacey chuckled quietly, as she knew this was studying, but in a very different way, before commenting.
"But that's the whole point of this process and why it's so effective. There's no real pressure and you feel it's just a quiz. I actually managed to get good GCSE grades by doing the stuff you'll do in this session."
Scott wasn't really listening, as he was so engrossed in the activity.
After a few minutes, Stacey began the video and the pairs whispered to each other, and checked their answers. Scott talked to himself really, mainly congratulating himself on how well he was doing.
When the video finished Stacey spoke again.
"Okay, one of you swaps your sheet with one from the pair next to you, one of you will mark your own sheet and one of you will mark the other pair's attempt."
The sheets were swapped; Scott swapped his with Hannah next to him.
Stacey continued.
"Alys, would you be so kind as to read out what you think are the correct answers, and the rest of you can let her know politely, whether you agree or not. If you disagree, can you explain why you think it is wrong, thanks."
Alys began reading out the answers, and the rest just keep agreeing with her, until she had finished.
"Okay can you give back the sheets to their original owners, please."
Again the students did as they were asked. Scott looked at his score and was amazed that he got full marks.
"Could you please raise your arm if you scored 12 or more."
Everyone raised their arm.

“Excellent, the next activity is another one you are probably familiar with, MC Jigsaws. Again, I have the sheets printed off here, please could you take one and pass them to your right, as before, thanks.”

The sheets were passed around and Stacey continued.

“Basically, you will see you have a photocopy of a page on ‘The Solar System and Earth In Space’ from a text book. However if you look closely you will see the numbers 1 to 10 scattered around the page, these are to replace the key words that have been removed and placed in the box at the bottom of the page.”

At the bottom of the page there was a table like the one below.

‘The Solar System and Earth In Space’ Missing Words

Place the number behind the word that you think has replaced it in the big picture above

MERCURY	DAY	SUN	VENUS
EAST	POLE	WINTER	
PLUTO	YEAR	SUMMER	

“As you’ve just done, in your pairs, try to workout where you think each of the words should go. Anyone unclear on what to do? Again you’ve got 5 minutes to decide on your answers.”

As with the previous activity, the pairs completed it then swapped one sheet with the pair next to them. Claire read out the answers this time, they marked the sheets and returned them as before. Again Scott struggled to believe he had got full marks. Stacey resumed talking to the group.

“Very well done, all of you. The next activity uses these Quizcards; you will all need a set, take one and pass the rest on.”

The sets of cards were passed around the table. Then Stacey continued.

“Place your cards on the table in front of you, with the questions facing upwards and in number order, please.”

They all did as requested and had the cards set out similar to this below.

1. How many hours does the Earth take to do one complete rotation?	6. What is the name of the star that does not appear to move?	11. How many planets take more time to orbit the Sun than the Earth?	16. What force from the Sun causes all the planets to orbit it?
2. In which season is the North Pole tilted AWAY from the Sun?	7. What is the planet that is closest to the Sun?	12. Which planet orbits the Sun quickest?	17. What is the type of moon that is seen when it is the opposite side of the Earth to the Sun
3. In which season will the North Pole have sunlight at midnight?	8. What is the planet that is just closer to the Sun than the Earth?	13. What S is the name given to smaller objects that orbit around a much larger object?	18. What is the type of moon that is seen when it is the same side of the Earth to the Sun
4. To the nearest day, how many days does the Earth take to do a complete orbit around the Sun?	9. What is the planet that is furthest from the Sun?	14. Which is the nearest natural satellite to the Earth?	19. What E is the moon blotting out the sun?
5. Does the Sun appear to rise in the east or the west?	10. What is the name of the star that is closest to the Earth?	15. How many days does the moon take to orbit the Earth?	20. What G is a large cluster of stars?

"If you turn over each card you will see the answer to that question is on the other side. You are going to use these quizcards to play a version of 'The Weakest Link'. I will demonstrate with Scott, how to play it first, okay?"

Scott was both baffled and intrigued as to what this was all about. So far he'd done a quiz, watched a video and completed a jigsaw, so he felt playing a game was no longer a surprise.

"Scott and I need to collect up our cards, keeping the questions facing upwards, and place them in a pile on the table in front of us.

We are both going to ask and be asked questions, alternately. I'll go first, I shuffle my cards, Scott does the same and we place them back in front of us."

They both did as Stacey said.

"Right the first question in front of me, I will ask Scott. What G is a cluster of stars, Scott?"

Scott looked at Stacey blankly, and just about managed to say.
"I dunno."
"Now I turn over that card and show it to Scott and read it out, 'Galaxy'. Because he did not get the right answer, I put it back in front of me to the left of my pile, Scott, now you need to ask me the question at the top of your pile."
Scott felt uncomfortable and previously would probably not have taken part, but in this environment he was not so worried at making a mistake, so he attempted to read out the card.
"Which planet orbits the Sun quickest, Stacey?
"Oooh, that's an easy one, Scott. We've just been doing that in the MC Jigsaw, the answer is 'Mercury'. Turn over the card, Scott."
Scott turned over the card and he said.
"Correct."
"Because I got it right, he puts it to the right of his pile, and that's how many I get correct. We just carry on for about 3 minutes, asking each other questions. Once we've finished the pile, if we've got time, we can start attempting the ones we got wrong or didn't know. Do you think you understand? Anyone want more explanation? No, okay your 3 minutes starts now!"
All the pairs began their game asking and answering questions, alternately, for 3 minutes.
"Three minutes are up! You need to count how many you got correct."
Stacey shouted. She had to shout because they were all so wrapped up and excited by the activity. They quickly calmed down and worked out how many they each got correct.
"The person in each pair that got the highest score will stay seated where they are. If you both got the same total correct, the one who answered questions second, stays where they are, the others are called 'the weakest link' and as it says in the programme, 'take the walk of shame', with their cards to the next position on their right. They will compete against a new opponent."
Most of the group were familiar with this game, so followed the instructions comfortably. One person in each pair got up and moved around the table. Alys came across to sit next to Stacey, in the space that Scott had left when he moved to his right, to compete against Hannah. Scott normally would be struggling if he had to sit next to a girl, but because he felt this activity was easy to do, and he was very competitive, it didn't bother him.
"Okay, same as before, this is your second round. Place your pile on the table in front of you, and the person who has not moved, asks the first question. Your three minutes, starts now!"
The same process was repeated several times, each time one person getting up and moving round. Eventually Scott ended up sitting next to Grace.
"Can you all now put your cards into the plastic money bag, and pass them around the table back to me, please."
Everyone did as Stacey requested.

"For the next activity, you are playing, 'Head To Head', and in a moment, you will all receive one of these large cards that are being passed around. Please leave them on the table, face down in front of you."
They all did as Stacey asked and had a large card in front of them.
"This time, your quiz is to correctly answer more questions on the card in 3 minutes than your opponent. You will need the pencil in front of you for this. In a moment, I'm going to ask you to turn over the card and start attempting the questions. Any problems before we start? No? Good, your three minutes starts now!"
They all picked up their card and turned it over and smiled, some even chuckled. The questions were exactly the same as those on the quizcards they'd been using for the last activity. They all frantically wrote down answers, some finished after only two minutes.
"Okay, times up, swap your cards with your opponent. You will mark the card you now have. Hannah could you read out what you think are the correct answers, and as before, if anyone disagrees, please let us know, and why you think it is wrong."
Hannah did as she was asked, and nobody disagreed, and they passed the cards back to their opponent.
"Did anyone manage to get 20 out of 20?"
Stacey asked.
Everyone's hand went up, including Scott's. He was amazed and delighted, he'd never been any good at Science, and could never remember getting full marks.
"Great effort everyone, well done. Can you please hang on to these cards and in a moment you will receive a large envelope. Please leave the envelope on the table in front of you. The second part of this 'Head To Head' is as you've just done, to try to correctly answer more questions on the cards in the envelope in 8 minutes, than your opponent, again you'll need your the pencil."
Since this was much as they had just done, Scott and the others understood.
"In a moment, I'm going to ask you to take out the cards and start attempting the questions. Any problems? Good, your time starts now!"
They all grabbed their envelope and took out the two large cards in it. A few smiled this time, but also some confused faces, including Scott. These questions were a little different from the previous ones, but not too much, he looked around the room and everyone was reading and writing. He started to study the questions, and felt they were fairly simple, some were multi-choice much like the MC Jigsaws he'd attempted earlier. He got to the end and was just about to check it through when he heard Stacey's voice.
"Okay times up, swap your cards with your opponent. You'll see there are yellow cards being passed around, please take one. They are the mark schemes for these questions. Again, you'll mark the cards you now have, using the mark schemes on the yellow cards. Aron, could you just let us know

how the answers on the mark scheme are worked out. If anyone has any questions please let us know and we'll discuss it."
They all did as they were asked and Aron explained the answers to the group, a few questions were asked, not by Scott, of course, but he did manage to understand and mark all the questions. They returned the cards to their opponents. Grace and Scott had both got the same score 18 out of 20.
"Did anyone manage to get 15 or more, out of 20?"
Again everyone's hand went up.
"Brilliant effort! You all managed to get at least a grade C at GCSE for Science. You just attempted two questions from recent Science GCSE exam and that was the mark scheme used by the examiners."
There was suddenly a bombardment of noise, as everyone commented. Scott's chin lowered and he sat there open-mouthed in astonishment. He looked across at Stacey who was smiling at him at him, and his expression changed into a huge smile. He was really struggling to believe that he had done so well, it had always seemed far too difficult for him, previously. Suddenly his thoughts were interrupted by Grace, his opponent, who spoke to him.
"Well done Scott. You seem to be good at Science."
Scott was startled, not only by Grace speaking to him, but also what she had said. Normally, he would've avoided looking at a girl like Grace, a girl who was in her late teens, especially as he thought she was very attractive. He could feel his heart quickening and his face reddening as usual, his impulse was to look down or away, but he didn't, he looked at her bright blue piercing eyes and stayed looking. She had pale almost white skin, apart from a slight blush on her cheeks. Her black hair was cut in the five point bob style introduced in the sixties, which seemed to make her black spectacles even more fashionable that almost hid her very petite nose. The redness of her lips contrasted with her white skin and faultless teeth, giving the appearance of that Andy Warhol had painted them. This gaze from Scott lasted only a few seconds, but it seemed much longer to him. In the past he would not have replied but this was not the past, this was now.
"Er, thanks Grace, you also did well. I've always been rubbish at Science in the past, I can't believe I've done so well."
Scott could barely believe that he actually said all that, a full sentence, and throughout it, he kept focused on Grace's face.
"It's this place, Scott. It has that effect on all of us as far as I can see. You seemed to suddenly have all sorts of talents and abilities, it's why so many think it's a school of magic. I felt just like that when I came here about 5 months ago, I can't believe how much I've improved in that time. I was in so much trouble when I came here, you just wouldn't believe. I was an absolute mess, but somehow, this place has saved me, and given me a real chance of success."

Scott looked at Grace, while she was talking and trying to imagine this very attractive girl, probably a few years older than him, as a 'complete mess'. He desperately wanted to keep chatting to her, but he was struggling to do so, he just couldn't think of what to say. His mind wrestled with different alternatives, but was too unsure how she might react, and so didn't say anything, as usual. Grace detected his internal struggle, and helped him by adding a further comment.

"I do hope the magic works for you, as well Scott, I'm sure it will."

Scott was still trying to speak again, when he heard Stacey speak.

"It's time for your next session, thanks everyone, well done."

Grace got up, and held out her hand towards Scott.

"Bye, Scott, it's been really good to meet you, perhaps we'll meet again sometime."

He also stood up, and somehow, his hand moved forward and shook hers. He was determined to speak to her again.

"Thanks Grace, er I mean goodbye, er yes."

She smiled, and made her way out of the room. Although Stacey had been putting the envelopes, cards and pencils into her plastic box, she had been trying to watch Scott with Grace, and went to Scott.

"I was very impressed with you, Scott."

Scott could still feel his heart pounding hard, and was clearly extremely excited, and responded enthusiastically and very rapidly.

Absolutely brilliant, Stace. I can honestly say that I have never enjoyed a Science lesson so much. I can't believe I could've done so well in the GCSE questions. That hour went so quick it was nothing like anything at school."

Stacey laughed loudly.

"Actually Scott, I was referring to you with Grace. I thought you did really well in chatting to her."

Scott also laughed when he realised that Stacey is invariably focusing on his eight success skills.

"Thanks Stace, you're right I did do quite well there. It was difficult, but I was determined to look at her and talk to her. Perhaps more of this magic is working on me."

Chapter 16
"exam success and without the need of a specialist teacher!"

"As well as an improvement in your social skills, you seem to be very motivated throughout the whole session."

Stacey was talking to Scott as they made their way back to Scott's room, with Scott carrying the box of resources they used in the session.

"It was nothing like I imagined."

"So what did you think?"

"Brilliant. As you know I am very competitive, so playing games and activities like that was great fun."
"I thought you'd feel that way, but do you think you learnt much?"
"I cannot believe how much I learnt. I have never done that well on any GCSE Science questions."
"You did seem to be studying throughout the whole session."
"Studying? How can that be studying? It was just good fun!"
They were just entering Scott's room, Scott placed the box on his bed and they sat in their usual positions.
"I asked the same question when I first came here, I think we all do. There's a session on the website that helps to explain why it is so effective."
"Good, cos I really don't understand how I could've done so well with so little effort."
"It is important to remember that JC struggled to learn as a kid and when he became a teacher he was determined to discover as much as he could about the science of learning and apply it to help everyone learn to succeed. What you've just experienced is a superb example of SUPERlearning and I reckon you will use it to learn academic stuff for school and college in the future, I certainly have!"
"Definitely, if I can succeed in exams doing that sort of stuff."
"I'll start by asking you who was the teacher in the session?"
Scott looked at her and thought for a few moments and replied.
"Well, I was going to say, 'you'. But then you didn't actually tell us anything to do with science, did you?"
"No, and I'm certainly not an expert in Science."
"So did we have a teacher?"
"That depends on what you think is the meaning of a teacher. It may help for you to look at this definition."
Stacey moved and clicked the mouse and tapped a few keys and the following appeared on the screen.

A teacher is anyone or anything that helps you learn

"But there were lots of people in the session that helped me learn, were they all teachers?"
"I would say so."
"What about the Videostudy, MC Jigsaws, Quizcards, are they teachers?"
"Well did they help you to learn?"
"Definitely, so I suppose they could be considered to be teaching me. I see your point, I've not thought of it like that before. So why was it so effective?"
Stacey pointed to the poster on the wall.

THE FIVE LEARNING REQUIREMENTS

MOTIVATION	Unless we are keen to learn, we will lack the determination to overcome the difficulties that will occur.
CONCENTRATION	If we do not focus on the task, our brain cannot receive or store the information needed.
ENVIRONMENT	Distractions can cause concentration to become too difficult to allow us to learn,
ATTAINABLE TASKS	Unless the task to be learnt is broken down into small steps ('bitesize chunks') they are too difficult to grasp ('too large to digest').
FEELING SUCCESS	If we do not feel we are making progress it becomes too difficult to keep motivated.

"I'm sure you recall that poster. In your session, were all five occurring?"
Scott studied it carefully and replied.
"I spose they were. So why have I been so poor in school?"
"This slide answers that for you."
Stacey moved the mouse and clicked it a few times and this slide appeared.

WHY we often struggle to learn in lessons

MOTIVATION	Most of us do not understand WHY learning is so important and are unaware of our own learning styles that can help us overcome our barriers to our learning, so we struggle and give up
CONCENTRATION	When we are born we are not able to concentrate very well, a lot of practice is needed to develop this, but many of us do not do this so we struggle and give up!
ENVIRONMENT	The closeness of other students is often too distracting for us, so studying in groups is often too difficult. Many of us get embarrassed when we appear to struggle and give up!
ATTAINABLE TASKS	When we look at some of the tasks we're given many of us think 'it's too difficult' or 'I can't do it', and give up!
FEELING SUCCESS	Many of us rely on teachers to check on our progress, so it occurs too infrequently to encourage us and maintain our motivation, and give up!

"That's it! That's why I've been unable to learn in lessons, But why was it so different in the CAI session?"
"Just consider each of the five requirements. You were motivated because from the start there was little pressure on you. You felt you were involved in a quiz and part of a team, supported by your peers. Because of this, your environment was unlike the usual lessons and you were able to discuss and concentrate comfortably with your partner. Each activity was carefully planned so that it was done in small steps, none seemed to difficult on their own but added together meant you did a lot. You were continually assessing each of these activities or steps so you kept feeling you were achieving success. In the end you did two exam questions that normally you would not even have attempted but you just carried on as before and got almost full marks on them."
"That's so cool, Stace. I suppose all you had to do was make sure we had the resources and understood what we had to do."
"JC was very keen to develop a process that helps us to learn effectively and achieve exam success and without the need of a specialist teacher!"
"Why?"
"Remember the first of the 8 skills is effective learning and the earlier we can develop as effective independent learners the greater our chances of success."
"That's brilliant. Why don't all schools do it this way?"
"Excellent question Scott. It's a very different from the traditional approach and developing people to do it this way will take time, but hopefully one day they will, but at the moment too few know about it."
"Is this how we are going to learn all our school subjects in here?"
"English, Maths and Science. This section on our successfeelosophy website on 'SUPERlearning and Exams' is what we use all the time, I'll show you some of it and I'm sure you'll do the same."
Again Stacey moved the mouse and clicked it. Scott was very impressed by all that he'd heard and adjusted his position on the chair so he could be more attentive and show Stacey he was interested.
"This slide is crucial in realising what is needed to succeed in exams."

To have exam success you need to be good a these 6 exam skills

1	CONCENTRATION	as the level increases the time expected for intense concentration, IN SILENCE, also increases (up to 3 hours)
2	READING	At GCSE this usually presents less of a problem than at Key Stage 2 or 3
3	UNDERSTANDING	as the level increases the questions and information provided become more complicated and difficult to understand
4	RECALL	GCSE requires much less of this than the Key Stage 2 and 3 or 'old fashioned' exams.
5	MATCHING	GCSE has an increasing emphasis on this skill which is connecting the information with the question, "like putting a jigsaw piece in the correct place."
6	WRITING	As the level increases the quantity and quality expected in the answer increases

Scott looked at the slide carefully trying hard to understand it. Stacey continued. "The CAI sessions are cleverly planned to help practise and develop these skills, usually so that that we don't even realise it. The videostudy required a little of all of these, especially the matching, that's why the answers were provided to reduce the reliance on recall. The MC Jigsaws are brilliant at developing these skills without realising it, they are superb practise to develop our cognitive skills, our skill at matching the solutions to the problems. The quizcards are outstanding at developing our recall, as you saw, Having the mark schemes immediately after doing the past exam questions meant that writing exactly the correct answers could be learnt, it is essential that it is done in this way."

"It certainly worked for me."

"It works for all of us, Scott. But you also need to be aware of these slides."

The screen changed and this slide appeared.

Whatever the subject or your ability in it, you will be assessed like this

If you don't practise it you will struggle to do it!

A new slide appeared.

This table helps identify your exam difficulties - For each question tick the reasons that you think best explains your loss of marks

REASON **QUESTION No.→**		
POOR **CONCENTRATION** (CARELESSNESS)		
MISUNDERSTOOD QUESTION OR INFORMATION (THOUGHT IT MEANT ...)		
UNABLE TO **RECALL** INFORMATION (DID NOT KNOW ...)		
UNABLE TO **MATCH** INFORMATION (DIDN'T REALISE THAT...)		
ANSWER **WRITTEN** TOO UNCLEAR (COULDN'T BE READ OR INACCURATE WORDS)		

"The last activity you did in the CAI session was attempting the exam questions, but gradually you need to practise doing more and more questions in one go, so you can cope with a full exam. Also you need to get used to using this to analyse you exam papers."

"I've used this table so many times in the last 18 months, it has been absolutely brilliant in identifying what I should concentrate on in exams, Using it stopped me wasting time on stuff I've already learnt. Since I've been using this process I improved so much in exams that I managed to get much better grades in GCSE in Maths, English and Science."

"What were your grades, Stace?"

"I got grade B in English and Double Science and a C in Maths, in a year."

"That's impressive, Stace"

"Especially when you consider I had not attended college or done any studying for almost two years before I started it."

"Do you think it could do the same for me? I'm supposed to take my GCSE's next year and I've just had predictions of grade F in all of those subjects."

"If you follow this SUPERlearning process, yes, I'm sure you will, Scott."

"Well I've got six months here, so I can make a start."

"Virtually everyday you'll have a CAI session in Maths, English or Science, so you'll get lots of practice and almost everyone in here is in the same situation, so you'll get lots of encouragement."

"It's really weird, Stace. Probably for the first time ever, I'm actually feeling positive, even looking forward to it."

"I know, Scott. Most of us have felt like that, It's another reason why so many of us talk in terms of this place being a 'school of magic'.

"The more I experience in here the more I believe it!"

"What is also important to note, Scott, is that the sessions are designed to develop the 8 skills and it was wonderful to see you displaying and developing the skills in it. It should also help us to complete your initial evaluation of the skills."

Chapter 17
"as my success skills developed my self esteem has improved."

"We can now complete our initial evaluation of your 8 success skills."
Stacey moved and clicked the mouse again and this table appeared.

Empathy	Grade
Works out how people are feeling through their words, body language, gestures, and tone.	
Able to see the world from other people's emotions, beliefs and points of view.	
Able to show respect (care and consideration) for people from all cultures, backgrounds, interests, attainments, attitudes, and values.	

"Empathy! I've heard the word, Stace, but I don't know what it means"
"Empathy is the skill of understanding other people, it is often confused with 'sympathy' which is 'feeling what other's are feeling'.
"Let's have a look at what the three parts are on it. Works out how people are feeling through their words, body language, gestures, and tone, How do you do that?"
"I'm not surprised that this is difficult for you as it is dependent on our communication skill. We saw earlier that during puberty this usually becomes very poor, so you are like most teenagers that you struggle to work out what others are feeling."
"We've already seen that I'm struggling to understand my own feelings so how can I possibly work out what others are feeling?"
"Excellent point, Scott and I wish others were aware of that, especially parents and schools. There are few learning opportunities provided to help children and teenagers develop this in the home and in schools."
"So what is done here then, Stace?"
"Mainly through collaborative action inquiry sessions and one-to-one discussions like this, Scott."
"I've never had anything like these discussions before, Stace and I've already found them very helpful."
"Good to hear that and I'm sure the collaborative action inquiry sessions will do the same."
"Can I have a grade of one, Stace? Otherwise it would have to be zero."
"Okay, Scott, one again."
"The next one is how well do you think you can see the world through other people's eyes? I don't think I've ever thought about it,"
"Again, you are a typical teenager there, Scott, just like I was. Because we don't get learning opportunities involving listening to other people express their thoughts and feelings, we are unable to develop this very well. Also, research shows that if you read a lot of wide-ranging fiction you can also develop this skill quite well. Unfortunately, as a teenager I only read magazines about celebrity and fashion, which only really caused me to concentrate on superficial and material things. I don't suppose you read much either, do you Scott?"
"I sometimes look at football reports and league tables, otherwise no."
"What I realised 18 months ago, Scott, was that I only ever listened to people who had the same view as me. First, Arthur started to show me a different view, and then my sister and family, followed by JC and then the collaborative action inquiry sessions here, so since then I've really improved in this."
"Until that happens, I reckon I should give myself another pathetic score of one."
Scott put down his grade on the computer and read the next one.
"This one mentions 'Respect', I've heard this word many times from my dad and teachers but I don't really know what it means. What is it all about, Stace?"

"Another good point, Scott. There are lots of words used by people who don't actually really understand them and it just adds to the confusion and problem. If you respect someone, it means that you are prepared to consider their thoughts and feelings and actually care about them. I used to find that teachers said I didn't respect them and basically I couldn't care less about them and I thought their comments were a waste of time, so they were probably right, in that I didn't respect them."

"I'm the same with my teachers. I reckon the only one I respect is Mr Cole, my PE teacher, I think he does care about me, he gives me some good advice and I try not to upset him."

"A good example, Scott. Why do you think you respect, Mr Cole?"

"Well he has spent some time trying to help me and understand me, I think he thinks I'm not as bad as everyone else does, and I feel he actually wants to help me, I suppose."

"And that's because respect has to be earned. It usually takes time and effort to gain people's respect especially with typical teenagers like you and me. We have not learnt the skills of communication, self-awareness and empathy very well and we are often reluctant to trust or appreciate others and so 'disrespect them'.

"Since I respect you and Mr Cole, Stace can I give myself a score of two here?"

"Of course Scott, and I appreciate that comment, thank you."

Scott felt a warm glow inside that he had made the comment about Stacey and that she'd appreciated it, he could feel the usual embarrassment creeping up on him so he moved on quickly.

"I get a total of 4 out of 30 for empathy then, much the same as the others. I'll put that grade in and let's move on to the last skill."

The screen then changed and the next table appeared.

Social/Relationship	Grade
Works and learns well in groups and teams, taking on different roles, cooperating with others to achieve a joint outcome.	
Displays an appropriate level of independence from others, while maintaining positive relationships with others.	
Gives and receives feedback and uses their experiences to help make decisions to improve their and other people's achievements	

Stacey spoke immediately.

"I think this one is very tricky. When I first saw it, I thought I would do well because I liked socializing with my mates. Once I started to study and think about it, I realised that it was much more than that."

"I can see that with the first part."

"Yes, I used to struggle to work with anyone or cooperate with others, I couldn't stay in a job particularly because of that."

"I've already pointed out in football I kept getting into trouble and sent off, but sometimes I'd have arguments with my team mates as well. Not so good in

school, in lessons I suppose, so I'm going to give myself a four here, my best so far."
"Good start, but what about the next one. I was unable to maintain any positive relationships with others and I'd not managed to have any long term close friends, boyfriends or jobs. I was so easily influenced by my friends, peers and the media?"
"Peers and the media? What do you mean by that?"
"The television, films, newspapers, magazines, adverts all keep telling us what we should like, how we should appear and behave, what to wear, what to buy. Our peers, kids of our age and our friends, can exert lots of pressure on us to follow these fashions and fads so that we think and behave like 'sheep', or like a 'pack animal', frightened to stand out and be an individual."
Scott felt that Stacey was describing him perfectly. She continued.
"Extensive research indicates that now most teens and people in their twenties have low self esteem, and unable to display an appropriate level of independence from others. There's a section in the website which you'll find very helpful, I think I can quickly find a slide that shows how common low self esteem is in young people in the 21st century."
Stacey moved and clicked the mouse and this slide appeared.

Self-Esteem is the **belief** that they are **capable** of overcoming difficulties in their lives to achieve success and happiness.

People with High Self-Esteem have a positive attitude to life and believe they are capable of overcoming the difficulties they meet. They are keen to take on new experiences, seeing them as challenges, not problems.

People with Low Self-Esteem have a negative attitude to life and do not feel they are responsible or can overcome their difficulties. They will often show the following characteristics:

- Focus on trying to prove themselves or impress others.
- Tend to use or put down others for their own gain.
- May act with arrogance and contempt towards others.
- Repeatedly try to convince themselves of their worth.
- Reluctant to take risks to expose themselves to failure.
- Frequently blame others for their shortcomings rather than take responsibility for their actions.

Scott studied the slide very carefully and then spoke.

"I've heard people talk about self esteem a lot but never understood what it meant. It looks like me and most of the kids I know have low self esteem."
"I definitely had low self esteem when I came here, but as my success skills developed my self esteem has improved."
"I wish I'd known about that stuff before. Back to my usual grade of one, here"
"The last part is about learning from others, Scott."
"I'm definitely not good at coping with criticism or 'feedback' as it says here but what's the rest mean?"
"Uses their experiences to help make decisions to improve their and other people's achievements' is in a way to highlight the importance of open discussions, or collaborative action inquiry, as we call it. Before everyone had televisions, families and communities had much more discussion about their experiences and why they occurred, this helped people to learn from each other. This rarely occurs now and so the learning tends not to occur."
"We don't even sit in the same room at home, Stace."
"I was the same with my family, I was in my bedroom if I was in."
"There is a famous quote on that poster."
Stacey pointed to the ceiling again.

The most important single ingredient in the formula of success is knowing how to get along with people.
Theodore Roosevelt

"I can only give myself a grade of one on that part and a total of six out of 30 in this skill section, almost my highest grade I think."
"And more than I got 18 months ago."
The screen now showed Scott's whole self-evaluation on the skills we need to succeed and they both looked at it closely. Scott felt ashamed and commented.
"That's rubbish, ain't it?"
"Very similar to mine and most other teenagers in the 21st century!"
"I can see why most teenagers would do as poorly as you and me."
"So what do you think about the process of going through this report together?"
"Great, much more use than the reports we have at school, they don't tell you nothing. I actually understand what needs to happen for me to succeed."
"Another superb comment, Scott. That's why we believe mentors are so much more use than teachers. We feel that most of the expertise in any area or subject can be obtained from the website but accessing and applying it is the key part of learning and this is where a mentor can help. The importance of 'Assessment for Learning' has been known for years but still only applied

occasionally in schools, but as you can see, learning through assessments in this way is incredibly useful."
"This has been so helpful, Stace."
"I felt the same doing this evaluation with JC when I came here."
"So how often do we do this, Stace?"
"About every ten days. The next time we do it, we'll have lots of video clips of you to refer to."
Scott thought about that for a moment before replying.
"That'll be helpful."
"I've found it absolutely brilliant. It helped me develop my self-awareness a great deal and identify my priorities."
"Yeah, I s'pose it would, never thought about it like that before."
Stacey smiled as she thought how many times Scott had said that.
"Right, now we need to sort out your timetable."
"Okay"
Scott moved and clicked the mouse and opened up his timetable.
"It looks as though my next CAI session is later today and it's called 'The Trouble With Boys', will you be there?"
"I will Scott, but after today, I'll be coming to less of them, I think you're making so much progress that I can spend more time with some of my other students."
Scott was clearly pleased that Stacey would be in his next CAI session but disappointed to hear that it would become less common. However, He felt good that she considered he was making good progress.
"I'm amazed at how much I've enjoyed my first days here and staggered by how much I seem to have learnt already. What's been most strange has been how different everything is here and how positive everyone seems to be."
"Interesting that you should've said that, because the next session is on 'boys' and quite a few of the CAI sessions you'll do in the first few days will help you with that."
"Good"
"I think you'll find the section on 'Adolescence and Men' in the website very interesting and useful. Our CAI session is at 1800 hours, so you've got some time to prepare for it. We could go for some food before that, at about 1730 hours. Shall I call for you then, Scott?"
"Yes please, Stace, thanks."
"Well done, Scott. A please and a thanks, you are learning."
Scott felt really pleased with himself as Stacey left the room.

Name: Scott Spicer	The Skills We Need To Succeed Report

GRADES
10 – DEFINITELY/EXCELLENT- OCCURS ALL OF THE TIME
8 – VERY GOOD – OCCURS MOST OF THE TIME
6 – FAIRLY GOOD – OCCURS SOME OF THE TIME
4 – O.K.- - OCCURS OCCASIONALLY
2 – VERY WEAK - 0CCURS RARELY
0 – NO – DOES NOT OCCUR AT ALL

	Grade
EFFECTIVE LEARNING	
Comfortable with change and learning new things.	2
Effective independent learner, who does not rely on someone to teach them.	1
Readily practices to develop new skills.	5
COMMUNICATION	
Concentrates intently despite distraction.	4
Verbal skills (speaking, listening, reading, writing)	1
Non-verbal skills (visual gestures, body language, touch)	1
COGNITIVE	
Understands 'cause and effect' and detects the key information or factors needed to make the decisions (Analytical thinking)	4
Puts information into context so is able to understand and relate the information to the particular situation (Conceptual thinking)	2
Able to realise the likely outcomes or consequences of decisions.	2
SELF-AWARENESS	
Knows and accepts what they are feeling, and can label their feelings.	1
Can identify their strengths and weaknesses, and feel they know themselves well.	1
Can reflect on their actions and identify lessons to be learned from them.	1
MANAGING FEELINGS	
Expresses their emotions to others and in ways that are clear and appropriate to the situation. (suitable/good behaviour)	2
Understands that how they express their feelings may have a big effect on others and how they are treated. (knows how to behave)	1
Has strategies to manage their impulses and strong emotions (eg. anger, anxiety, stress, jealousy) to avoid them behaving in ways that has negative consequences for them or for other people.	1

MOTIVATION	
Views errors as part of the normal learning process, does not 'fear failure' and bounces back from disappointment or failure (Resilient)	1
Uses their and other's experiences, including mistakes and setbacks, to change (improve) their thinking and behaviour.	4
Takes responsibility for their lives, believe that they can influence what happens to them and make wise choices. (growth mindset and Internal locus of control)	1
EMPATHY	
Works out how people are feeling through their words, body language, gestures, and tone.	1
Able to see the world from other people's emotions, beliefs and points of view.	1
Able to show respect (care and consideration) for people from all cultures, backgrounds, interests, attainments, attitudes, and values.	2
SOCIAL SKILLS	
Works and learns well in groups and teams, taking on different roles, cooperating with others to achieve a joint outcome.	4
Displays an appropriate level of independence from others, while maintaining positive relationships with others.	1
Gives and receives feedback and uses their experiences to help make decisions to improve their and other people's achievements	1

Chapter 18
"it was like being with my mates but much better."

Almost as soon as Stacey left the room Scott began talking to himself as he moved and clicked the mouse.

"So the CAI session is an inquiry into this question –'Why do so many boys struggle so much in the 21st century'. There's the one I studied with Stacey on being a teenager. Ah, there it is 'The Trouble With Boys', I like the title. Good, lots of videos and slides, perfect."

Suddenly this slide appeared on the big screen.

Suicide is the most common
cause of death in men aged under 35
(Men's Health Forum, 2002)

Teen male suicides hit 'crisis' levels

Suicide among the teenage male population has reached "crisis" point with a 72% increase in reported cases over 20 years.

Health psychologist Dr Rory O'Connor believes the growing suicide rate reflects the urgent need for society to address the wider underlying issues.

He said: "We place higher expectations on our young people and we are not training our young people with the skills needed in a changing society.

Fifteen to 19 is a very vulnerable age and it is everyone's responsibility to help them."

"Blimey I'm amazed at that and I don't like the sound of it. There's a video clip on this, I'll get myself comfy."

Scott adjusted his position and started watching the video. Gradually his chin began to lower and he sat there open-mouthed, struggling to believe what he saw and heard. It was about a seemingly 'happy-go-lucky' typical 18 year old suddenly who commits suicide. His parents and friends had absolutely no idea how he felt, he never talked to them about his feelings and were shocked at his death after an evenings drinking with his mates. His suicide note made no sense to them.

Scott eyes began to water, as they did when he watched sad videos, on his own, of course. He realised that this could've been him. No matter how upset or depressed he felt he would never let anyone know, no way would he do that, especially not to his mates. As one of the boys said in the film, 'it's not the sort of thing you do in front of your mates'.

Suddenly the screen changed and a new slide appeared in front of him, causing him to comment.

"That's incredible!"

Wednesday, 2nd September 2009

Depression looms as global crisis

The World Health Organization predicts that within 20 years more people will be affected by depression than any other health problem. According to the WHO, depression will be the biggest health burden on society both economically and sociologically.

- **About half of mental disorders begin before the age of 14**
- **Around 20% of the world's children and adolescents are estimated to have mental disorders or problems** *Source: WHO*

"How can there be so many kids suffering from depression, I know I have, but these are ridiculous numbers."

Then the next slide appeared on the screen.

INQUIRY QUESTION

The next video clip focuses on a 16 year old boy, Lee.

1) Why do you think Lee thinks and feels like this?

2) What skills does he most need to develop?

3) How would you try to help him learn them to succeed?

Scott read the slide carefully and continued talking to himself.

"From those questions it looks as though this kid ain't gonna kill himself, this time."

The video clip began and this time Scott smiled as he watched it. Lee, the 16 year old boy, was very much like him, but wanted to be a professional rugby player rather than a footballer. He kept smiling and laughing because he thought Lee was just a lazy, 'waste of space', who couldn't be bothered to do anything he didn't like and just making excuses. However, as the film progressed Scott began to realise that this could be him in the near future and it ended with Lee being very depressed and helpless. Scott began to imagine Lee committing suicide like the 18 year old had done in the previous film, and the smile disappeared from his face to be replaced by a very concerned expression.

"This could be me, this is me! Am I becoming Lee? Would I commit suicide? I s'pose so."

Scott's discussion with himself ended when a new slide appeared on the screen.

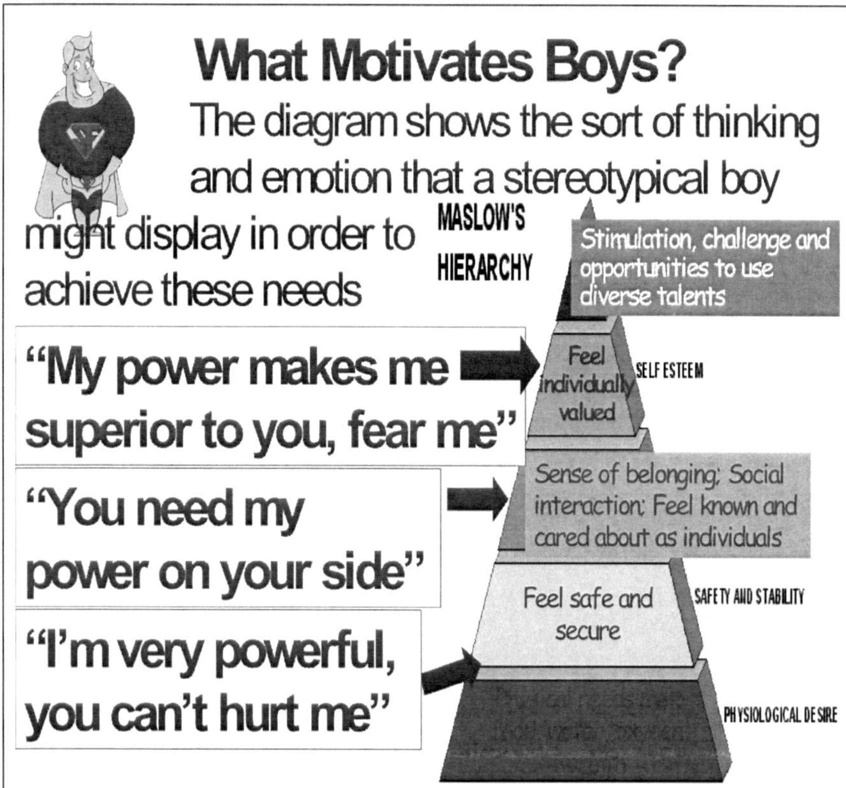

"I remember this, Maslow's Hierarchy, from the other day with Stace."

Scott studied it closely and his face frowned, reflecting his thoughts. He realised that this diagram showed his obsession with being 'macho', he'd spent many years desperately trying to show everyone how 'big and tough and strong' he was. His fights were usually to show that 'my power makes me superior to you' and showing any form of weakness was to be avoided at all costs. Having just watched two videos of boys very similar to him, he was feeling very uncomfortable; he had been almost as foolish as them.
Again the screen changed and this next slide appeared.

Key difficulties in the 21st century that boys have to overcome if they are to succeed.

1) The traditional 'macho man' is now at a disadvantage – physical power can now be done by machines.
2) The skills of communication, self-awareness, managing feelings, motivation and empathy have become essential in all aspects of life.
3) These skills have to be learnt during and following puberty when frontal lobe of the brain is responsible for developing the skills is reduced (depressed) in effectiveness, so thinking rationally and good decision making becomes difficult and emotions are in control.

Scott was now thinking very deeply and thoroughly engaged with what he was seeing, this slide continued to increase this effect. His eyes began to water again and his throat felt as though he was going to choke - all of this was about him! Stacey's mentoring him and the effectiveness of the applying the five learning requirements in the centre was really having this magical influence on him. He actually felt that some 'spirit of awareness' was entering his body and he was seeing himself in a very different way.

Scott actually felt excited, a very unusual emotion for him considering he was sat in room with relative strangers, all teenagers, in what could be described as a 'lesson'. However, his experiences in the few days he'd been in the centre meant he was confident that the group would be supportive and the topic was extremely relevant to him, he even felt he knew enough to contribute!
"Who wants to start?" Stacey asked.
Ben, a 16 year old bespectacled boy with striking resemblance to Harry Potter at that age, with short dark spiky hair, dressed entirely in black, including his success feelosophy 'T' shirt, was very quick to respond.
"Lee is a very typical 16 year old boy, which means after puberty, the frontal lobe of his brain has probably not developed the neuron pathways enough to the emotional part, to manage or control his emotions. His self-awareness seems poor in that he thinks he needs to be 'macho', the old-fashioned traditional man, and he seems to believe this is his only real asset, which is reflected by his desire to be a professional rugby league player. However, he does not seem aware that his poor skill of managing feelings means his repeated loss of temper and control is a real liability to his team and costs them dearly on many occasions, even though it seems his coach repeatedly explains it to him. Also he clearly has poor motivation skills and has a fixed mindset, because he keeps blaming everyone and everything for his lack of success."
Throughout Ben's comment, Scott was thinking he could be talking about me, and then suddenly he was shaken out of his deep thinking by the round of applause that spontaneously broke out when Ben stopped talking.
"Well put, Ben." Said Alys. "His poor communication skills are clearly shown throughout the video, especially in the interview, he can't maintain attention or eye contact. He struggles to listen or speak clearly and it shows him repeatedly texting on the phone."
"He's just like I used to be before I came in here." Dave commented. "I just couldn't communicate at all except with my mates or electronically. He doesn't seem like a particularly bad kid, but like me, his 8 success skills are very poorly developed."
"And me, Dave." Ben replied
"And me" said Sam, then Tom, then Andy.
"And me" said Scott.
Stacey just glanced and smiled at Scott, touched the back of his hand and he felt she knew how much of an effort and improvement it was for him to have said those two words in front of a group of teenagers. The 'strange magical feeling' he has experienced several times since he'd been in the centre flowed through him again.
The discussion continued with everyone very keen to take part and although Scott did not make any major contributions, on several occasions he made

supportive comments and agreed with various people. He was both shocked and disappointed when Stacey pointed out that the session needed to end, and he still had this 'strange magical feeling' when he and Stacey arrived back at his room.

"Incredible, Stace, absolutely incredible." Scott said as he sat down in his usual chair.

"What do you mean, Scott?" Stacey replied with a smile.

"I have never felt like that in a classroom before."

"Well it's not actually a classroom, but carry on what do you mean?"

"It's difficult to describe but I felt as though some sort of drug was injected into me and flowed through me. Almost from the start I felt comfortable in the group and it was like being with my mates but much better."

"What do you mean it felt better than being with your mates?"

"Well, with my mates I'm always trying to take the pee out of them, or going one better, I'm always on my guard that they may take the pee out of me so even with them I don't relax completely. But in there once I saw who was in the group I felt they were going to support me because they support everyone. I've not seen any of them put anyone down or try to upstage them."

"It's an amazing feeling isn't it Scott? I remember when I started to get that feeling and like you I struggled to believe how good it felt. We've looked at Maslow's Hierarchy and this feeling comes from the fact that we have a sense of belonging and our esteem needs are being met, because we feel we are being valued by everyone. What is really remarkable, magical even, is that we adjust and do the same very quickly."

"I can definitely see why you describe it as magical. I've never experienced anything like this before and it's so difficult to explain."

"And that is quite a good description of the term 'magic'. What about the topic, 'the trouble with boys', what did you think about that?"

"Outstanding! To have that session after the 'Good Will Hunting' one, was so helpful. I really understand now why I've had so many difficulties and why I'm here."

"Brilliant, I thought and hoped you would. What about overcoming these difficulties?"

"That's learning the 8 skills we need to succeed, that's going to take some time."

Stacey immediately moved towards Scott and hugged him. Scott was surprised initially and then again he felt that 'magical glow' go through him.

"That's so wonderful to hear, Scott. You've made so much progress so quickly. To have developed you're self-awareness so much in just a few days is staggering."

Stacey noticed that Scott was smiling and his eyes were watering.

"Tears of joy Scott, tears of joy! How great to see them on you. It shows again how much you've improved, you've started so well."

Probably for the first time in his life he was actually not ashamed of crying, in fact he actually realised he was pleased with it. His throat had such a 'lump' in it that he just couldn't speak initially despite desperately wanting to. Finally he managed to say something.
"Thanks Stace, this has been the most incredible few days of my life. Somehow, I think I now understand why I did what I did and what I've got to do to change."
"Well that was my hope in bringing you here, it certainly transformed my life, I'm sure it can do the same for you. I just wish everyone could have this sort of opportunity. Anyway, I'm off for a swim now and I think you are off to the soccer skills room again, aren't you?"
"I am, Stace. When you first talked about the Learning For Success Centre you described it as being 'magical. You said it was like having a Hogwarts in the real world, a holiday camps or health centre having the power to transform people, I just didn't believe you but I think you are right, it is certainly a magical place."

Chapter 19
"We could certainly do with some of that magic in our schools"

"What time is she due to arrive, Stace?"
"About 1000 hours, Scott, we've got plenty of time."
"This is the most nervous I've felt for a very long time."
Scott said to Stacey as they sat in the food hall to have some breakfast.
"Is it common for head teachers to visit this centre?"
"You've been here for almost six months, Scott, have you seen many people visiting?"
"I suppose I have, especially in the last couple of months, but are many of them head teachers?"
"Yes. The word has spread about these 'Learning For Success Centres', and head teachers are particularly keen to find out what they are like."
"I do remember when I was in Mrs Lucas' office with mum and dad just before I came here, that she said JC Learner was one of her heroes and she'd heard that these centres were excellent. She was very keen for me to come here and said she'd like to visit. But that was nearly six months ago and I'd forgotten all about it."
"Well clearly she hasn't and since you will be returning to her school after Christmas, she probably wants to see you and the centre before you leave."
"Stace, don't you mean, I hope to be returning to her school. After all the trouble I caused, she may not have me."
"Once she spends any time with you she'll know you are a completely different person and will be keen to have you back. In fact, I bet she will struggle to

believe who you are. In the six months you've been here you've made incredible progress, she probably won't recognise you in any way."
"That's kind of you to say so, Stace. I know I have improved a great deal, our continual assessment of the 8 skills has ensured that I kept on my journey to success and I'm amazed at my improvement."
"Mrs Lucas will feel the same. How has your presentation gone?"
"I'm pleased with it, but that's what I'm probably most nervous about, especially as JC will be there as well."
"I've seen you do quite a few presentations recently Scott, in various CAI sessions and I'm confident that both JC and Mrs Lucas will be very impressed."
"I think Mrs Lucas will be shocked that I'd actually do anything like that, I certainly wouldn't have until I came here."
"Exactly, Scott. Her memories of you will not be good so I think she'll be impressed by everything you do today. It's almost time for us to go and meet her so we'd better get our skates on."
Scott and Stacey finished off their breakfast and made their way to JC Learner's room. When they got to the main entrance, Angela was sitting the receptionist's seat as she had been when Scott first arrived almost six months before.
"Hallo Ange, how are you?" Scott said cheerfully, staring straight into her eyes, a complete contrast to his 'rude, non-greeting, when they first met.
"Hi, Scott, hi Stacey. Good to see you and excellent timing. Mrs Lucas arrived early and she's already in with JC."
"Thanks Ange, does he want us to go in?" Stacey asked.
"Yes, he said for you both to go in as soon as you arrived."
They went past Angela, tapped on JC's door, and entered his room.
"Ah, Stacey, Scott, excellent, come in!"
JC was on the sofa wearing a yellow success feelosophy T shirt, black track trousers and trainers opposite pouring tea into a cup for Mrs Lucas. She who was sat on the end of the other sofa, dressed in a silky white blouse, dark blue skirt with matching shoes and spectacles. Mrs Lucas looked up at Scott and Stacey as they entered, the expression on her face was one of shock, almost as though she'd seen a ghost. JC had been expecting this reaction and looked at her immediately.
"I think you'll find Scott's changed a bit." He said, knowing he was making a huge understatement.
Mrs Lucas had automatically tried to stand up, but the shock of seeing Scott had momentarily weakened her muscles and she couldn't move. The reason for her shock was that the boy in front of her looked very different from the one she last saw in her office only six months ago. His hair was now long and curly, just brushing his shoulders and his natural light brown colour. His shoulders seemed huge, his chest much broader and very muscular as a result of regular exercise. His bright blue success feelosophy T shirt was fairly tight and tucked into his black track trousers, showing he was carrying very little fat and his face

was so much thinner. Scott walked straight over to the stunned Mrs Lucas and held out his hand for her to shake and greeted her.
"Good morning, Mrs Lucas, great to see you again. How are you?"
The very polite and pleasant greeting from Scott only added to Mrs Lucas' surprise, she used the arm of the chair to help her stand up and still open-mouthed in amazement moved her hand to shake his. His firm handshake and friendly gesture added to her surprise but gradually she began to restore her composure and she replied.
"Good morning Scott. I'm fine, just recovering from shock. You look so different, so much fitter, healthier."
"I am different, Mrs Lucas. I hope you'll find I'm very different, much better than you remember. I'd like to introduce you to my cousin Stacey, she's been my mentor for the last six months and has helped immensely with my journey to success."
Stacey and Mrs Lucas shook hands and greeted each other.
"Journey to success, that sounds good. My first impression is that you've certainly done a good job." Mrs Lucas replied.
"Please sit down all of you and I'll pour us some tea." JC commented.
They did as he asked and he continued speaking while pouring the tea.
"Mrs Lucas, we've arranged for Scott to give you a tour of the centre, and then to meet Stacey and I, in a CAI room, where he will give us a presentation to demonstrate how much he has developed in the skills we need to succeed. Is that okay with you?"
"That's sounds excellent, although I don't know what you mean by CAI room or the skills we need to succeed, but I'm sure the new Scott will explain them to me."
"Of course, Miss. It will be my pleasure."
The politeness of Scott's reply caused the surprised look to reappear on her face. JC then continued talking.
"Mrs Lucas has been telling me that she's been keen to visit one of our Learning For Success centres for quite some time and has been hearing some very positive feedback about them. Stacey came here as a student about 18 months ago and then returned as a mentor. Many of our mentors are ex-students, they have learnt the skills to succeed very well and fully understand what we are trying to do here. I think you will find that we have such a radical approach here, for the mentors to be effective they need to embrace this approach completely and Stacey is an excellent example."
Stacey looked embarrassed at the compliment, but managed to respond with a 'thank you'. Scott then spoke.
"I agree with that completely. The six months I've been here have been absolutely amazing, nothing like anything I've ever had or even heard of before and Stacey has been truly wonderful."
"Thank you, Scott, that's very kind." She replied.

"I can see you've both finished your tea, If you are ready, Mrs Lucas, it's time for Scott to start your tour." JC commented.

"I'm ready, let's go, Scott."

They all got up, Scott opened the door, Mrs Lucas left with Scott following.

As soon as they entered the reception area Scott began his commentary.

"Mrs Lucas, as we walk around you'll see that the walls are covered with posters, they are to inspire us and keep us motivated."

"Yes I noticed them as soon as I walked in, do you think they help?"

"They have been a great help in developing my self-awareness skill, continually helping me to identify my strengths and weaknesses, and sometimes how to improve them."

"Self-awareness skill, what do you mean by that?"

Scott stopped walking and pointed to this poster on the wall.

Successful people have learnt the skills they need to identify and overcome the difficulties they meet in life to achieve success and happiness.

"The 8 skills we need to succeed are central to the success of this place. Until I understood the importance of the 8 skills, I was not really aware of why I was struggling and having so many difficulties. In a way I was like one of the people that poster refers to."

Scott pointed to another poster.

"I'm too busy drowning to learn to swim!"
If we don't take time to learn,
we won't succeed

"I can see that I have a lot to learn from this place, Scott. Already it is clear why JC Learner said there is such a radical approach here which needs to be embraced completely."

"People like me, who've spent time in here and changed so much, find we can't really explain what happens to us very easily, so we tend to use the word magic a lot."

"I can see why, just looking and listening to you. I can't believe you are the same person."

Scott laughed.

"That's because I'm not the same person, Our personality is how we think, feel and behave, and because I've developed the 8 skills so much since I've been in

here I think, feel and behave differently, my personality has changed, I'm a different person."
Mtr Lucas was incredibly impressed with the quality of his answer and shook her head in disbelief.
"Well I wouldn't argue with that, Scott. So what are these 8 skills?"
Scott looked around and pointed at another poster on the wall.

The skills we need to succeed

- **Effective Learning**
- **Communication**
- **Cognitive (thinking)**
- **Self-awareness**
- **Managing Feelings**
- **Motivation**
- **Empathy**
- **Social skills**

"My journey in here was to improve as much as possible in each of these skills."
"Your journey?"
"Journey to success is the term we use in here to describe what we are trying to do. When I do my presentation later on I'll be trying to explain it."
"I must say I'm looking forward to that a lot."
That comment prompted Scott to realise that if they were to complete the tour in time, they had better get moving. He moved to the door and pushed it open so that Mrs Lucas walked forward into the corridor. Scott watched her face closely and waited for her face to show surprise, which it did.
"Everyone is astonished when they first enter this corridor, the lighting and decor gives the impression that it is always daylight. The traditional day and night does not apply in here."
"It's wonderful. With all those colours and posters as well on the walls, it is such a cheerful and bright place. What's behind those doors?"
"They are the rooms where we sleep and study, I'll show you mine when we get to it, I'm number 25."
"You have your own rooms for sleeping and studying?"

"Yes, it is one of the important features. The first of the 8 skills is effective learning and so encouraging us to become effective independent learners is vital."
"So Scott, you mean you did a lot of studying on your own."
Scott laughed when Mrs Lucas made this comment because he knew this was so difficult for her to believe.
"Yes, probably at least 6 hours each day."
"Six hours each day!"
Mrs Lucas exclaimed with a look of complete astonishment on her face and momentarily stopped as though she was unable to walk while coping with the surprise.
"Maybe more than that, Miss. But studying in here is enjoyable, a lot of it is watching videos, playing computer or video games, doing quizzes and puzzles. We use a process called SUPERlearning and have a website called successfeelosophy.com."
"Will you be able to continue with this when you leave, Scott?"
"Of course, Miss. The website is available to everyone, it actually says on it, 'Helping Everyone Learn To Succeed'."
Just as Scott finished this sentence they reached the central atrium and it was time for another look of complete amazement to appear on Mrs Lucas' face and for her to stop and have a good look around.
"You're probably thinking it looks like a shopping mall. Another key feature is having a place that does not look or feel like the traditional schools which were based on the 19th century model. It is important in here to feel that learning can be enjoyable. I'm actually going to mention a bit on this in my presentation."
"That's the second time you've linked learning and enjoyment."
"I think that is such a key part in my journey to success, the magical way in which I can now learn effectively and enjoy doing it."
"We could certainly do with some of that magic in our schools, Scott."
"I wouldn't disagree with that, Miss. Anyway, here is my room, number 25."
Scott pushed the door and held it open for Mrs Lucas.
"Don't you lock the door, Scott?"
"No. We don't have any valuables in here, so there's no need. There is a big huge emphasis on the negative effects of the brand culture and fashion. It's amazing how quickly we get used to not having mobile phones, i-pods, labelled clothes and so on."
"Very impressive, that is a major problem schools."
Mrs Lucas entered Scott's room as he held the door open and again her mouth lowered to express her surprise, but Scott said nothing this time, he just waited for her to comment.
"What an amazing room! I've never seen so many posters, you've covered every possible part of the walls and ceiling. That's a large screen on wall, what TV channels do you get?"

"None, that's for our computer, TV is too much of a distraction. I haven't seen any actual television since I've been in here. We do get to watch lots of television programmes and films, but they are all on the succcessfeelosophy.com website. They've been carefully selected to help us learn to succeed and that's also where we get our lessons in Maths, English and Science."

Once again Mrs Lucas' face expressed her surprise, but it turned to bewilderment when he mentioned the lessons.

"Well I fully understand and agree with the distractions and problems caused by much of what's on television, but I don't understand what you mean by getting your lessons from the website."

"I thought you'd struggle with that, Miss. Perhaps if you sit down there I will try to explain."

Mrs Lucas did as she was asked and Scott sat at his desk and operated the computer so that the 'SUPERlearning For Exam Success' slide appeared on the screen. He then carefully explained how the process is applied and outlined the effectiveness of Videostudy, M.C.Jigsaws, Quizcards and the Exam Papers with Mark Schemes are to the process.

"Incredible, absolutely incredible, Scott"

Mrs Lucas said when he'd finished his explanation.

"So you've been learning GCSE English, Maths and Science in here without having specialist subject teachers."

"We've had brilliant specialist subject teachers, Miss. But not in person, they've been teaching us on the screen, a bit like watching a film instead of watching a play. I prefer having the teacher on the TV screen, I can stop rewind and replay as much as I want, I couldn't do that in class."

"It certainly is a very radical approach and the exam results from the students that have been in these centres has been remarkable, it is how I first came to hear about them. You've got your mock GCSE exams in the new term after Christmas, you'll have a chance to show how much you've learnt in those."

Scott realised with that comment, that Mrs Lucas was saying he would be allowed back into school, but asked for confirmation.

"Do you mean that I will be allowed to return, Miss?"

"Yes, Scott. I've already seen and heard more than enough to realise that your six months in here have been very effective."

Scott was very relieved and pleased, such that he could feel a lump forming in his throat, so he continued.

"Thanks, Miss. I won't let you down. I think we should continue our tour now."

"Okay Scott, lead the way, please."

They left the room and returned to the central atrium and then into the food hall, where Scott explained how it operated. Once again Mrs Lucas was amazed and asked to sit down for a deeper explanation.

"Scott, there's a couple of things I'm struggling to grasp. First of all, I don't think I understand this 24/7 situation. Do you mean the whole centre is always open, nothing ever closes?"

"Yes. Another key feature in why it is so successful. It took me and everyone else a while to adjust to this sort of timetable, and Stacey helped me a lot at first to organise and plan. However, very quickly I found with the wrist monitor and computer in my room prompting me, I developed my self-awareness and cognitive skills so much that I was able to organise and plan quite easily. Before I came here I couldn't organise my life at all, I had what we call a 'chaotic lifestyle'."

Mrs Lucas took off her very smart designer glasses and began cleaning them, her eyes showing the strain of trying to understand and accept what she was hearing.

"Most of the students in our school struggle with organising and planning their lives, I think the term 'chaotic lifestyle' probably describes many of them. But what exactly did you plan to do, what did you do each day, when did you sleep?"

"It's okay Miss, I appreciate it is difficult to understand, life is so different in here. I would say after the first few days I had a very regular 24 hours. Probably on most occasions I slept from about 0100 hours to 0900 hours, since most of my CAI sessions were either at 1000 and 1900 hours. I tended to eat just before those sessions, so that leaves about 12 hours which I used for SUPERlearning, studying you might call it, soccer skills and fitness sessions."

Mrs Lucas replaced her cleaned glasses, but her expression still showed a level of confusion.

"I've heard the term CAI sessions several times now, but I have no idea what they are, yet they seem to have been central to your day."

"CAI stands for Collaborative Action Inquiry, and these sessions are really enjoyable discussion groups. They are a great way of learning and I suppose you might call them lessons, but there's no traditional teaching. We have key questions that are the focus of the inquiry, most of them relate to English, Maths and Science, but also what you would call PSHE, Personal Social and Health Education. In these sessions I learnt from the others in the room as well as from the videostudies, puzzles and games we have in them."

Scott was enthused with what he was saying and Mrs Lucas was clearly surprised and impressed with his enthusiasm, but still struggling to grasp the complexities of what he was saying. Just then a short stocky boy in his mid-teens, with a round face and bright ginger hair, wearing a light blue success feelosophy T shirt, track bottoms and white trainers walked into the food hall and greeted Scott.

"Hi, Scott, how are you?"

"Hi Sean. I'm fine, are you okay? Can I introduce you to my head teacher, Mrs Lucas."

"Pleased to meet you."
Sean held out his hand, Mrs Lucas stood up and shook it.
"Good morning" She replied
"Sorry to have to leave you Sean, but we'd better carry on with our tour, Miss."
"That's fine, I've got to rush anyway, see you."
Scott and Mrs Lucas said goodbye and left the food hall. As they left Mrs Lucas commented.
"Scott. This is all so fascinating and I have so many questions. But seeing that boy in there prompts me to ask something that is really bothering me. Since we've been on our tour we've hardly seen anyone, but everyone we've seen has been very polite. I thought that this centre would have lots of students who have had lots of problems like you. Where are they?"
Scott smiled and then laughed.
"I asked Stacey the same question when I first came here. There are in fact over 100 students in here, but with the 24/7 approach, the facilities are shared over a long period of time and everyone is kept so busy that you tend not to meet many people except in the CAI sessions."
"And why is everyone so polite?"
"One of the first priorities is for the mentors to help us focus on our self-awareness and to improve our communication skills. We have CCTV cameras everywhere which are used to help our self-awareness skill develop by illustrating how important our communication skills are and how to improve them."
Scott scanned the walls and then pointed to one above the door in front of them. He then spotted a poster near to it and pointed to that.
"That poster might help. There is so much importance placed on being positive and supportive, having so much support from the other students and no negativity is absolutely amazing, almost the complete opposite from in school."

Remember everyone here is your ally
- not your enemy!

Mrs Lucas had the look of surprise that had become commonplace now and commented.
"Getting rid of the bitching, slagging off, verbal and emotional bullying that seems to have become part of every school would be incredible, I can see that if that's occurred here, it must feel like a magical place."
"As I've already said, right from the start, the emphasis is on using mentors to help us identify the difficulties we've had in life and how we can learn the skills we need to succeed to overcome them. We are continually praised for the effort we apply in trying to overcome these difficulties, like maintaining eye contact or being polite, each of the small steps on our journey to success that are actually very difficult for us. When you've got everyone around you being so positive

and encouraged to praise and support, you get sucked into it. Yes, it does feel as though a magical spirit is taking you over."

"Well, there's no doubt from what I've seen so far, it does seem magical. I keep thinking I'm in a Disney movie or Harry Potter will appear any minute."

Scott laughed and realised he'd better continue the tour.

"You can probably see that this section was the old primary school, with what used to be the classrooms either side. The ones on the right are the CAI rooms, we'll use one of those for my presentation in a little while. These on the left have been converted into skill development rooms, the first two are for soccer skills. This one is empty, so we can pop inside."

Scott set up the programme as he had done many times before and watched Mrs Lucas as it began. As he expected, she was again amazed and struggling to grasp what she was observing. Scott continued.

"I've spent many hours in the soccer skills room during the last six months, it's cleverly designed to help people develop their soccer skills extremely quickly. Apparently research has shown that the top experts in sport, music, art etc have had about 10,000 hours of 'deliberate or purposeful practice'. JC has created a room that provides a very effective feedback loop and opportunity for concentrated practice, so that this time can be greatly reduced."

Mrs Lucas was now not only amazed by the room but also Scott's language and knowledge, and although she was conscious of the time, she felt impelled to ask for further information.

"You sound so different as well, Scott. You seemed to know so much and use such complex language, how come?"

"I quickly found so much in here that interests me, I've tried to find out as much as possible. I've also researched lots of stuff on effective learning of skills by people like Matthew Syed, Malcolm Gladwell, Anders Ericsson, and Carol Dweck."

"I've never heard of any of them, but I do know that JC Learner has been very successful."

"JC is an expert in sport, computer programming and most of all learning and this room has been heaven to me. I worked out that I've spent about 1000 hours in here in six months, that's supposed to be worth over 10,000 hours of normal deliberate practice, so I reckon I've improved enormously."

"Well it is certainly a remarkable room, it reminds me of the holodeck they had in Star Trek."

"That's it, Miss. Apparently JC used that as his inspiration but I've never seen Star Trek."

"Oh I've watched all of the series over the years, I'm a huge fan."

Scott then felt the vibration on his wrist monitor reminding him that he only had ten minutes left to complete his tour.

"Oh sorry, Miss. We've only got ten minutes left to complete our tour. We'd better get a move on."

"That's okay, Scott, I understand, it's just that this is all so amazing."
They left the soccer skills room and walked along the corridor, Scott briefly stating the purpose of each room.
"This one is for cricket, this for golf, for tennis, for hockey, and for martial arts."
As they got to the end of the corridor they went through the double doors on the left into 100 metre long corridor.
"The sports hall is on the right and on the left they are cardiovascular training rooms."
Mrs Lucas stopped and stared through the transparent plastic wall, first at the big flat screen TV at the front, then the running, cycling, rowing, and cross training machines.
"What a brilliant idea, having your own personal training room."
"Yes, I've spent many hours in them. All the equipment is linked to the internal internet, so it keeps all your records and helps your plan and keep an eye on your training."
They continued walking along the corridor and Mrs Lucas stopped in her tracks when they got to the swimming rooms.
"This is an unbelievable place, such a clever use of space and the old buildings. It looks nothing like a school, or anything I've ever seen before. This bit reminds me of a health centre."
They briefly looked into the sports hall on the right and then Scott held open the double doors on the left so they could see into the corridor for the offices and admin rooms.
"There are various offices along here, the one at the end is where we met JC earlier. This one on the left is the monitoring room, as you can see there are lots of screens for the CCTV, which are continually monitored by people and electronically, so that any problems are quickly detected and also clips are collected and used to assess and support students."
"What do you mean, 'used to assess and support students'?"
"Miss, I'll answer that on our way back to the CAI rooms, if that's okay? I'm afraid we're very short of time."
They turned around and walked back through the double doors and along the long corridor. Scott began his reply.
"A key feature as to why these centres are so successful is the focus on continual assessment of the 8 skills we need to succeed. About every 10 days we attempt to assess ourselves, with our mentor's help, in these 8 skills, using video clips of ourselves whenever we can to help with it. I will show you in the presentation in a moment my journey to success over the last six months."
As Scott finished his explanation they went through the double doors at the end of the corridor, and he pointed at the room in front of him.
"We're in this room, Miss."
"Thank you Scott, so much of this is so fantastic and difficult to believe, it has certainly been a magical tour!"

Chapter 20
"the World Health Organisation considers that the lack of resilience is central to the growth in depression worldwide"

As Scott and Mrs Lucas entered the CAI room, JC Learner and Stacey were just sitting down at the front of the usual U-shape, to the right of the screen. JC spoke first.
"Brilliant timing, Scott, well done. Have you had a good tour Mrs Lucas?"
"Absolutely wonderful, thank you. This is a remarkable place and Scott has been a superb guide. Both have been just too good to be true. I keep hearing the word 'magic', and I can understand why. Scott seems to have undergone some form of magical transformation and this centre is nothing like anything I've ever seen before."
"You've been impressed with both Scott and the centre?" He asked.
"I think that classifies as a gross understatement. Incredibly impressed by both!"
"Excellent, and I think Scott will impress you further with his presentation. Please sit yourself down."
Scott felt really proud and six months ago he would've gone red and been paralysed with it, but his skill at managing feelings had improved so much that he was able to cope with it. He politely moved a chair for Mrs Lucas to sit down and got her a drink of water from the machine in the corner. He then moved to the front, placed his large cards with prompts on them on the table and began his presentation, clicking the portable computer mouse in his hand.
"Good morning, everyone. Following a discussion with my mentor, Stacey, I have created a presentation that I hope you will find useful and enjoy. Since I, and probably all the students in this centre, have struggled to cope with secondary school, my presentation attempts to provide an understanding using scientific research, of why so many young people struggle to cope with secondary school and how they can be helped to learn to succeed in them.
The screen had a slide on it with the title 'Preparing For Success In Secondary School'. Scott continued.
"We will start with a brief video clip to explain and emphasise that the hormones produced during puberty usually have a major effect on the brain. They usually cause a big effect on thinking and emotions resulting in a big change in behaviour."
Scott clicked the mouse and the video played which demonstrated clearly how the stereotypical behaviour of teenagers could be explained by the influence by hormones on the brain, using neurobiology. The MRI scans of the brain appears to illustrate that these hormones can cause the neuron pathways to the frontal lobe of the brain to be weakened, such that they have much less influence on how they think. When the video finished Scott gave a conclusion.
"Basically the part of the brain that is responsible for planning, organising, reasoning and problem solving becomes almost ineffective and the emotions

have a much greater influence on behaviour. Because of the way our secondary schools operate, this change occurs at a time that can cause big problems for many young people."
JC and Stacey were, of course, already very familiar with this video and the information, but Mrs Lucas was not and her face reflected her fascination. Scott clicked the mouse and the following slide appeared.

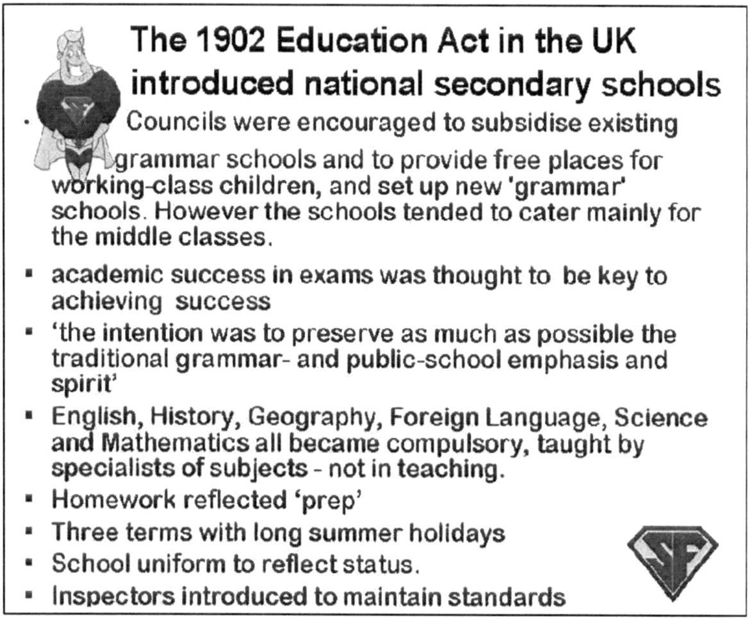

"It is essential to understand that we have only really had secondary schools for about 100 years, and as you can see from this slide, they basically copied the traditional public schools, focusing mainly on achieving exam success and preparing students for university. You will see that virtually all the key parts have not changed throughout the 100 years."
Again it was clear from Mrs Lucas' face that she was quite surprised by this information, Scott was watching her closely and asked.
"Do these all still occur in your school, miss?"
"Yes, Scott, they do and I'm afraid it is many years since I thought why we do."
Scott clicked the mouse and the next slide appeared.

20th century schools

- 1900 Alfred Binet a gifted psychologist, was asked by the French Ministry of Education to discover the 'dull and defective children'
- Binet posed many questions to youngsters of different ages which he believed predicted success or difficulties in school, the first 'intelligence test'.
- The test was used in the USA to determine who was fit to serve and to lead in the Army. it was soon used to assess "normal" children, to identify the "gifted".
- By the 1920s the intelligence test had become a fixture in educational practice in the United States and much of Western Europe.

"This slide illustrates that having secondary schools focusing on testing by exams also occurred in other countries about 100 years ago. In the UK, this intelligence testing occurred in the form of exams called the 11plus in the last year of the primary school. The result of this test decided which children were capable of going to grammar schools. Towards the end of the 20th century virtually all secondary schools focused largely on exam achievement and tended to use them as a measure of how good the secondary school is. This next video clip shows how the 1944 Education Act caused this situation to occur."

Mrs Lucas watched the video carefully and found it both amusing and worrying, as she realised that the perception of the importance of exam achievement as a measurement of success was based on some very traditional ideas and values. When it finished Scott continued.

"Although our secondary schools have largely remained unchanged in 50 years, in their structure and emphasis on exam achievement, in contrast, our society and everyday life for young people has changed enormously. The next slide attempts to briefly illustrate the extent of the concerns with young people in the 21st century."

In the UK in the 21st century

- 1 in 10 young people now suffer from mental health problems
- 1 in 15 young people have harmed themselves, most 11 -25
- Suicide is the most common cause of death for young men
- 41% of 15 year olds had drunk alcohol in an average week
- 25% of 15 year olds were regular smokers
- 17% of 11-15 year olds had used 'illegal drugs'
- Young people almost bottom of Europe's wellbeing table.
- 90% suffering from depression in their teens.
- 90% having low self-esteem.

World Health Organisation

- About half of mental disorders begin before the age of 14
- Around 20% of the world's children and adolescents are estimated to have mental disorders or problems

Mrs Lucas was clearly surprised and appalled at what she was reading, and Scott watched her carefully and waited before he continued speaking.

"Everyday the news is filled with concerns relating to vast numbers of young people, that even a few decades ago could probably not have even been imagined by the previous generations. It is important to remember that when secondary schools were introduced they were to prepare children for the 20th century not for the very different world of the 21st century. Life for most young people in the UK bares no resemblance to the one they have now. For example, Mrs Lucas, what skills do you think are the most needed and in short supply according to the employers in the UK?"

Mrs Lucas thought for a few moments and replied.

"I suppose it must be Numeracy and Literacy, we keep hearing how important Maths and English grades are at GCSE."

Scott then clicked his mouse to reveal the next slide.

In the UK, in the 21st Century, the skills most needed and in short short supply according to the employers are - in order of importance

1 Teamwork
2 Customer-handling skills
3 Technical & Practical skills
4 Oral communication
5 Problem-solving skills
6 Written communication
7 Management skills
8 General IT skills
9 Literacy skills
10 Numeracy skills

(Source: Learning Skills Council)

Mrs Lucas' face reflected her surprise and Scott commented.
"For many years now, employers in the UK and internationally have been much more concerned about the lack of development in the 8 skills, they often refer to them as communication, soft or social and emotional skills."
He clicked the mouse and this next slide appeared.

'In the 2004 Enterprise survey of 20,000 employers in the UK, employers were most worried about lack of skills such as customer handling, problem solving and teamworking. In fact, research has shown that social and emotional skills had more correlation with success in the labour market than cognitive skills, IQ and formal qualifications' (Cunha et al., 2005)

'many young people today are left simply incapable of succeeding in the current socio-economic climate.'

'in just over a decade, personal and social skills or "capabilities" became 33 times more important in determining relative life chances'

("Freedom's Orphans" Raising Youth In A Changing World – IPPR Research Nov 2[illegible])

"This next video clip is an illustration of the importance of one of these skills, 'managing feelings'. It shows some children taking part in a famous experiment called 'The Marshmallow Test', which was first performed several decades ago, in the USA, and repeated numerous times since then. It demonstrates clearly why it is one of the 8 skills we need to succeed."

They watched and enjoyed the video clip, especially Mrs Lucas, who had not seen it before. Scott continued talking when it finished.

" In the second half of the 20th century, a huge amount of scientific research was carried out and published demonstrating that successful people have learnt the skills to identify and overcome the difficulties they meet in life to achieve success and happiness. There appear to be 8 key skills, actions and activities that need to be learnt, that are well developed in successful people in areas as widespread as sport, music, books, film, science and business. This next slide tries to simply summarise these 8 skills."

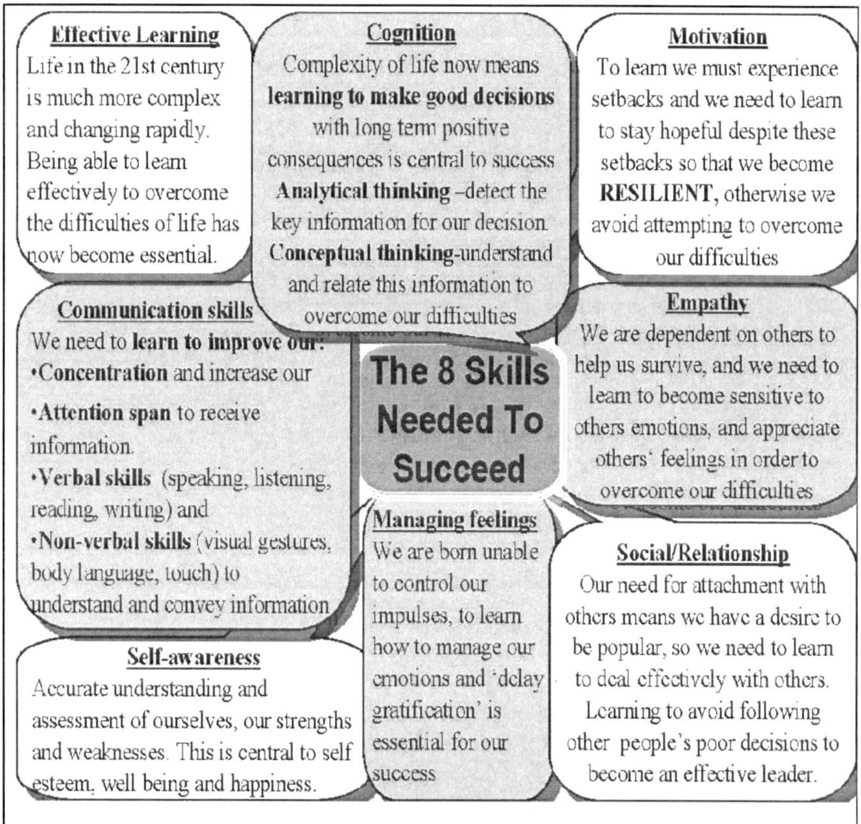

"All five year olds are now basically assessed in these skills when they start school. Research throughout the last 40 years shows that thousands of hours of deliberate or purposeful practice of skills are needed to become an expert. We are not born able to do any of these skills, but have the potential to learn them

with lots of practice. Unfortunately, most children in modern society no longer get the opportunities to practice these skills for the hours needed. Childhood and growing up in families is so very different to previous centuries that learning opportunities and practice of them have become quite rare for many at home. As we've already seen, the secondary schools in the UK,, based on the Victorian concept, have not changed their structure or priority on exam achievement. Not only do they provide few opportunities to practice and develop these skills, they actually tend to expose the weaknesses of the students in them."
Mrs Lucas kept his eyes on Mrs Lucas as he caused the next slide to appear on the screen, before he continued talking.

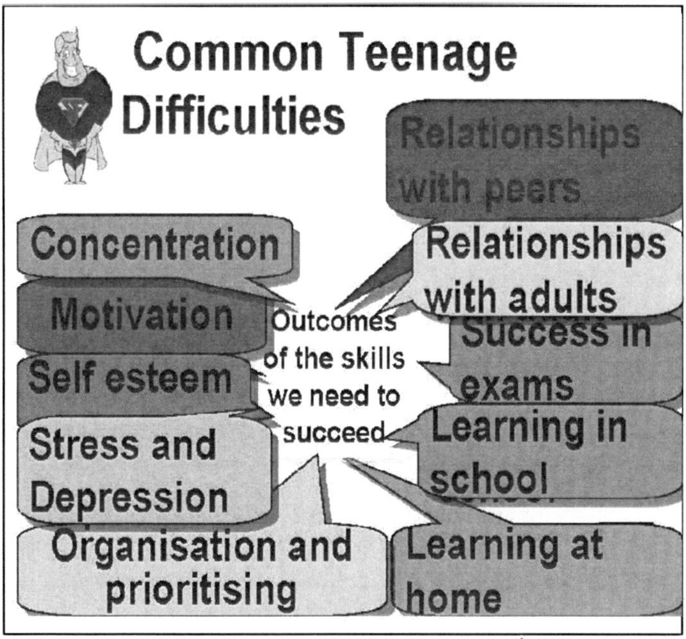

"These difficulties experienced by teenagers in the 21st century are shown repeatedly in surveys and research. Do any of them surprise you, miss?"
Mrs Lucas paused before answering.
"No, I don't think so, Scott."
"I think I probably suffered from each of them. Not only can each one be explained in terms of the poor development of the skills, but I think it also illustrates why secondary schools need to be changed to help children develop the 8 skills."
Scott could see JC and Stacey smiling and nodding in agreement with this comment, Mrs Lucas looked much more confused with a deep frown on her

face and Scott allowed a few moments for her to think about it before continuing.

"Possibly why most of these difficulties are outcomes of poorly developed success skills may be obvious but I will attempt to clarify or explain them anyway. I'll start with 'concentration', this is a key part of the communication skills and we are born with poor concentration and a lot of interaction and stimulus with people in our early years particularly is necessary to help us learn to focus and avoid distractions. A lot of research seems to indicate that many of the children with ADHD may be due to a lack of these learning opportunities. Since students in secondary schools are usually taught in traditional classrooms with many other students, they are prone to distraction and with so many students having poor development in concentration, they struggle to cope in lessons. I certainly found this to be a problem, but I've discovered since I've been in here, I can concentrate under the right conditions, especially when I'm on my own."

Scott looked at Mrs Lucas and could see from her face that what he had said seemed to be making sense to her, and he continued.

"The skill of motivation is one of the 8 skills and as we saw in a previous slide, the World Health Organisation considers that the lack of resilience is central to the growth in depression worldwide. We are not born resilient, able to cope with setbacks, but with lots of opportunities and support we can learn from them and not to fear failure. In fact, we can learn to view setbacks as challenges or learning opportunities that will help us succeed in the end, this is called a growth mindset However, too few children develop this mindset and in the competitive environment of secondary school many just opt out or crumble. Until I came here I definitely had a fixed mindset and stopped me trying anything in which I thought I might fail."

Scott paused at this point and looked at Mrs Lucas and asked.

"Miss, are you aware of Dr Carol Dweck's stuff on mindsets?"

Mrs Lucas felt embarrassed by her lack of knowledge and replied.

"No, Scott, I'm afraid not, but I will do some research on it as soon as I can."

"Good, I think you'll find it very interesting and useful. We saw in an earlier slide that probably at least 90% of teenagers suffer from low self esteem and I was certainly one of those. Self esteem is our belief that we are capable of overcoming the difficulties we meet in life. It is clear that self esteem is highly dependent on three of the 8 skills. The skill of self –awareness, determines how accurately we assess ourselves and with most young people being so poor at this, they tend to use stuff which is very superficial. From an increasingly young age, their appearance seems to dominate what they use for their self-assessment and have come to rely heavily on the media, adverts and fashion. The other two key skills are managing feelings and motivation, their poor development in these skills means they often focus on 'superficial quick fixes' such as fashion items, make up, tattoos, piercings, even cosmetic surgery.

They become extremely insecure, being very 'sensitive and fragile' to comments or support. This means that for many young people, stress and depression have become a social norm."

This time Scott looked at Stacey, knowing how relevant this symptom had been to her, and saw her nodding in agreement then Scott continued.

"Since secondary schools are based on the traditional public school model, they are structured very differently from most primary schools. Students suddenly have lots of lessons with different teachers in different rooms, most have homework with a big emphasis on reading and writing to focus on exam achievement. This means that these 11 year olds need to be organised and be able to prioritise their lives, probably for the first time. With such poorly developed cognitive skills they find this impossible and many quickly give up and opt out. I suspect Mrs Lucas, you've seen a lot of students in year 7 struggle to cope with this, I know both Stacey and I did."

Scott glanced between Mrs Lucas and Stacey, smiling as he did so.

Mrs Lucas replied.

"I certainly have, Scott. We've tried a variety of transition projects to help with this problem. With what you've already shown us today, I can see why we've had such limited success so far."

"The next three, success in exams, learning in school and at home, are linked to the first of the 8 skills, effective learning. In the few days in this centre I improved so much in this skill because for the first time I studied the science of learning. This meant I understood about effective learning and how I could learn successfully and enjoy it. Very few young people are able to do this when they start secondary school so learning at home or in the classroom is very difficult for them. Even if they try hard, because it is not effective learning, they make little progress, get frustrated and give up."

So far, Scott had not looked across to JC Learner very much as he was aware that virtually everything had been taken from his successfeelosophy website, but he felt he needed some reassurance from JC, with such expertise in this area. JC detected Scott's feelings and gave him a subtle 'thumbs up'.

"I have been absolutely amazed at how much I've improved in exams in such a short period of time. In fact, for the first time in my life I'm actually confident about the exams I've got in school after Christmas."

All three had a look of surprise on their faces at this comment and Scott had a huge grin on his.

"The last two, relationships with adults are very dependant on empathy and social skills. As we saw in the first video, during puberty, these skills seem to really suffer. The term adolescence is actually a stage of development and it is often the poor empathy and social skills which explain their anti-social and unpleasant behaviour. Bullying and vandalism in gangs are easily explained because these people simply do not have the skills needed to show the care and consideration that is referred to as respect. They desperately want to feel the sense of belonging shown in Maslow's Hierarchy, so behave in ways that make them part of the mob or gang. We've seen a lot of this recently with riots in London and large towns, and over the years with gang violence at football matches."

JC, followed by Stacey and then Mrs Lucas applauded Scott at this point, feeling he had very clearly explained these ten symptoms very well indeed. Scott was very moved by this response, but his managing feelings skill had improved so much he was now able to respond politely.

"Thank you, I very much appreciate that. But having identified the difficulties, if we are to succeed, we must now focus on how they can be overcome. Hopefully, it is now clear that for people to succeed they need to have better development of the 8 success skills. With Stacey's help, I have been assessing myself in these 8 skills every 10 days during the six months I have been in the centre. The next slide shows how much I've improved in each of the skills in the time I've been here."

Scott's development of the	score out of 30	
skills needed to succeed	day1	day 170
EFFECTIVE LEARNING	8	24
COMMUNICATION	6	20
COGNITIVE	8	18
SELF-AWARENESS	3	24
MANAGING FEELINGS	4	22
MOTIVATION	6	22
EMPATHY	4	16
SOCIAL SKILLS	7	16

Scott specifically looked at Mrs Lucas when this slide appeared to study her reaction. As he expected she showed surprise, but he was aware that she probably did not actually fully understand the skills and their significance.

"As you can see in the space of six months, I think I have managed to make sufficient improvement in the 8 skills to be able to cope in the outside world."

"And succeed, Scott." Stacey added.

"Thanks Stace, I hope you are right."

Scott clicked the mouse to show the next slide.

All three looked closely at this slide as none had seen it before.

Key factors in my journey to success

•A 'mentor' who could understand, support and help me learn effectively
•Ensuring the 5 Learning Requirements were continually in place to help with my effective learning
•Focusing on the effective learning of the 8 skills needed to succeed.
•Starting with the skill of self-awareness to realise how I could succeed.
•Regular frequent careful self-assessment of the 8 skills needed to succeed, so I could see how I was continually improving.
•Providing a lot of learning opportunities to develop each of the 8 skills.
•An environment that encourages effective independent learning and avoids distractions, especially having positive peer pressure.
•Tasks and activities that develop effective learning of the 8 skills needed to succeed, and also improves exam success.
•Resources (**successfeelosophy.com**) that provide effective and enjoyable learning,and also improves exam success.

"This final slide shows what I consider to have been the key points that have helped me learn to overcome my difficulties and prepared me for success in secondary school. It was actually quite easy to prepare, as we recently had a CAI session for students like me, who had been in the centre for at least 5 months. Our inquiry question was, 'What are the key factors that have caused you to succeed in this centre and could they occur in secondary schools?' We ended up with a list virtually identical to this."
Mrs Lucas studied each point very carefully. Scott was expecting this and kept silent while she did this, then he spoke again.
"Are there any points or questions you want to ask Mrs Lucas, or JC and Stacey for that matter?"
Mrs Lucas was desperately keen to respond.
"Today, I've seen how different this centre is to anywhere else, the results clearly show that it is effective and I'm very impressed, but how much of it do you think could occur in secondary schools?"
"I think JC is more able to answer that question than I or anyone else, miss. But I will reply as well as I can. Everyone in the CAI group that discussed this, felt secondary schools were a major factor in our difficulties. If I quickly go through the points on this slide it may help to answer your question. We thought that we

could be mentors in schools and we felt if we'd had one in year 7 when we started secondary school it would've helped us immensely. We could see no reason why schools could not focus on the 8 skills and assess them regularly and starting with effective learning and self-awareness like we do in here is so much better. All the resources are on the website so they could be used in schools. The points that we thought would be most difficult in schools would be getting the staff to teach so differently and creating a more positive environment and attitude to learning."

JC and Stacey were smiling and nodding in agreement while Scott was talking. Mrs Lucas was fidgeting in her chair, trying to think and apply what he was saying to her own school. Scott again kept quiet to give her time to process and reflect on these points, finally she spoke.

"I am aware that schools in Finland have a very different approach like this and they are considered to be the most effective in the world, so I'm sure it is possible to apply most of this in school."

JC decided this was a good time to comment.

"I'm delighted you said that Mrs Lucas and that you are already aware of the effectiveness of the schools in Finland. I am keen to help and support schools to adopt this sort of approach, so perhaps we can discuss this in the future."

With Mrs Lucas' high level of admiration for JC, she was delighted and excited with this offer and responded accordingly.

"Yes, please, I'd very much like that, You are welcome in my school anytime."

"When Scott has settled back in school, I'll contact you and arrange a visit and we'll discuss it further."

Mrs Lucas was struggling to hide her excitement at this prospect, and decided to manage her feelings by returning to Scott's presentation.

"That slide is a great finish to an outstanding presentation."

She began clapping, JC and Stacey quickly joined in.

"Scott, JC, Stacey, I would like to thank you for this remarkable visit. My experience this morning has been absolutely incredible and has caused me to totally rethink almost everything, especially my school. I can fully understand why so many refer to this centre as a school of magic."

Chapter 21
"something like 'A Super Christmas Carol!"

"I'm feeling quite nervous, Stace. I haven't been out of the centre for six months. Life is so different in there, it is so strange being in the outside world. I suppose this must be like returning home from prison or being away in the forces."

Scott was talking to Stacey as she drove up outside his parents' house.

"Except that you have been developing the skills you need to succeed while you've been away and you're now able to overcome the difficulties in this life." Stacey replied.

"I do hope so, Stace. It's going to be so strange though, but I think I'm ready. I'm actually looking forward to the surprise everyone will have when they meet me, just like Mrs Lucas did. She just couldn't believe it was me, it was so funny."

"Yes, I must admit, I really enjoyed meeting people as the 'new me'. People kept thinking I was messing about and would return to my old unpleasant self,"

They both got out the car and walked up to the front door, Scott rang the doorbell.

Scott's mother opened the door, hugged him as tightly as she could, trying to kiss him as much as possible. Over her head he could see a banner draped across the hallway ceiling saying, 'Welcome Home, Scott'. Under it he could see his father, brother and both sisters, Scott's eyes began watering.

During the six months he'd been in the 'Learning For Success Centre' he'd had regular visits from his parents but not his brother and sisters. They were now all in their twenties and had moved away from home, but this was special, Christmas and Scott's homecoming.

"Who the hell is this and where's my brother?"

This was Adam, Scott's 'big' brother, as usual trying to crack a joke. Although he was still eight years older than Scott, he certainly wasn't bigger any more. Adam was about six foot and Scott was now several inches taller, he was also much darker and quite stocky, and always wore the latest brands.

He grabbed Scott's hand and shook it firmly.

"Blimey, Scott! What you been doing in there? You been on steroids or something, you've got arms like Popeye's"

"Popeye! He looks more like Superman. Come on give us a hug"

Kate, his eldest sister grabbed hold of him tightly.

"Dad said you looked different, but he didn't say you'd become a pin-up. I can't believe I could say that about my little brother."

Commented Diane as she pulled Scott away from Kate and hugged him herself.

Scott was overcome with emotion, he was so pleased to see his family again, the tears were rolling down his face, the lump in his throat stopping him from being able to speak.

Throughout all of this, Stacey had been standing just outside the front door, keeping out of the way, but smiling broadly. Adam caught sight of her.

"Is that Stacey? It is, it's Stacey. You've also changed so much, I barely recognised you either. Is this place you've been in a super health centre, doing plastic surgery or something, you look terrific!"

Kate and Diane hadn't seen Stacey for a long time either and turned to look at her, both of them looked on in amazement and perhaps a little envy at how attractive she had become.
"That's very kind of you Adam. Long time no see, all of you."
Stacey came in and she greeted them all with a hug. The hallway was now very crowded.
"Go on through to the lounge all of you, we were just about to have a cup of tea, you've timed it just right." Scott's mother said as she tried to usher them into the lounge, which was covered in Christmas decorations with the traditional trimmed tree in the corner. They all gradually sat down, Scott had recovered his voice and joined with the furious chatting that ensued. After about ten minutes, Stacey began to move to leave.
"Well it's been great to see you all again. I'm sure you'll enjoy your time with Scott and be very impressed with him. Scott, phone me if you need to and I'll keep in contact as we arranged. Bye, everyone."
"I'll see you out, Stace." Said George.
Stacey and George left the room and as they went outside the house he spoke.
"Stace, I can't express how grateful I am for all you've done for Scott No, all you've done for us! I must say I was very worried I'd lose my temper with him before he went into the centre and we'd end up fighting. He's so different now, so pleasant, such a contrast to what he was like before. I do hope he doesn't go backwards now he's home."
"I don't think he will, Uncle George. His change is very much like mine, he sees the world differently. He's developed so much that he's nothing like the person he was before, it's like trying to compare a four year old to a mature adult. We've had lots of discussions about what may happen and he's already planned and well prepared how to handle it. I'm confident you'll be amazed by him and enjoy being with him."
"I hope you are right, Stace. Thanks again. Have a safe journey, a happy Christmas and my regards to your family."
"Bye, Uncle George, happy Christmas."
For the next hour, Scott's brother and sisters interrogated Scott as though he'd been abducted by aliens. In fact, after about an hour Diane actually joked.
"Well I still can't believe you are our brother, I think some aliens have taken over your body.
"No, Di, they've even radically changed his body as well, I think this is probably a sophisticated robot, like a male version of a Stepford Wife."
"Whatever, it is, he's much better than that obnoxious slob of a brother I used to have, he was a complete waste of space."
Throughout all this banter, Scott and his parents were laughing, but he thought it was time to comment.
"Alright, that's enough, I know I was a thoroughly unpleasant person but it is Christmas, think of me as the new young Ebenezer Scrooge."

"Well you're certainly too big to be Tiny Tim" Adam quipped.
Ann had been quietly soaking up this rapport and for the first time in many years felt really proud of her youngest child.
"No matter how much he's changed, he's still my little baby." She commented.
They all laughed, but Scott quickly commented.
"A baby is helpless and that's what I've been. I've got to do stuff for myself now, mum. I've had you people doing everything for me for too many years and I now know I've been spoilt. I think I've got the skills to cope for myself and succeed from now on."
Scott was sitting between Kate and Diane, and they both squeezed and kissed him when he said this, but his mum responded.
"It's alright, Scott, we've discussed this over the last few months and I know what I've got to do, but I know I'll find it difficult. Anyway, I think its time for us to have some dinner, I hope it's alright for me to do that."
She had a huge grin as she said that and they all laughed and got up to move to the dining table.
The jokes continued throughout dinner, most emphasising the amount of change in Scott, which included his table manners. After dinner, Scott went up to his bedroom with his sisters, who sat on his bed which was against the wall in the corner. Scott pulled out the chair opposite them from underneath the table on which his computer, DVD player and playstation was placed. The video screen was not as large as he had in the centre but attached to the wall in the same way. The walls were covered with posters and pictures of footballers. He started to unpack his bag.
"Is that all you had in the centre, Scott?" Kate asked.
"Yes, it is such an incredible place, sis, that I find it difficult to describe or explain how remarkable it is. We all tend to keep using the word 'magic', because nothing else seems to explain it. It is incredible that I should come out on Christmas eve, because the two stories that I think can give you an idea of what has happened to me are Christmas ones. 'Christmas Carol and It's A Wonderful Life'."
"Why do you think that, Scott?" Diane asked.
"They both show a person undergoing a magical change, they both have a major development in their self-awareness and realise how stupid they've been. Especially with Scrooge, the ghosts help him develop his self-awareness so that he becomes a completely different person, we had mentors to do that in the centre."
"How you going to continue that now you're home, Scott?"
Diane responded.
"Stacey and I have discussed and planned for this for quite a while. I know it will not be easy. Life is so much different in the centre from being home, but I aim to bring as much of the centre into my life here."
"What do you mean by that?" Kate was clearly puzzled.

“First I’m going to transform this room so that it is as near to my room in the centre. Mum and Dad have bought me lots of stuff for me to make my own posters, my room was covered completely with posters.”
“What sort of posters, Scott?”
“Lots of inspirational and informative stuff like ‘Success in life requires short term pain to achieve long term gain.’ and ‘If we don’t learn to control our emotions, they will control us.’ I’ve got loads of them to make and put up. My room in the centre was very much about encouraging me to learn but this one has been about playing video games and watching videos or TV. I’ve actually already got internet access so I shall be able to carry on using the successfeelosophy.com website.”
Scott pointed to his ‘successfeelosophy.com’ T shirt as he said this.
“I’ve been meaning to ask you about that shirt, Stacey had one on as well.” Kate asked.
“This website is absolutely brilliant, it is what we used all the time in the centre, but anyone can use. It means all the studying I was doing in the centre I can continue here.”
“Can anyone use it?” Diane asked.
“Yes. In fact, when we come out of the centre we are asked to publicise the website as much as possible. It’s got an incredible amount of excellent videos and resources that’s completely changed my view of learning.”
Both Kate and Diane were fascinated by Scott’s enthusiastic attitude and wanted to understand it. Diane responded first.
“What do you mean, Scott, ‘changed your view of learning’?”
“Almost everything I observe now, I am thinking ‘why or how’, and trying to understand or explain it. As I pointed out, one of the first things Stacey helped me with as my mentor, was to develop my self-awareness skill, and I am becoming an ‘effective reflective practitioner’.”
Scott was confident that his sisters would not understand this term, and smiled broadly as he said it, studying their amazed facial expressions as he did so.
“What I mean is that I am now able to think more deeply about what I’m seeing, hearing, feeling and doing while I’m doing it. It means that I’m able to question, analyse and learn much more. It has meant that I’m actually practising and developing my effective learning skills much of the time, so my learning has not only become more effective but easier and enjoyable.”
Kate and Diane were clearly ‘gobsmacked’ at what they were hearing and were a little ‘dumbstruck’, but eventually Diane spoke.
“The more I hear and observe you Scott, the more amazed and impressed I get. When I last saw and heard you, you could barely speak a full sentence, now you sound like a real boff.”
“Thanks, sis, I never imagined I’d be called a boff, but it must mean my communication and cognitive skills have improved a lot.”
“It’s like listening to professor or something.” Kate added.

"I think the phrase, 'you aint seen nothing yet' could be applied here. I was in the centre for about 170 days, and I think I developed more than most would normally in about 20 years. Everything in the centre is focused on effective learning, every day we had a collaborative action inquiry session, which has been essential in helping me develop."

Again Scott was confident that his sisters would not understand this term, and had another huge smile as he said it, he looked closely at their faces.

"I've become quite flash with all these terms, haven't I? These sessions are basically groups that we had every day to discuss all sorts of things, often using videos we'd watched. It meant that we were practising and developing all of the 8 success skills. I found these groups absolutely brilliant because I was so poor at all those skills six months ago, I think these made more difference to me than anything else."

"Well, it helps me understand how you now appear so confident with us. You used to say nothing positive, always moody, big chip on your shoulder, grunting and not even looking at us. You are the complete opposite now and it's happened in only six months. Diane commented.

"But, how have you changed so much physically, Scott. When I last saw you, you were a fat slob, with short spiky bleached hair, looking like a right yob. You've gone from being an obnoxious waste of space to becoming Clark Kent from Smallville, how?" Kate asked.

"Thanks, both of you. Throughout my time in the centre I wore a wrist monitor, which as well as acting as a prompt to help me plan and become organised, also measured my pulse rate and blood pressure repeatedly. It helped develop my self-awareness towards my health and fitness, I gradually learnt to eat healthily and exercise regularly. I've actually lost over 20 kilograms of fat, about 3 stone, and managed to develop both my muscles and cardiovascular fitness."

Kate turned to Diane and commented.

"He is now so fit that if he wasn't my brother, I'd actually admit to quite fancying him."

Scott smiled.

"I heard that! That's very kind of you. I'm hoping to continue my fitness training and that I'll get a cross trainer and rowing machine for Christmas, they fold up easily so, I think there's enough room in here for them "

Since Kate and Diane had been asked to contribute to these presents for Scott, they both smiled and commented.

"I think Santa Claus may be kind to you,"

"So, when do you go back to school, Scott?" Diane asked.

"Tuesday week. I've got my mock GCSE exams straightaway, so I've got to try to do lots of exam preparation. For the first time in my life I'm actually going to make a real effort to succeed in them rather than focusing on making excuses why they don't matter. I've improved my effective learning skills so much in the

last six months and I can now use the successfeelosophy website very effectively, I'm going to superlearn GCSE English Maths and Science."
Kate shook her head to express her amazement and joked.
"There you are, he is Clark Kent, he's now able to do superlearning!"
Diane then commented.
"So our little brother has changed more than Scrooge to become Superman, something like 'A Super Christmas Carol!"
They all began laughing uncontrollably, as this comment seemed to sum up their delight at having discovered a wonderful brother.

Chapter 22
"Yes, I am Scott Spicer, but not as you know him."

"Scott, can I come in?"
"Yes, of course, Dad. I've just finished."
George tried to enter Scott's bedroom, but the door was stopped halfway.
"Just a minute, Dad, I need to fold up the rowing machine."
Scott did just that, and George entered the room. Scott was moving the cross trainer from in front of the TV screen into the corner. George sat on the bed, Scott was wearing only a pair of black shorts and dripping with sweat, began wiping himself down with a large black towel. His dad stared at and admired Scott's physique, barely an ounce of surplus fat, his 'pecs and six pack', better than most male models, his six foot three inch broad shouldered frame towering over him like a Greek god statue.
"I just wanted to have a brief chat before you go back to school tomorrow, Scott."
"As I've said many times recently Dad, after the way I've treated you over the years, the more we can find time to chat, the better. I've got a lot to make up for."
George just smiled.
"I'm sorry, but I'm still struggling to believe it, Scott. I watched you change each week when Mum and I visited you in the centre, that was amazing in itself, but when you came home last week on Christmas Eve, I was still worried the magic would wear off and you'd change back. Stacey said I'd be amazed by you and enjoy your company, she was completely correct. It's a long time since I've enjoyed a Christmas and New Year as much as this one."
Scott wrapped the towel around his neck, sat down on the bed next to his dad and hugged him.
"Thanks dad, it means so much that you are able to say that to me. We've spent so many years just shouting and scowling at each other, it makes these moments even more precious."
George had spent his life being the 'traditional macho man', trying to hide his 'soft emotions' as he called them, but this comment from Scott broke through

his shell and he hugged Scott with tears forming in his eyes. Scott recalled having a similar experience with Stacey in the centre only a few months ago. George was clearly uncomfortable expressing his emotions and attempted to deflect from his embarrassment by asking.

"Why haven't you contacted any of your mates since you've been home, Scott?"

"A good question, dad. Stacey and I discussed this before I left the centre. We decided that I would continue my journey to success in stages, the first one being to sort myself out here, at home. We felt I needed to ensure that I focused on creating a room for learning and establishing a routine for study and training, first and getting my family to trust me again."

"Well you've certainly achieved that part of your journey. This room has been transformed, it is incredible now, a bedroom, study room and a mini gym. I also really appreciate the way you've hidden the need for redecoration by covering every inch of the walls and ceiling with posters!"

George had a huge smile on his face as he said that and Scott spotted the joke and responded.

"Only too pleased to help, dad. But I couldn't have done it without you and mum's support, it's been a team effort."

"But what about contacting your mates and going back to school?"

"Oh yeah, I was talking about my journey to success. The next stage was to identify and prepare for the difficulties I will probably need to overcome with my mates and everyone at school. Stacey and I decided that this would probably be very difficult as everyone remembers me as I was and will not understand or even believe who I am now. I'm expecting a lot of pressure to wind me up and tempt me to go backwards, but I'm ready for it, dad."

"Me and your mum had a chance to get used to you changing from Mr Hyde into Dr Jekyll each week when we visited you in the centre, but as you saw with your brother and sisters, you will be a huge shock to everyone at school. How do you feel about it?"

"I must admit I'm quite nervous, especially as I'm sure there will be quite a few kids who are going to challenge me and staff who will be just waiting for me to cause trouble. Fortunately, I've not got my normal lessons for a while as we've got our mock exams."

"What about your mock exams? I know you've been doing some studying but you haven't actually been to school since June."

"I didn't learn much when I was at school before, anyway, so whatever I've done in the last six months I'm sure will be much more than if I'd been at school. I've certainly done a lot of exam questions."

"But you haven't actually had any teachers. I don't really see how you could've done the learning."

"We'll see dad, when I get my results."

"What about your football, Scott? You haven't played at all this season, are you going to try to get in the school team and what about your club side?"
"Another good question, dad and this is the third stage of my journey to success. I've got to try to convince my coaches at school and my club that I've changed, I know they will be reluctant to take a chance with me because I caused so many problems."
"I think that's a bit of an understatement, I reckon you have the worst disciplinary record of any footballer ever at any level, you made Wayne Rooney seem like an angel!"
"That's a bit harsh, dad, but sadly you may not be far from the truth. I'm just hoping that I'll be given another chance in both teams."
"Do you think, you'll be able to control your temper on the football field, now?"
"Yes, yes I do. I really feel that I won't get wound up any more, especially in football matches."
"I hope you're right, Scott. I may even start watching you play again if that happens. I used to get so embarrassed at your behaviour, getting involved in fights and being sent off all the time."
"I know, dad, I'm so sorry, it won't happen again. I know I've said that many times before but please believe me this time it's true."
"From what I've seen recently Scott, I actually believe you."
George stood up, ruffled Scott's curly mop of hair and left the room.

*

"I'm off now, mum. I think I'll be home for lunch, I don't think I've got an exam this afternoon."
Scott yelled to his mother as he was leaving and she shouted back.
"Okay, son. Have a good morning, best of luck."
Scott had 'butterflies' at the apprehension of the day ahead. He decided that he'd try to make the mile walk to school as quick as possible to keep his nerves to a minimum. As he got within about 500 metres of the school, he spotted four girls, each with different coloured hair, in front of him. As he got closer he realised that they were from his year group, much more focused on talking than walking. Scott had only a few seconds to decide what to do and who they were. He had never been very good at socialising with girls and didn't really even know the ones in his classes very well, but that was then, this is now.
"Hi girls, looking forward to the Maths exam."
All four girls visibly jumped when they heard Scott's deep voice, they had engrossed in chatting and messing about with their mobiles, They stopped what they'd been dong and turned around in unison. Each looked surprised, then confused, then very interested. Several seconds passed before any of them said anything. Scott had been expecting this so said nothing, but used this time to study their faces, especially their eyes, trying desperately to apply his greatly improved communication skills.

"Scott?" Remarked the girl with the bright red hair tied in a pony tail.
Scott studied her face and looked into her dark brown eyes. He could see she wore lots of make-up, especially mascara and lip gloss similar in colour to her hair.
"Yes, Judy, Scott. Good morning,"
Judy was shocked and delighted that such an attractive boy should know her name, and struggled to reply but commented.
"You don't look like him."
The girls' eyes lit up in recognition, they stepped back to get a better look at him, clearly eyeing him up and down. Scott continued his focus on their faces and eyes, smiling broadly as he did. His much improved non-verbal communication skills and empathy meant he knew they liked what they saw but were extremely surprised at such an incredible change.
Scott was wearing his school uniform for the first time in six months, he'd always been uncomfortable in a tie and his worn out blazer had been too small for him for a long time and exposed his well-developed chest. His body had completely changed shape and his trousers were now too big and the belt trying stopped them falling down, merely made them look comical. His shirt was tight across his chest, an although his clothes did not flatter his now muscular and healthy body shape, the girls could make out enough to be both amazed and impressed. Scott's sisters had given him some warning and preparation of their reaction.
"Yes, I suppose I have changed a bit since you last saw me." Scott replied smiling, knowing he was making a big understatement.
"Changed a bit, you're joking. You look nothing like the Scott I remember."
This comment came from a very thin girl with long straight blond hair. Scott looked at her closely, recognised her but not her name. He could see she had bright blue eyes but he felt the thick black mascara tended to spoil their effect as did the thick pink lipstick and orange tanned skin. He immediately thought that her self-awareness was probably based heavily on her appearance and she'd spent a lot of time and money trying to improve it, yet she was clearly quite attractive.
"What's happened? We thought you were chucked out. You look as though you've been staying in a health centre for six months."
This comment came from a girl with orange hair and she stepped back to take photo of him on her mobile phone. Again Scott studied her face and eyes closely; he recognised her but did not know her name. She also had lots of make-up but it was her huge earrings that distracted Scott most, since it had been a long time since he'd seen huge earrings. Again he started to think why a girl would wish to have them and reflected on her self-awareness. Is it to deflect from her face, she's quite pretty but with so much make-up, perhaps she does not feel that way. His reflection was broken by all the girls now trying to take photos on their phones.

"In a way it was like a health centre, but it had much more." Scott replied continuing to smile broadly.
"Where have you been? There were all sorts of rumours going around, nobody seemed to know anything. Most of us thought you'd been locked up in some sort of juvenile prison or something."
This comment came from the girl with the long straight jet black hair, Scott studied her face and eyes carefully but did not really recognise her at all. She was a few inches shorter than the others, with less make-up, and he thought she may be Asian and very attractive
All the girls were studying Scott closely, 'checking him out', the old Scott would've crumbled under this sort of attention but the development of his 8 skills meant he was actually enjoying it.
"So what did happen, Scott? Where you bin'?
The red haired girl asked.
"And how do you come to look so fit?"
The girl with short spiky orange hair shouted, they all giggled and nodded in agreement.
"Alright girls, I'll tell you as much as I can while we walk to school. I've got to check in with Mrs Lucas secretary before I can go to the exam, so I've got to get a move on, sorry."
They started walking, much faster than they had before, but delighted to be walking with Scott.
"Right girls, I'll try to be brief. You probably know I got knocked out in a fight in the school do and went to hospital. I thought I'd be thrown out of school, as I had to go and see Mrs Lucas with my parents a few days later. Fortunately, I was offered a place in a very unusual learning centre for six months where my cousin is a mentor. She became my mentor and took me there the following day and I came home on Christmas Eve."
They were now at the school gates, the girls were struggling to keep pace with him but listening intently and bursting with questions.
"What sort of centre?"
The girl with long black hair asked first.
"Very difficult to describe or explain. It's called a 'Learning For Success Centre' and looks a bit like a shopping mall, You have your own room and have to stay there for six months."
They were now at the doors to the school's reception area.
"But what happened to you in this centre? How come you've changed so much?"
Scott looked at his watch and realised it was time for his appointment with Mrs Lucas' personal assistant.
"I'm sorry girls, I've got to go now, I'll see you later."
"Oh No, you can't stop now. Please Scott, it won't matter if you're late."
The blond hair girl pleaded.

"I'm sorry, but it does matter. I'll see you later, bye girls."
The old Scott would never had thought or said that. He went through the doors into the reception area. The girls had a look of astonishment on their faces as he left them as though they'd just met Brad Pitt or Johnny Depp. They were buzzing and itching to know more, and even more importantly to tell everyone one else. All four girls had their mobiles out and were texting furiously.
Scott passed through the reception area and entered the waiting area for the Head teacher's room, where he'd been many times before and six months previously. Mrs Lucas personal assistant, a very pleasant woman in her fifties with curly auburn hair and glasses, saw him immediately and spoke to him.
"Goodness me! Mrs Lucas said you'd changed Scott, but I had no idea how much. She said she'd like to have a quick word with you before you go into the exam. She's out of the office at the moment but she'll be back soon. Could you sit there please, Scott."
"Of course, Mrs Simpson, no problem."
Scott sat down on the padded chairs he'd been on many times before. But this time he put his hand into his inside blazer pocket and pulled out his Maths Quizcards and began testing himself.
"Good morning, Scott."
Mrs Lucas had surprised Scott, he had been engrossed in using his quizcards for almost 15 minutes. He looked up and she had new dark blue designer glasses, but wearing her usual white blouse, knee length dark blue A line skirt with dark blue shoes, to match the glasses.
"Morning miss."
"What you got there, Scott?"
"These are my Maths Quizcards, miss. I was just doing some last minute exam prep, these are brilliant."
Mrs Lucas looked at her watch and realised his exam was starting soon.
"I bet they are, Scott. Everything from the centre really impressed me, especially you and that's why I wanted to see you this morning. I just wanted to check that your week or so at home had gone okay and you were still alright to return."
"I'm fine, miss. I had a great Christmas and New Year. I have tried to prepare as much as possible for my exams and I'm pleased to be allowed back after all the problems I've caused. Thanks for giving me a second, well it's more than that, another chance, I won't let you down."
"From what I saw in the centre, I have a lot of confidence in you. I have never seen such an improvement in anyone in such a short period of time."
"Thanks miss, I won't let you down, I promise."
"I'm sure you won't, Scott. I think you'd better get a move on or you could be late for your exam, I was going to look in to check everything was okay, so I'll take you. We don't want you getting into trouble straightaway, do we?"
"No, miss, I'd appreciate that."

"Come on, let's go."
It took only a few minutes to get to the sports hall where the exams were taking place. Mrs Lucas pushed the door carefully and the hall contained about 250 students sitting at desks already quietly attempting the exam. Fortunately, the desks were facing away from the door which so their entrance was virtually unnoticed. A young smartly dressed male teacher immediately came to them and whispered.
"They've just started, Mrs Lucas."
"It's okay, Mr Warburton, I'm only bringing in Scott, so he can start the exam."
Mr Warburton looked at Scott and his face showed he had just recognised who he was.
"Scott Spicer?"
"Yes, sir. Where shall I sit, please."
Mr Warburton was clearly startled as he could not recall being spoken to so politely by Scott before.
"Er, there's an empty desk here with papers on it, you can sit here."
"Thanks, sir."
Very few students were very close to where he was sitting, a few that were disturbed looked round at Scott and frowned, as they did not recognise who it was.
Mr Warburton continued to look startled at this politeness and then became very confused as he watched Scott sit down carefully, place his pens etc. on the desk and started to write his name on the front of the booklet. He then turned to the back of the booklet, looked at the last questions and smiled. This question is meant to be the most difficult but it looked identical to many he had done over the last six months and began answering it comfortably. Mr Warburton had never seen anyone start an exam paper at the end and work towards the front. However, Scott had attempted so many GCSE maths exam papers in the last few months, he preferred to do the most difficult question first when he was fresh and finish with the easier questions at the front. Mr Warburton assumed it was Scott messing about as usual and couldn't really be bothered.
Scott worked his way through the paper, repeatedly smiling as he thought how many times had he done that question or similar before.
"You have ten minutes left"
Scott heard booming out as he was just completing question one, his last one. He was amazed at how quick the time had gone, but now he was familiar with the concept of 'flow' he was not surprised. He then began carefully checking his answers, something he had never done in an exam in school before, because that's what good students do!
"Times up, make sure your names are on the front page and then put your pens down." The middle aged male teacher in a suit said loudly.

For the first time, Scott was able to look up and look around the hall. He was at the back of the hall but several heads were turned and looking at him, he had a huge grin on his face, he knew that few, if any, would recognise him. The students were dismissed from the exam hall in rows and many stared at Scott when they saw him on their way out of the hall. Scott was now able to think about the reactions of the other students to him and started to become quite excited as his row was dismissed. As soon as he left the foyer outside the sports hall into the playground area he was confronted with a mass of students staring at him.
"It is him!"
"No it's not, it don't look nothing like him."
"Yes, it is, it is, Scott."
Scott heard a barrage of voices and noise, and started laughing. More students were pouring out of the hall behind him, and yelling at him. The old Scott would've just angry at this pushing and shoving and lashed out but not now. He realised he needed to explain as quickly and clearly as he could what had happened to him, so he yelled loudly.
"Hold it, everyone! Gimme a chance, I'll explain."
His voice was so confident and loud that there was a sudden hush as though everyone was in shock.
"Yes, I am Scott Spicer, but not as you know him."
He was actually paraphrasing Star Trek, but none appreciated his humour.
"I did get knocked out last summer, and they were probably going to throw me out of the school. I got sent to a special centre in East Anglia for six months. I was told if I improved enough by Christmas I might be able to return here, and here I am."
There must've been close to a hundred students trying to listen to what he was saying and many started talking about him following this.
"What type of centre?"
"Where was it?"
"Why do you look so different?"
"What did you do in there?"
These and many other questions were being fired at him and he tried to answer them all, the 'old Scott' would probably have lost his temper, and sworn or lashed out, but not now. Gradually, the crowd dispersed as their curiosity was satisfied and he was left with about ten of his mates.
"So have you played any footie, recently? A tall thin boy with very short hair asked.
"Smudger, I ain't played in a proper match this season. I did a lot of practising of me skills in the centre, but I ain't actually played for over six months."
Scott's friends were also mainly his team mates in their football club.
"Will you be able to play for the team at the weekend, Scotty?"

A boy with gelled spiky blond hair, who was about a foot shorter than Scott, asked.
"I think so, Tommy, but I can't see Stevo picking me."
Mr Stevenson, Stevo, is the coach of their football team, 'Ipsodonians'.
"We could do with you, mate. We've had a poor season so far. I think we need to contact Stevo today and see if we can get you to play at the weekend."
A boy with black short Mohican style hair and shoulders almost as broad as Scott asked.
"Good idea, Chopper. We all need to phone Stevo, this evening. We're going down the park for a kickabout now, you coming, Scott?" Tommy responded.
"No, I'm going home to prepare for the Science exam tomorrow, but I'll try to contact Stevo later."
All the boys looked at Scott in amazement. The Scott they knew would never have done any exam preparation and always been the first to go to the park for a kickabout.
"What! You're going to revise rather than footie, I don't believe it!
Chopper yelled.
"Is this a wind up, Scott? Or are you being serious? Smudger asked.
Scott had been waiting for this, he was very aware that his mates would be very reluctant to accept the new Scott and this was another of the key stages in his journey to success that he and Stacey had discussed thoroughly.
"Look boys, I've got to be honest and clear to you, I've changed. I don't only look different on the outside, I'm even more different on the inside. I was given a lifeline by going into the centre, it was a chance of a lifetime and I'm not going to waste it. I ain't going back to what I was doing before. I've spent the last six months trying to learn from my mistakes and how I can overcome the difficulties I've had and will meet in the future."
The boys were amazed, they weren't even used to Scott speaking in this way, so confidently, let alone what he was saying. None of them quite knew what to say. Dave, another boy with bleached blond spiky gelled hair spoke first.
"To be honest, Scottie, I'm just relieved to see you again, most of us thought we wouldn't see you again anyway. We didn't know what had happened to you, there were loads of rumours and some of us thought you may have had a serious head injury after being knocked out."
"Me and Chas thought you'd been put inside." Chopper said.
"A lot of us thought that. Your parents and the school wouldn't tell us anything. We thought they were too ashamed to own up to what had happened." Commented a boy who they called Ash, because he looked like Ashley Cole, the England footballer.
"I suppose they were, Ash. The centre I went to, is a place that kids go to rather than getting expelled or put inside. Although it is a brilliant place, you are sent away from home and have to cope with a very different life."

Scott's reply echoed his feeling of relief that his mates seemed to just appreciate him being there, despite all the changes in him. But he was very aware of the temptation he might feel to go with them so he thought he'd better leave.
"Right boys, it's been great to see you again. I'm off home now. I'll see you tomorrow."
With that, Scott began his walk home, leaving his mates 'buzzing', trying to cope with the sudden reappearance of Scott but also the fact that he was completely different.
Scott smiled as he reflected on his first morning back at school, feeling he had safely overcome some tricky obstacles on his journey to success.

Chapter 23
"you've got superpowers!"

"Scott! It's Stacey on the phone."
Scott pulse still quickened at her name, not so much because of the sexual attraction he had six months ago, but now more for the high level of respect and gratitude he felt towards her. Scott was handed the phone to him, she had walked with it, up the stairs to his room, he thanked her as he took the phone.
"Hi, Stace, how are things with you?"
"I'm fine, Scott, more students to help here, you know how it is. More to the point, how are things with you?"
"Brill, Stace. So far, so good. As you can see, I'm actually at home on a Saturday evening, at what time, 9pm or should I say 2100 hours."
"I hoped you might be, that's why I phoned. So how has your first week at school gone?"
"Much better than I imagined. As usual, you were right that they were so shocked that they just didn't know what to do. As you predicted, the girls have been the most amazed and they just don't recognise me, especially as I can actually talk to them comfortably. I must admit their interest in me has boosted my confidence even further."
"Remember what we discussed though Scott, be careful not to let yourself get carried with their interest in you."
"It's okay, Stace. Listening to your story and all the others in the centre has made me very aware of that pitfall. Again you were right about the advantages of now being an effective reflective practitioner, I'm analysing what is happening and why, while it is happening. It is just as you described, it is like being able to read their minds, like having a superpower."
"So your journey to success is still on course?"
"Definitely, Stace. Tomorrow morning I'm a sub for my football team, so I may get to play footie for the first time in over six months. I can't wait to see the

effect of my hundreds of hours of practice in the soccer skills room, I do hope I get a chance."

"What about your exams, how have they gone?"

"Incredible, Stace! I cannot believe how easy I've found them. I've done so many past exam questions that I keep smiling throughout them, they basically just keep asking the same questions, I've quite enjoyed doing them and I'm actually looking forward to the results. I've still got a few more to do though and this week I've got to do my option subjects, since I only studied Maths, English and Science in the centre, I know they will be very different, but I ain't worried, I'll just do what I can and guess a lot, as we discussed."

"Excellent, Scott. I'm so proud of you. Have a good week, I'll try to phone again when I get a chance."

"Thanks, Stace, I appreciate it. Bye."

Scott went down the stairs to return the phone to the lounge, where his parents were watching television.

"Did you chat with Stace, mum?" Scott asked.

"Yes, both me and your dad had a good chat with her, she is very pleased with what we said about how well you're doing."

"Thanks for that. It's still early days yet though, but it has gone well so far."

"What time you want to leave tomorrow, Scott?" George asked.

"It's a 10:30 kick off, it's an away game, but I reckon it will only take about 20 minutes to get there. I'll already have my kit on so about 9:30, is that okay, dad?"

"Yeah, that's fine with me. It's be a long time since I've been anywhere with you, let alone a match, I'm looking forward to it."

"Thanks, dad, I really appreciate it. Stevo said he'll try to make sure I get part of a game, but he ain't seen me for almost nine months and the last time he did, we had a huge bust up."

"You were always having 'bust ups' with someone, especially me. He's been good to give you another chance, even if it is as sub."

"I know, dad. The other boys had told him I'd been sent away and said how much I'd changed, I don't think he'd have risked me again otherwise."

"I can't blame him for that, it was like having to play with ten men, the number of times you got sent off."

"That was then, this is now, dad, it won't happen again."

"Having seen you here over the last two weeks, I actually believe you, son."

"Thanks dad, I won't let you down, I've done enough of that to last a lifetime, the old Scott is dead, long live the new Scott. I'm off to bed now, see you in the morning."

Scott, with a tear in his eye, went over to his dad and hugged him and then kissed his mum before he went upstairs.

*

"There they are dad, over there!"
Scott said to his dad and pointed across the field of about five football pitches, to a group of boys at least 100 metres away from them, in bright yellow football kit, kicking the ball in front of a goal. At the other goal there was another group of boys in an all red kit doing much the same. On the sidelines there were about a dozen adults, probably parents.
As they got closer to the adults, Scott looked at his watch and spoke again.
"There's Stevo, dad. We're in plenty of time."
A bald headed man with a pot belly, in a Manchester United track suit, looked across as he heard his name and stared at them as they got closer. When Scott and George were within a few metres they could see the astonished look on his face.
"Scott! They said you'd changed but I just thought they were winding me up, there always doing that, but you don't look nothing like you used to."
Scott held out his hand to greet him.
"Morning Mr Stevenson, thanks for giving me a chance. I've not just changed my appearance, I'm a different person as well. Do you remember my dad?"
Stevo shook Scott's hand and then George's.
"Yeah, I remember your dad, poor sod. I don't know how he didn't throttle you, in fact, I don't know how I didn't."
"He's not like that anymore, Mr Stevenson."
For the first time in many years George felt he was able to defend his son.
"So I've heard. Call me Bob. Well he certainly looks and sounds different but we shall see how he copes on the pitch. I'll bring him on at some stage, he'll have a chance to see if he can control his temper. I understand you haven't played at all this season, but you certainly look fitter."
Stevo looked up and down at Scott, who was wearing a black track suit that was baggy on him now that he was so much thinner.
"As I said on the phone, I've been able to do lots of training in the centre but I ain't played in a match since last April."
"When you got sent off, as usual. How many times have you been sent off? "
"I think about ten."
"Ten! I thought it was even worse than that. Anyway, we'll see. I've got a full side at the moment, but we ain't been having a good season, so hopefully you can help us."
"Thanks, Mr Stevenson, I really do appreciate it."
Mr Stevenson called the rest of the boys over to him and Scott, where they greeted him with yells, waves and hi-fives. They all sat down and Stevo gave them his 'team talk', as he'd seen the referee making his way across the field towards them.
When the match started, Scott spent a lot of time stretching and doing various exercises, while watching the game. Stevo shouted almost continuously showing lots of enthusiasm, though many of his comments were probably

misdirected or ignored. George said very little, but puffed his cheeks and shook his head a great deal and the other adults watching the game behaved in similar ways to these two. At half time, Scott's team, Ipsodonians, were losing 2-0, they came over towards Stevo, who moved on to the pitch, where he got the boys to sit down and he gave them another 'team talk'.
"Stevo, I think I may have pulled a hamstring." A tall thin boy with short ginger hair interrupted him after about five minutes.
"Do you want to come off, Ginge? We have Scott here who could come on." Stevo asked.
"I think I'd better, it seems to be getting worse."
"You're okay to play upfront, ain't you Scott?"
"Yeah, definitely."
Scott replied enthusiastically and started to take his track suit off.
The referee blew his whistle to let everyone know he wanted them to get ready to resume the second half. Scott took his track suit over to where his dad was standing.
"Ginger's pulled a muscle, he's coming off, I'm replacing him upfront."
"Okay, son. Good luck."
It was a January morning so George was very cold and relieved he was actually going to get a chance to see his son play.
Scott ran to the middle of the pitch and took the kick off, then ran up field towards the penalty spot. He curved his run towards the right wing as he got to the edge of the penalty area and Chopper, who played in midfield, attempted to kick the ball from his own half to Scott. Unfortunately, the ball was kicked too hard and went over Scott's head and was dropping in front of him to land on the right hand corner of the penalty area. As the ball came over Scott's head he twisted his body in an anti-clockwise direction and swung his right leg at the same time. Scott volleyed the ball perfectly as it was about to land and it rocketed against the nearest goalpost, almost instantly. The goal shuddered, the net shook as the ball bounced off the post so hard it went about 50 metres behind the goal line. Absolutely everybody, the opposition, the referee, Stevo, George and all the adults stood in complete amazement. Scott had executed an incredibly difficult soccer skill almost perfectly. Of course, none of them were aware that Scott had been practising that skill for many hours in the centre.
Scott smiled, pleased that he had at last had a chance to start displaying the hours of soccer skills practice, but disappointed he had not scored, and then he heard the clapping and yells from his team and the sideline. The ball was retrieved and the goal kick taken by the goalkeeper. He was aiming for his left winger but Smudger managed to stop it getting to him by heading it, just inside the half way line. Scott was still on the right side of the field, about 30 metres from the goal as the headed ball came towards him, this time on his left side. Once again, as the ball came over his left shoulder he swivelled his body and

swung his left leg to strike the ball cleanly with his left foot. The ball, as before, went towards the post but this time the other post. The goalkeeper was still to the right of the goal from taking the goal kick and nowhere near the ball as it went inside the left hand post into the net. As before, there was a momentary hush as everyone looked on in astonishment, which was broken with enormous yells and hard clapping. Scott was quickly surrounded by his team-mates, hugging and patting his back. Their congratulations contained a lot of swearing but largely consisted of unbelievable, incredible, remarkable, fantastic, absolute magic etc.

The second half had begun less than two minutes ago, and on the sideline, Stevo and George looked at each other both open-mouthed. Stevo spoke first.

"What kind of a centre has he been in? What has happened to him. Has he gained some superpowers? Wayne Rooney couldn't have done that!"

"He said he'd done some practice of his soccer skills but I had no idea that this had happened. They keep saying these centres are magic, I'm beginning to believe it."

"When he took his track suit off, I thought he'd had a body transplant. He looked like Superboy, having seen those two shots perhaps he is!"

The Red Scorpions, Ipsodonians' opponents, had been much the better side in the first half and were clearly shaken by this start to the second half. The match recommenced with a kick off and they set up a series of unsuccessful attacks on the Ipsodonians' goal, which meant the ball did not get near to Scott for several minutes. Eventually, Ian, their goalkeeper got the ball and attempted to punt it to Scott in the centre circle. Scott was in the process of trapping the ball with his thigh when suddenly he was hit hard in his back by one the Scorpions defenders and sent sprawling forward. The referees' whistle shrilled as Scott hit the ground, but his new athletic physique meant he quickly sprang up and spun round. Stevo, George and all the Ipsodonians probably all thought the same thing, Scott is going to hit the defender who did it. They had all seen this situation many times before and feared the worst.

Scott just smiled at the defender with as he run past him. Again, surprise and astonishment was felt by all that knew Scott.

"I would never have believed it, if I hadn't seen it with my own eyes. He just got up and jogged past him, I've never seen him do that before."

Stevo said to George.

"Neither have I. In fact I've seen it and I'm still struggling to believe it."

George replied.

Chopper took the free kick and aimed it towards Scott, who was on left hand side of the penalty area and running towards the penalty spot. The kick was too hard and too near the goalkeeper, but Scott still ran and jumped to try to head it. He had spent many hours practising jumping and heading the ball in the centre and being much lighter and stronger, his leap was incredible. Understandably, the goalkeeper had no reason to think that a boy of this age,

at this level, would get anywhere near it, but he was wrong. Scott just reached the ball and it flicked off his head, but since the goalkeeper had run out of his goal to simply catch it, the ball just looped over his head into the goal.
There had barely been 10 minutes in the second half, Scott had touched the ball four times and scored twice! The terms shock, amazement, astonishment barely describes the feelings of all the people who were there. Football commentators frequently use the term 'magic' to try to describe what they saw, and this was 'magic'.
"I just don't believe it! I have never, ever seen anything like this. How high did he jump there? He must've broken the world record! What has happened to him George, what did they do to him in that centre? He is Superboy!"
Stevo was clearly struggling to cope with what he was seeing.
"I don't really know Bob. It is a very unusual place but I had no idea how incredible the changes in him were."
George was a mixture of pride and shock.
Scott had ended up on the floor after his leap and as he got to his feet he was descended upon by his team-mates, hugging, slapping and yelling as before. The Scorpions' coach was shouting at his team and several of them grouped together, clearly discussing what to do about Scott, so the restart took some time. The Scorpions were still much the better side and Scott could rarely get anywhere near the ball, apart from him going back to defend corners. It was obvious that the presence of Scott had a big effect on how the Scorpions played, they desperately tried to prevent the ball getting to him and repeatedly kicked or crashed into him.
About five minutes before the end of the match, Ipsodonians managed to get a corner on the right hand side. Chopper took the kick and aimed for Scott, who was at the far corner of the penalty area with two opponents next to him. As Chopper kicked the ball, Scott started to run towards the penalty spot with the two opponents trying to push and run with him. However, Scott's strength, speed, timing and spring were all now of a much higher level, he jumped so that his head was high above anyone else. His head hit the ball perfectly, so that it flew into the top right hand corner of the goal.
"He's done it again, he's bloody scored again. He's incredible, George, incredible!"
Stevo was yelling, jumping up and down, glowing red and waving his arms in the air."
George just stood still as though in shock and totally speechless. On the pitch Scott had been leapt on by his team-mates, completely submerged under a swarm of bodies. The Scorpions were much like George, seemingly suffering from shock, until their coach started yelling from the sideline to 'sort themselves out' and take the kick off. This prompting caused them to start moving again and the referee started to usher the Ipsodonians back to their own half. The Scorpions kicked off again, but were clearly demoralised with so

little time remaining in the match, their passing, crosses and shots reflecting their deflation.
When the final whistle blew, Scott was on the wing in front of Stevo and George, his team-mates clearly wanted to mob him again but Scott's great development in empathy meant his first thought was to 'feel for the opposition' and he immediately started to jog around to all of them, shaking their hand and saying 'well played', the rest of the Ipsodonians started to do likewise. When Scott went to shake the referees hand he spoke.
"You don't remember me do you, Scott?"
Scott looked at him closely and shook his head.
"I've refereed you before and sent you off,. You've never been anything but a right pain, until today. You were absolutely brilliant, I don't think I've ever seen such a remarkable performance, well done."
"That's very kind of you ref and I do apologise for my previous behaviour, it won't happen again."
"From what I've seen today, I think you're right, congratulations."
Scott continued shaking hands with his opponents and started to return to where Stevo and his Dad were standing, but as he did so, his team-mates descended on him, swearing and yelling as they did so.
"What the f**** has happened to you?" Smudger asked.
"I told you, I've done a lot of practice while I was away."
"A lot practice, you're joking. I don't think Messi, Ronaldo or Rooney could do what you did!" He replied.
Stevo and George had now walked over to them. Stevo shook his hand violently, then hugged him and yelled at him.
"Brilliant Scott, absolutely brilliant. I have never seen anyone your age play so well, how the hell have you improved so much?"
"Superlearning, Mr Stevenson, and hundreds of hours of effective purposeful practice!"
Stevo stepped back and tried to think about Scott's reply, George and the other boys did the same, none of them had a clue what he was talking about. Chopper responded first.
"When you said this place you'd been sent to was magical, I thought you were joking, but you weren't, what we've just seen was impossible."
"They sent you to Hogwarts, didn't they Scott, you've got superpowers!" Shouted Smudger and they all laughed.

Chapter 24
"I ain't afraid of failure anymore"

"How did you get on?"
Scott's mum had heard the car pull up and was placing the Sunday dinner on the kitchen table as they came into the room.

"We won 3-2, mum."
Scott went over to his mum, grabbed her round her shoulders and kissed her on the cheek.
"Mum, we've now not only got a son who's got rid of his 'attitude', we've got a brilliant footballer. He came on at half time and scored a hat trick, he was absolutely superb."
Ann stopped what she was doing to ensure she was listening carefully, looked at Scott, then George and smiled broadly.
"You're winding me up aren't you? I bet he didn't play or he got sent off again."
"No, seriously, he really did come on at half time and score a hat trick, honest." George replied
Ann stared at both of them, searching for a smile, checking to see if they were trying to wind her up and when she was convinced it was true, she grabbed Scott and gave him a huge kiss.
"Well done, son! That centre has certainly had a great effect on you, I'm so proud."
"Thanks mum. But I've got a lot to make up for. Can I do anything to help with the dinner?"
Scott was just pleased that he was beginning to rectify some of the harm he had done over the years.
"No thanks Scott. Just wash your hands and it'll be on the table."
Scott and George did as they were told and sat down for a 'Sunday Roast' dinner.
George was still struggling to understand how Scott had made so much improvement in just six months in the centre and asked Scott a key question over dinner.
"You may not be able to answer this question, Scott, but I'm going to ask it anyway. I've just witnessed what I would describe as another miracle. Since you came home about two weeks ago, I have been so impressed by how much you've changed and in so many ways. Today, I saw yet another example of what I would describe as miracles, in how superbly you played and controlled your temper. How Scott, how has six months in that centre made so much difference to you?"
"I think I can answer it, Dad. I don't know how much you can recall when Stacey and Grandma came to us over six months ago, but Stacey tried to explain what the centre was like."
"I remember thinking I didn't really understand it, but to be honest, I was so sick of you, and Stacey was so enthusiastic, that I was keen for you to go. But apart from her mentioning that it was JC Learner's idea, I can't recall much." George replied.
"I was the same, Scott, it was Stacey's enthusiasm that I remember, but I didn't really understand what she was saying." Ann added.

"Your views are typical, mum and dad. The centre is so different from anything else that few people can understand it, even my head teacher struggled when she visited the place. However, I gave a presentation for her which contained the key parts in my journey to success. Basically the centre is specifically designed to provide the 5 requirements essential for learning, motivation, concentration, environment, attainable tasks and feeling success. Throughout each day, these 5 things were occurring which kept me learning. Having a mentor who understands and supports you was essential and Stacey was perfect for me. But also crucial was all the time we focused on the 8 success skills so I always knew exactly what I needed to focus on and why I was struggling. With this approach, together the brilliant resources on the website and in the centre, everyone seemed to be so positive and encouraging that I was being continually encouraged."

"But how did you manage to become so brilliant at football, in six months?"

"Well actually, dad. You may not have realised it today, but I don't think I have become a brilliant footballer, but I have improved my soccer skills a great deal, particularly kicking, shooting, heading and ball control. There are still a number of areas in football that I'm not so good at. Throughout the six months, I spent hundreds of hours doing effective purposeful practice of these soccer skills and so I've improved immensely in them."

"And what about your exams, son, you seem to have made a lot of progress there." Ann asked.

"Even I can't believe how much easier I've found the exams this week, mum. The Superlearning approach has been invaluable for this and it meant that again I've spent six months doing effective purposeful practice preparing for exams. The successfeelosophy website has been so brilliant in providing great resources and activities that once I was in that exam hall, I just did what I'd done so many times before in my room. For the first time in my life, I'm actually not dreading getting my exam results."

George was listening carefully to what Scott was saying and responded again.

"When Stacey told us about her teenage problems and said how JC Learner and his centre had helped her, I was surprised and impressed. But in my wildest dreams I never imagined it would it would have such an incredible effect on you and in so many ways, I thought you were a lost cause, I really thought you'd either end up inside or dead."

"We both did, son." Ann added.

"Knowing what I do now, you were probably right. Stacey is a typical example of how once you get on that slippery slope it gets more and more difficult to get off it and her suicide attempt is not unusual. Probably for me, it would've been a high risk activity like fighting, showing off or drugs that would've killed me, and possibly you're right, I would've gone into prison first.

"Can you do that, Scott?" George asked.

"Yes, in fact, I think almost everyone who's been a student in there feels so grateful that they are keen to spend time as a mentor. It is one of the reasons why these centres have such low running costs. There aren't vast numbers of staff as in the traditional schools or centres for kids with behaviour problems, and although they are obviously highly skilled, they don't get paid a great deal."
"So when could you do that, Scott?"
Ann was a little worried she may be 'losing' her son having just got him back.
"Don't worry, mum, not for a while. You've got to be at least 18 and demonstrated for at least a year that you consistently have high scores in the 8 success skills."
Ann was obviously relieved, but George was very curious.
"You keep referring to the 8 success skills, I vaguely recall Stacey mentioning them when she was here six months ago and posters of them were everywhere in the centre and in your bedroom. It is obvious that these 8 skills are very central to your journey to success as you call it but otherwise I've never heard of them, why?"
"Brilliant question, dad, and one we discussed in one of our action inquiry sessions in the centre. As far as I understand it, at the moment, education and schools in this country have not yet realised how important they are and stick to what they've been doing for centuries. There are some countries, mainly in Scandinavia, I believe, like Finland and Sweden, that do place more emphasis on these skills."
"I've never read about them in the papers or magazines, or even come across them on the telly or radio, yet they are obviously extremely important in being successful. It seems ridiculous."
George was clearly getting annoyed.
"I feel the same dad, all of us from the centre feel like that, and what everyone in there says is 'spread the word'."
"Good point, son, we can all do that, I suppose."
"I also reckon with someone like JC Learner being involved it may not be too long before the 8 skills and the 'Learning For Success' centres do become well known." Scott added.
"And with outstanding examples like you and Stacey spreading the word, you might be right."
"That's very kind of you, dad. I'm hoping that Mrs Lucas will help with this particularly, she seemed very impressed with the centre and my progress."
"I've always thought she was a good head teacher and if she can learn from your experience that will be good news." George replied.
"When will you get your exam results, son?" Ann asked.
"Not until tomorrow week, at the earliest, mum. We've still got another week of exams remember and we don't have normal lessons until next week. I have Maths first period on Monday, so I reckon we'll get our results then.

Unfortunately, I have exams on my option choices this week and I've not done any studying on them for six months."
"So what you gonna do about them?"
"I discussed this with Stacey and we decided that I should apply Superlearning to them anyway. We thought that it would be a good opportunity to discover if I can still get a grade C in them, in the few months I've got left. Fortunately, there's loads of stuff on the success feelosophy website that I can use to prepare for them, so I'm gonna have a bash."
"How will you feel if you get a really low mark?" George asked.
"Motivation is one of the 8 skills I've really improved in, dad. I've managed to develop a growth mindset, which means I'm now resilient and can use setbacks as learning opportunities, I ain't afraid of failure anymore. This has made so much difference to me in so many ways. In fact you saw an example of this today in the match. My first kicks in the game were volleys, one on my left, the other on my right foot. I would never have tried those difficult kicks in the past, in case I made a right monkey out of myself, but now with a growth mindset I think, 'nothing ventured nothing gained' and had a go."
"And you should've seen them, mum. They were absolutely brilliant shots, one almost broke the post, and the other went into the corner of the goal!"
George said to his wife, proudly.
Scott smiled and patted his dad on the shoulder.
"Thanks, dad. I really appreciate your praise, I've caused you so many problems over the years that I'm determined to be able to repay you and mum from now on."
Mum gave Scott a hug and a kiss, crying as she did so.
"And if you'll excuse me, I've got to go and have a shower and then get on with my exam prep."
Scott got up and left his parents amazed and glowing with pride.

Chapter 25
"I have a lot to make up for"

"So why ain't you gonna sit next to me, Scottie?"
Smudger asked as they were lining up outside their Maths classroom. Lining up was not an accurate word, more milling about really. this was a year 11 class and set 4 after all. Since it was first period, Monday morning, they were still quite docile, half asleep really.
"You know why, Smudge. If we sit together we'll get into trouble, we always do, and I ain't going down that road anymore. You must've sussed that by now."
"Having seen who you've become over the last two weeks, I reckon you'd be too boring to sit next to anyway. I bet your gonna go in there and be a right boff, ain't you?"

"That's certainly my aim, Smudge. I ain't never been a boffin in my life, but it's never to late to start. Hopefully in time, I might even progress to geek level. Scott smiled broadly and Smudger laughed as well.
"I hear you've become a star at football as well as becoming a right hunk, a right David Beckham, aren't you Scott?"
Judy, the girl with bright red hair tied in a pony tail, that Scott had met on his way to school on the first day of term, was standing in front of him.
"He ain't a bad role model is he Judy? Sadly I don't think so."
Scott was able to actually talk to girls now, and actually felt quite comfortable, no redness or looking down.
"No he's better looking than Becks, perhaps Christiano Ronaldo."
Commented one of Judy's friends.
Scott studied her face and eyes carefully as he'd learnt to do. She was a tall thin girl with long straight bleached blond hair, he thought her pretty face was spoilt with lots of make-up, especially mascara and lip gloss, with large gaudy earrings. His thoughts were that she, like so many others, had poor self-awareness based on her appearance. Even though he'd been in her Maths set since the start of year 10, he still didn't know her name.
"That's very kind of you, but I don't think so, but thanks anyway."
Scott could see she was chuffed by his reply and he felt pleased with how he'd handled it.
"Scott's a better player than them." Smudger butted in.
"And better looking."
Added a short girl with short jet black gelled spiky hair. Again Scott carefully studied her face and eyes, and as before thought her excessive make-up and jewellery were symptoms of her poor self-awareness, he didn't know her name either and was about to reply in a way to boost her esteem when a loud voice interrupted him.
"Okay in you go!"
This was signified the arrival of their maths teacher, Mr Bevan, a thin six foot, middle aged balding man, wearing a dark three piece suit and red Wales RFU tie. Scott waited for everyone else to go in and then spoke to his teacher, .
"Mr Bevan, I'm sorry for all the hassle I caused you last year, I think you'll find I've changed."
"It's very obvious you've changed Scott. Thanks for apologising."
Scott assumed Mr Bevan was referring to his huge change in appearance and politeness. They moved into the room and Scott looked to see if there were any spaces at the front, previously a 'no-go area' to him. Just in front of the teacher's table, he spotted a space next to a girl whose name he did actually know. He moved towards her and studied her face carefully in his usual way, now! Even though she was seated he could see she was fairly short, slightly overweight, with brown curly hair and glasses. He was pleased that she didn't have a face caked in make-up or wearing huge earrings, he recalled her as

being quite quiet but pleasant (not bitchy!) and thought she was she wasn't very good at maths but tried hard.
"Okay if I sit here, Lynn."
Lynn cricked her neck to look up at his six foot four inch frame and was clearly surprised, delighted and struggling to speak, but eventually managed to say.
"Yes"
She wanted to say please at the end, but thought she shouldn't.
Scott's broad shoulders and long legs meant he didn't fit in very well, but carefully sat down beside her. It had been almost two weeks since Scott had returned to school and word had spread about him but Lynn and the rest of the class were still quite surprised that he would sit at the front What surprised everyone even more was he sat next to a girl, he had never done this voluntarily before, and this, in particular, caused a buzz of chatter to go around the class.
"Right, welcome back everybody. You'll be delighted to know that your papers have been marked and I'm about to give them out. You'll get both paper one and two, they've each got a percentage mark at the top together with a grade. It was last year's exam and we've used the mark scheme from the exam board and their grade boundaries. Therefore, these are the marks and the grades you would've got if this had been the final exam. Hopefully, you can improve on these in the next few months by at least a grade."
Mr Bevan walked around the room giving out the papers, as he did so, for the first time in several years, Scott felt some excitement at getting his papers and marks. He had actually made some effort for these exams and cared about the result. Annoyingly, he seemed to be one of the last to get his paper, no, he was the last! Mr Bevan dropped two sets of papers in front of him with a smile on his face and moved around to the front of the room to study Scott's reactions.
At the top of the front paper there was written 96% Grade C, Scott then looked at the other set of papers underneath it, which had 98%, Grade C. Scott stared and several seconds elapsed for the information to really sink in with him and then he looked up to see Mr Bevan staring at him with a huge grin on his face, who then spoke to the class.
"As I said, you all took last year's Foundation level papers, which means Grade C is the highest you can get. Normally, with decent practice over the next few months, you should be able to improve by two grades."
The interactive white board behind him showed the same information that he was saying.
"An average of 70% or more is a grade C,
57 to 69% is grade D,
44 to 56% is grade E,
32 to 43% is grade F and
19 to 31% is grade G"

The room was then full of noise as all the students tried to find out the grades of as many people as they could.
"How did you do so well, Scott?"
Lynn asked having looked at his papers, she had an average of 45%, a grade E written on the paper.
Scott was still 'in shock' but Lynn's question brought him back to reality and answered.
"Superlearning and lots of effective deliberate purposeful practice."
"Superlearning, that's a good name and it seems to work. Any chance you could share it with me, Scott?"
"Of course, Lynn, it ain't difficult, in fact, once you get the hang of it, it's a doddle."
They were then interrupted by Mr Bevan speaking again.
"For the rest of the lesson we're going to go through the paper and use the mark scheme to ensure you know the right answers and can learn from it."
And that's precisely what the class did for the remainder of the lesson, with Scott helping Lynn throughout. When the bell rang to signify the end of the lesson, Mr Bevan spoke to the class again.
"Your homework is to select which three questions or topics you found most difficult and would like us to go through first. Scott, can I have a quick word with you, please."
Scott was used to having to 'stay behind' usually because his behaviour had been so bad, but he'd not done anything wrong today, so this was a bit of a surprise. Scott packed his stuff into his kit bag as Mr Bevan walked over to him.
"Incredible result, Scott. I had no idea you were capable of it. How did you manage it?"
"Superlearning and lots of effective deliberate purposeful practice."
Scott said for the second time that day
"Well I don't know what that means but it seems like some sort of miracle to me, It also means you can't be in this class anymore."
Scott was confused with this comment, in recent years he'd heard this before when he'd done something wrong, but why this time?
"You are clearly too good to do the foundation level, so you need to move into a class that does the higher level paper. From tomorrow you need to go to Mrs Morgan's class, set two, okay?"
Scott had not thought about this before and was very surprised with this information. Mr Bevan had finished the remark with a question but it had not really registered with Scott, so he asked again.
"That is okay with you, isn't it Scott?"
"Oh sorry, yeah, that's fine, sir."
"You'd better go to your next lesson now, Scott, well done again."

Scott was still trying to think about what had been said and how he was 'too good for the foundation level'. But then he realised he would be late for his first English lesson for six months and rushed off, thanking Mr Bevan as he did so.

"I do apologise for being late, Miss Naisbett, I had to see Mr Bevan after the lesson."

Scott arrived at his next lesson as the last student was entering the room.

Miss Naisbett, a petite young pretty woman with long wavy hair, wearing discreet make-up and earrings, a white blouse, black knee length skirt and patent black shoes with high heels, was very surprised at seeing and hearing Scott. He looked and spoke very differently to the one she recalled in year 10, who had caused many problems for her in the past. Scott now had good non-verbal communication skills and was able to detect the surprised look on her face and he spoke again.

"I also want to apologise for my behaviour last year, miss. I know I've had lots of chances but I do hope you'll give me one more chance, I think you'll find I have changed and improved a lot."

This politeness was in stark contrast to the repeated rudeness she had encountered last year and only added to her astonishment, but she did manage a short reply in a quiet voice with a Scottish accent

"Oh er, Scott, well your change in appearance and manners supports the other radical change I've already witnessed. Please go in and sit down."

Scott did not fully understand what she meant by 'other radical change' but entered the room as she requested. He stood just inside the room and scanned it for empty chairs. There were four rows and four columns of tables, with two chairs at each table, and the only empty chairs were in the front rows. Scott saw an empty seat next to a little Asian girl just in front of him.

"Is it okay if I sit next to you?"

The girl was already staring at him, and was surprised to hear him speak, especially so politely, he had never spoken to her at all before. Scott analysed her face and eyes in his usual careful way. She seemed to wear no make-up and just stud earrings; her long jet black hair was platted and tied in a long tail behind her. He thought she was extremely pretty but shy probably due to her social skills being weak.

"Of course." She muttered.

"I'm Scott, I'm afraid I can't remember your name."

"I know you're Scott, we've been in this class since the start of year 10, I'm Saira."

Scott was more ashamed rather than embarrassed at not knowing her name, but he had been preparing for these situations before he left the centre.

"I do apologise for my ignorance and rudeness last year then, Saira."

Saira's face clearly reflected her surprise at Scott's politeness as she moved her chair slightly to allow room for Scott's broad shoulders.

There was quite a lot of chattering in the room which was interrupted with Miss Naisbett speaking very loudly, almost shouting.
"Good morning class, welcome back, I suppose I should even say happy new year but we're over halfway through January. I'm delighted to say that your exams papers have been marked and I've got them here."
The class were interested in what she was saying and went quiet.
"In case you didn't realise, everyone in the year took the same exam, which was basically the one last year's year 11 took in the summer. We've also used the mark scheme the exam board provided and given you a grade using it. Both papers have been put together and your mark as a per cent and grade are written at the top of the front paper. On the board you will see the grades for each percentage mark, they are called grade boundaries."
Miss Naisbett touched the computer mouse on her desk, this table appeared on the whiteboard and the class looked at it.

English GCSE Grades

%	90+	77-89	68-76	57-67	46-56	36-45	26-35	16-25
Grade	A*	A	B	C	D	E	F	G

As in the Maths lesson the teacher walked around the room, giving out the papers, and as before Scott was last. Miss Naisbett had a smile on her face as she passed the papers to Scott and quietly said.
"Well done, Scott."
At the top of the front paper he had two things written large and clearly in red, 82%, Grade A.
Getting a grade C in Maths may have been a surprise but a grade A in English, that's unbelievable!
Scott had never been one for reading, possibly comics, but he's never been able to get any reasonable marks in almost anything in English, this really was a miracle as far as Scott was concerned. But he was not alone, Saira saw his face first, then his paper and asked.
"Is that a grade A, Scott?"
Scott was still too stunned to even hear her, let alone reply.
"It is, it's an A."
Saira then turned to her friends behind.
"He's got an A, Scott got a grade A!"
The two girls behind stopped what they were doing and both said.
"You're joking, don't be ridiculous, what did he really get?"
Saira grabbed Scott's paper and showed it to them.
"Look there, in red, 82%, grade A!"
"You're right, it is an A. Scott, how did you get a grade A, you've never got any decent grades before in English, how did you do it?"
The girl with short red hair, named Kelly, sitting right behind Scott asked.

Miss Naisbett was watching and listening to these responses and decided to get involved before Scott had a chance to respond.
"Scott, I think we all feel the same as Kelly. Would you be willing to let us all know how you did it?"
Six months ago Miss Naisbett would never have asked Scott something like this and although there was no reason then, he would never have done it, anyway. But that was the 'old' Scott who was only prepared to act the fool or be negative in English. Scott was still in a daze but with Miss Naisbett's request he had a chance to reflect on the miracle and 'spread the word'.
"Of course, miss, no problem, if the class wants me to."
Miss Naisbett was shocked again, she had made the request but didn't really think he would be so positive, he never had been before! Fortunately, she was distracted by the positive response of the class, yelling and encouraging him to speak.
"Is it okay to use your computer, miss? I would like to show the class a website."
Scott looked at Miss Naisbett, whose face showed some apprehension, she still bore the scars of Scott's abuse last year.
"Don't worry, miss, it's not porn or anything like that, it's a brilliant website that will help everyone learn to succeed."
"Er yeah, that's alright, go ahead."
Miss Naisbett was still a little nervous and moved over to her laptop.
Scott stood up, walked over to the laptop and used the mouse and keyboard until the whiteboard had the homepage for www.successfeelosphy.com displayed. Miss Naisbett relaxed and moved to the side and sat on a chair to watch and listen to Scott. The class had gone very quiet, which was quite unusual for them, studying the screen and waiting for Scott to speak.
"I think most of you know now that I spent six months in a place called a 'Learning For Success Centre'. Basically it is an extremely unusual place that tries to help kids like me, who were a complete pain and waste of space."
Scott looked at Miss Naisbett and smiled, the class laughed.
"The aim of the centre is given away in it's name, to try to get the students, or inmates if you prefer, to learn to succeed. I had a mentor who help me a lot at the start and convinced me that unless I changed I would end up in all sorts of trouble and be lucky to see my twenty first birthday. She also persuaded me that I could change and learn to succeed by a very different approach called 'Success Feelosophy' and this is the website that I used everyday I was in the centre."
The class looked at the screen and Scott continued.
"This website has virtually everything on it that I needed for learning when I was in the centre and I've continued using it when I came home a few weeks ago. It has loads of stuff on it, especially videos and brilliant resources so that I could learn. I'll show you some of it."

For well over half an hour, the class sat staring and listening intently to what Scott was showing and telling them. Sometimes sitting open-mouthed showing their amazement, but also often commenting to the people next to them. Finally Scott said.

"So basically, as far as my exam marks are concerned, I managed to get a grade 'A ' by applying SUPERlearning and spending many hours using the brilliant resources on the website for purposeful practice. Any questions?"

Before anyone could ask any questions, the class began clapping. Scott had never felt like this before in a lesson in school, possibly for the first time in a lesson he actually felt proud of what he'd done and believed he had some ability in it.

Miss Naisbett had loads of questions and was itching to ask them, but the bell rang.

"Thank you Scott, that was so good, in fact, it was brilliant. Thanks again Scott. Okay class off you go!"

Some students had already begun to move and towards the door and the rest began to do the same.

"Could I have a quick word with you please, Scott?"

Asked Miss Naisbett.

"Of course, miss."

Scott was more prepared for the request this time. He returned to his seat, collected his bits and pieces and put them in his bag, Miss Naisbett walked over to him and since Scott towered over her he decided to sit down.

"Scott, I just wanted to say how absolutely amazed I am with you. I can honestly say I have never seen such an incredible change in anyone in such a short space of time. Your improvement is miraculous, in your exam and character, and your presentation to the class was fantastic."

"Thanks, miss. I have a lot to make up for and I apologise again for my behaviour last year. Will I have to change class like I have to for Maths?"

"No, we don't really set in English, you'll stay with me."

"Good"

Miss Naisbett looked pleased, yet ironically last year she had spent a lot of time trying to get him put in another class.

"I'm pleased you feel that way, I'll see you tomorrow."

"Yes, miss, all the best."

Scott stood up politely and left the room proudly.

Chapter 26
"it's definitely a miracle what's happened to him!"

"So how was your day, son?"

George enquired as he and Scott were hungrily sitting down at the kitchen table. Mrs Spicer was busily placing the bowls of peas and broccoli on the table, to join the dishes of sausages and mash potato already there.

"Brilliant, dad, absolutely brilliant!"

Since Scott had only just got in from school, neither of his parents had had a chance to talk to him, and were eager to hear how his first day of lessons had gone, and discover if he'd got any exam results.

"Why, what happened?"

Mum quizzed as she carefully sat down, delighted by his enthusiastic response.

"It began with Maths; I got a grade C, which is the highest grade possible in that exam. So they are going to put me in for the higher paper and move me into set 2. In English I got a grade A, which means I'm also going to be entered for the higher level in that, but I'm okay to stay in Miss Naisbett's class. In Science, I got a grade C, again that's the highest grade possible in the papers I took, so I've got to go into set 2 for Double Science and do the higher level."

Both parents had begun to put food on their plates but stopped instantly, barely able to believe what they were hearing.

George was first to recover his senses and speech.

"Just a moment, son, did I hear you right? Did you say you got a grade A in English and C in Maths and Science? And you are entered for the higher level in all of them?"

"Yes, dad, but I ain't finished yet. In the afternoon, I got a grade C both Business Studies and P.E."

His mum had been motionless for several seconds, but finally managed to utter a few words.

"I thought you said you didn't study any of your option subjects in the centre?"

"That's right, mum. Stacey suggested I should try to prepare for those exams using the SUPERlearning approach, and I did just that, using the stuff on the successfeelosophy website."

His dad had ignored his meal to concentrate on what he thought he was hearing. Finally convinced he could believe that he had heard correctly, leant over and shook Scott's hand.

"Those grades are incredible. I don't think your brother or sisters did as well as that in their mock exams."

Mum's eyes were watering as she leant across and kissed Scott on the cheek.

"You really are a marvel, son."

“I’m not the marvel, mum; it’s the magic of the centre, SUPERlearning and the successfeelosophy website.”
Dad had resumed dishing up his dinner, but also commented.
“You’re probably right, son, but it still requires you to make use of it.”
“I s’pose you’re right, dad and one of my tasks is to become a disciple for it.”
Scott had now begun to dish up his food, and smiled as he said this, knowing his parents would be confused.
Mum was first to ask.
“What do you mean?”
“You’ve already seen what Stacey does, as well as being a mentor in the centre; she acts as a disciple for it, successfeelosophy and superlearning. Everyone who’s been in the centre is encouraged to act as a disciple, to act as a good role model for it, to help others learn and spread the word about it.”
“That’s a bloody good idea; it’s obviously such a great centre and effective approach and website.”
Dad interrupted his eating to comment.
“At the end of school today, I had to go and see, Mr Edwards, the Director of Leaning for my year.”
“What’s a Director of Learning?”
Mum asked immediately.
“I think it’s another name for Head of Year. Mr Edwards is the one for year 11. He wanted to see me, to talk about my exam results, and asked me how I’d managed to do so well. He showed me this table of predicted grades on his computer that used previous SAT results and teacher assessments. He said all schools are now expected to do this tracking, as he called it, and when the Government inspect schools they use this stuff to assess them. He was amazed at how I had done so much better than predicted from that information.”
Dad was eating but clearly fascinated with what Scott was saying.
“What did you tell him, son?”
“Same as I just told you, dad, successfeelosophy, superlearning and lots of effective deliberate purposeful practice. Obviously he’d never heard of it and didn’t understand it all. That’s why I’m so late, it took me ages trying to explain it to him.”
“Did he understand it all in the end?”
Dad enquired between mouthfuls.
“I’m not sure to be honest. If he did understand it, he still didn’t seem to believe it. He just couldn’t seem to accept that I had not actually had any ‘proper teachers’, as he called them, since July. It helped a lot when I showed him the website, and told him that Mrs Lucas had visited the Learning For Success Centre. But he was obviously still struggling to believe me. In fairness, I’d not really met him before, and all he’d ever heard about me was how much of a pain I was.”

Both parents chuckled, prompting Dad to comment.
"I think you are going to have a lot of that, son. I reckon most teachers will struggle to understand or believe what you've done and how you've done it. Perhaps that's why you've been asked to be disciples, as you call them."
Mum was getting concerned that Scott had not had a chance to eat much, but wanted to add a comment.
"Obviously since you've done so well, everyone, not just teachers, will struggle to believe or understand it. I think we all feel that what has happened to you is like a miracle and that centre does seem to work magic. Now eat your dinner before it gets cold."
"Very true, okay mum, I will."

*

"Hallo Mrs Simpson, I believe I've got an appointment with Mrs Lucas"
Scott was again in the waiting area for the Head teacher's room, a place he now knew well. He was speaking to Mrs Simpson, the head teacher's personal assistant, on Friday afternoon, after school, at the end of his third week back at school.
"Oh hallo, Scott. Yes, Mr Edwards is in with her at the moment, she said for me to take you in as soon as you arrive."
Mrs Simpson came out from behind her desk and moved towards the head teacher's office, she always wore a smart suit, this one was red. She knocked on the door and opened it, Scott was almost a foot taller than her so was clearly visible to Mrs Lucas as the door opened.
"Thank you Mrs Simpson, please come in, Scott."
As usual, Mrs Lucas was wearing, a white blouse and a knee length carefully tailored skirt, with matching shoes and spectacles, this time black. She was sitting in her padded swivel chair, behind the large modern desk, and Mr Edwards was sitting in one of the three chairs in front of it.
"I know you've already met Mr. Edwards, Scott, please sit down."
She pointed to the chair next to Mr. Edwards, who was a white haired man in his fifties, wearing a plain black suit, white shirt and a school tie.
"Good afternoon, Mr. Edwards."
Scott said politely as he gently sat down.
"Scott, I think you know Mr. Edwards is the Director of Learning for year 11. He is also our Assessment Manager, which means he responsible for tracking of our students; he closely monitors the progress of them. I know you went to see him at the start of the week, but he is still very confused about your progress. He says you told him you've not had any teaching or subject tutoring since July, and he cannot understand how your exam results are so much better than your predicted grades."
Scott was studying her eyes and face closely, detecting some confusion in her also.

"I was amazed and impressed with the Learning For Success Centre you were in, and have been incredibly impressed with the change in you since July. But I'm struggling to believe these results. Can you try to explain them for us, please?"

Scott's face broke into a broad smile, as he had been doing this repeatedly throughout the past week. He recalled the discussion with his parents about becoming a 'disciple and spreading the word'.

"I'll do my best, miss. When you were with me in the centre, do you recall I told you about 'SUPERlearning For Exam Success', and explained about the process, and how we used Videostudy, M.C.Jigsaws, Quizcards and the Exam Papers with Mark Schemes in it?"

"Yes, I do Scott, but although you were very enthusiastic about it, I had no idea it could have this effect."

"To be honest, miss, until I sat in the exam room and got the results, neither did I."

Scott grinned and looked briefly at both teachers for their reactions, before continuing.

"In the centre I became aware that to get good grades, I needed to put down the answers that were on the mark scheme, and having attempted so many exam questions and marked them in the last six months or so, I was aware I had improved a lot, but not as much as my results showed."

Mr Edwards was obviously very sceptical, clearly still struggling to understand or believe and immediately asked a question.

"I've never heard of and have no idea of what Videostudy, M.C.Jigsaws, or Quizcards might be. But are you saying that you did lots of exam questions and mark them?"

Scott could detect Mr Edwards' frustration and incredulity.

"Yes sir, in fact, the Videostudy, M.C.Jigsaws, and Quizcards are great ways of doing past exam questions, they are great fun as well as being very effective. I did have teachers, they just happen to be on video, and the videostudy allowed me to stop and rewind them when I wanted, and keep replaying them as often as I wanted. I learnt the English, Maths and Science from them and then I had to try to get good at answering the exam questions on it. The successfeelosophy website had loads of past papers and mark schemes on it and because I'd learnt how to use them for effective learning, I just spent many hours of effective deliberate purposeful exam practice."

Scott smiled again as he'd used this phrase so many times in the last few weeks and was confident they wouldn't really understand it.

"What about your option subjects?"

"I just did the same for them, when I got home. The videos are on the website and I made my own resources."

Mr Edwards still looked disbelievingly at Scott, but responded positively.

"I've been teaching for almost 30 years and I can honestly say I've never heard or seen anything like it before. You've not only made a mockery of your predicted grades, you appear to have done it without teachers or tutors."
Mrs Lucas had been listening very carefully and still looked stunned, but commented.
"Congratulations Scott, again you've been quite remarkable. I wonder, would you be prepared to spend some time in the near future, with Mr Edwards, explaining all this in in more detail, please?"
Mr Edwards responded positively to Mrs Lucas' request, despite continuing to struggle to be completely convinced. Scott looked at his eyes, his improved communication and empathy skills meant he was able to detect that Mr Edwards was slowly becoming convinced.
"Yes, of course, miss. When would you like me to come to your office, sir?"
"Is after school on Monday, okay for you, Scott?"
"Yeah, that's fine with me, sir."
Mrs Lucas was aware that Scott had been kept quite late, so suddenly stood up and held out her hand.
"Thanks for that, Scott, and for coming along this afternoon. Have a good weekend."
"Thanks miss. I'm pleased to be able to help. As I've said before, I've a lot to make up for."
Scott grinned widely as he shook her hand and then swivelled to shake Mr Edwards hand, who was surprised by his politeness and clearly wasn't used to shaking hands with a student, but copied his head teacher.

*

"Shall I get it, mum?"
Scott was watching some sport on TV with his dad in the living room, when he heard a knock at the door.
"Yes, please, son."
Scott shot up and went to the front door promptly. As he opened it, a huge smile went across his face.
"Stace! What a surprise, so great to see you!"
He held out his arms and hugged her very tightly.
"Careful Scott, you'll crush her."
His dad exclaimed from behind him.
Scott let go and stepped backed to study her more carefully. Her unzipped jacket displayed her usual black, figure hugging successfeelophy.com T shirt and black track bottoms and trainers. Her huge smile, beaming across her pretty, make-up free face, underneath her black curly hair.
"They didn't tell you I was coming then?"
"No, we wanted it to be a surprise."
A grinning mum replied as she joined them.

Stacey carefully stepped inside, then hugged and kissed her aunt and uncle on the cheeks.
They all greeted each other and moved into the living room, dad immediately switching off the TV. Mum had been preparing some tea in the kitchen, expecting Stacey to arrive, brought in the tea tray.
Scott was a mixture of excitement at seeing Stacey, but also curiosity as he wondered if there was a particular reason for her visit. Scott and Stacey sat on the sofa; dad spoke as he sat in his usual chair,
"Stacey spoke to us on the phone the other day, and asked if it was okay to visit now, being a school night we thought it would be fine."
Stacey smiled at Scott, realising he was very curious as to why she was visiting.
"It's almost May and over four months since you came home. You've only got a few more weeks in school before your GCSE's and I wanted to do a bit of 'catching up' and also to tell you some important information."
"Ever since you spoke on the phone, and told us what was planned I've been dying to tell Scott about it."
Mum responded excitedly.
"I'd better start with that, then, hadn't I?"
Stacey replied with a huge grin.
"As you know, JC Learner has taken a particular interest in Scott's progress, partly because he's my cousin, but I think mainly because he sees close parallels with himself in Scott. Anyway, when your head teacher, Mrs Lucas, visited us at the centre he said he would try and visit her, and you, at your school and he has a meeting with her tomorrow. Afterwards he wants to come here a visit you and your mum and dad."
Scott had a huge look of surprise, and looked around at his mum and dad, both of whom were smiling.
"Yes, we're finally going to get to see the great man. I've got time off of work specially."
Dad said excitedly and mum added with as much excitement.
"And Stacey is going to stay with us tonight."
"Brilliant, absolutely brilliant. I've often wondered if I'd see him again, and if he knew how much I've improved."
Scott was equally excited.
"He knows, Scott, he knows. As I said, he's taken a special interest in you, but he tries to keep track of all the students who've been in his Learning For Success Centres."
Stacey took a sip of her tea, sat back in the chair and looked at the beaming Scott, before continuing.
"So that's my news, but what about you? Give me a brief summary of your journey to success since you left the centre, and what are you planning for the next part?"

Scott had a quick slurp of his tea and began talking.
"Right, I'll try to sum it all up as best as I can, perhaps mum and dad, you'll comment whenever you want. At home, I can't recall any serious unpleasant arguments at all. We've had lots of family forums where we've discussed loads of things calmly and in depth, usually over tea, but no bust ups like we had all the time before I went to the centre."
Scott looked across to his dad sitting in his favourite armchair, for reassurance. George was smiling and nodding, keen to comment, clearly proud of his son, at last!
"Stace, you said when you brought him back on Christmas Eve that I would enjoy living with him, and you were so right. The family forums, as you call them, have been invaluable in sorting out problems early on, and seeing each others views, I wish we'd have done that, years ago. I can honestly say I've really enjoyed them, and the last few months with him in the home."
It was possible to detect some watering in George's eyes as he said this, much as he still tried to conceal it. However he had also learnt and become more comfortable with this since Scott's return.
Mum, of course was also keen to comment.
"It's not only been a great pleasure, I've learnt so much from him, especially in these forums."
Scott felt proud and a little embarrassed already and decided to continue promptly.
"In school, I could never have imagined in my wildest dreams that I could do so well. I'm entered for the higher papers in all my GCSEs, and they are predicting A's and B's."
Stacey did not look surprised, but very pleased.
"That's brilliant, but I'm not surprised, you improved so much with Superlearning in the centre. Have you had a chance to spread the word about it all, at school?"
"Very much so. I've got loads of kids in my year using both Superlearning and the successfeelosphy website. I also spent a lot of time with the teacher who is responsible for Assessment and Exams in our school, explaining Superlearning, Videostudy, MC Jigsaws and Quizcards to him. It took a lot of time, he really found it difficult to believe."
"I'm not surprised at that either Scott. JC said a lot of teachers seem to find the Superlearning resources and approach so different to what they are used to and very difficult to cope with. What about in lessons how have you got on in them?"
"Much better. I've not been sent out at all, and I've kept my mouth firmly shut whenever I felt annoyed or angry."
"Have you felt annoyed and angry often?"
"To begin with, quite a few of the kids did try to wind me up, but because my self-awareness and managing feelings skills are so much better now, I never

responded. After a while they stopped because they knew I wouldn't react. Actually, I've found some of the teachers in lessons most annoying, they want me to waste my time by taking notes or doing stupid tasks. However, I've managed my feelings and just stuck with Superlearning despite them sticking with their out-dated, old fashioned teaching."
"I'm really pleased to hear that, because I felt you'd find that really difficult. I think most students struggle with traditional lessons and teaching, after they used Superlearning in the centre. I think you've acted as a really good role model and disciple there."
"He does lots of studying at home now, Stacey."
Mum was keen to point out.
"It's not really studying, mum, it's fun, its Superlearning!"
"Whatever it is, son, I'm bloody pleased you are doing so much of it."
She replied with a huge smile on her face.
"What about your mates and social life?"
Stacey felt this could be a big problem.
"Very different, now Stace. I've still got my mates from the football team, but I haven't out getting pissed since I came out of the centre. I have had the odd beer, but no binge drinking. I have managed to continue doing quite a lot of practising of my soccer skills and cardiovascular training."
"I can see that you have kept yourself very fit, in fact, you look more muscled than when I saw you at Christmas."
"I have done more weight training than I did in the centre. It was very funny watching people try to recognise me at first, especially the girls. I never used to have much contact with girls at all, and could never speak to them but the interest they've shown in me has been amazing."
"I'm not surprised, you are very fit now, Scott."
Scott was particularly pleased to hear that sort of comment from Stacey. He knew that although she was complementing his appearance, she was really more interested in his skill development.
"But more importantly Stace, my social, emotional and communication skills have improved so much I can cope with that, and talk with them comfortably. I have been able to be an effective reflective practitioner with them, it's been so useful to be able to do that."
"I thought you would. I found it made so much difference to me as well."
"Stacey, he's left out how good he's become at football."
George looked at Scott and realised he was probably not going to mention that, so he continued.
"Stacey, he's become an absolutely brilliant footballer, or as he insists, a striker. In all my years of watching football, I don't think I've ever seen anyone who has such great ball control and can strike the ball with both feet so clean and hard. I reckon he can now jump higher, heads the ball harder and sprints as fast as almost any players in the premier league."

Scott was clearly embarrassed with such glowing praise and interrupted his dad.
"But I'm rubbish at tackling and dribbling, dad."
George looked at Scott and shook his head.
"Okay, you may nor make a world class defender or dribble like Messi, but I think you've become a top class forward."
Stacey was really enjoying the the praise and banter between Scott and his dad.
"So those hours you spent in the soccer skills room have paid off then, Scott. How many hours did we calculate you spent in there?
"Over 850 hours, Stace. But because the soccer skills room is so effective, its probably like having 8,000 hours of normal practice. That's why I've become a much better striker, because those were the skills I practised."
"A great striker!" George wanted to emphasise.
"What about being sent off?"
As usual, Stacey wanted to explore Scott's development of the 8 success skills.
George was desperately keen to reply to this.
"Another absolute miracle - No sending offs or bookings! Once the opposition realise how good he is, he gets kicked, pushed, tripped and they try to wind him up all the time, he never reacts at all, now. He's gone from one extreme to the other."
"It's great example, Stace, of how much my self-awareness and managing feelings skills have improved. I actually now feel that when they are trying to wind me up or kick the crap out of me, they are complimenting me. They think I'm so good they have to resort to cheating and unfair tactics. Perhaps that's why Lionel Messi never seems to get wound up."

Chapter 27
"Expect Nothing, Appreciate Everything"

"How do you prefer your tea, Mr Learner?"
Ann asked politely as she placed the tray of drinks and biscuits on the low wooden table in front of the long brown striped sofa. JC Learner was sitting in one of the armchairs; his broad shoulders, like Scott, are spilling over the top of its arms. He was wearing a blue T-shirt with the Successfeelosophy.com logo on it, causing him to look like a mature version of Superman, except for the black track bottoms and trainers.
George was sitting in his usual chair and clearly a little awestruck at meeting someone he'd admired for so long while his wife was clearly impressed at meeting such a fit mature man, as though he was George Clooney. Scott and Stacey were both amused at his parents' reactions.
"Thank you Ann, white, no sugar and please call me JC,"

Ann sat between Scott and Stacey on the sofa and began pouring the drinks, as JC began talking.
"Thank you for allowing me into your home, I suspect you are wondering why I wanted to have this opportunity to talk to you. First of all, I simply wanted to see Scott in his home environment, to see how you feel, as his parents, about his progress."
George was trying hard to overcome his 'awestruck reaction' and responded passionately immediately.
"Absolutely miraculous, in fact, I do not have the words to describe how remarkable his change has been. I can certainly understand why the term magic is used to describe the centre and what's happened to him. I'm still struggling to believe how much he has improved, and I certainly cannot explain it. We can't thank you enough for giving him the chance in your centre."
George's felt a huge lump in his throat and his eyes watering with this comment. JC immediately detected this and being aware that George might find it embarrassing, deflected attention away from him.
"That's great to hear and I'm just pleased to have been able to give him the opportunity. What about you, Mrs Spicer, what's your opinion?"
"I think you are a saint, Mr Learner, sorry JC. Your centre has transformed my son from a devil to a disciple, as he calls them. Like George, I cannot find the words to thank you enough or describe how wonderful his improvement has been."
Ann was also now very tearful, Stacey was prepared and handed her a tissue and cuddled her, and Scott squeezed her knee.
"Thanks both of you, but I must emphasise that the centre only provides a learning environment and opportunities, it has been Scott's response to it and Stacey's support that has been key. Well done, Scott."
"Thank you."
Scott instantly responded as JC continued.
"However, there is a second reason for me being here. I want to discover Scott's plans after his GCSE exams."
Scott sat up abruptly in the sofa surprised by the question and trying to focus on his answer. This new Scott had developed very good cognitive skills; able to think analytically and conceptually, so planning ahead had become 'natural' to him.
"Well if I get good results in my exams, and I am predicted grade Bs and above, now, I hope to go to our local college to study A levels."
"Which AS levels you planning to study, Scott?" "Chemistry, Biology, P.E. and Psychology."
"Why have you chosen those?"
"Well I'm very interested in sport, of course, so P.E. was obvious. I've discovered that because of my improvement in cognitive skills, I'm actually good at science. When I was in the centre, I found Chemistry and Biology

interesting, and seem to be very useful in so many areas. I have found the science of learning extremely interesting, and since Psychology is part of it, I thought I'd study it further."

"They are probably the choices I would've made if I was choosing now. I would also like to know if you've considered any careers yet."

"I have done some research, the Employability section on the successfeelosophy website has been very helpful in discovering the skills needed in employment. I have not really made any firm decisions, I'm trying to keep my options open with the A levels I've chosen."

"Good answer, Scott. You keep on impressing me. Have you considered a career in professional football?"

Scott's startled expression appeared as though JC had spoken in a foreign language, not really able to understand the question. George sat up in his chair suddenly as though he'd had an electric shock.

"Er, well, I suppose I've always had that dream, but I've just thought it would take a miracle for it to happen. Why did you ask, sir?"

"It's JC, Scott, I've not been knighted! I looked at some of the recordings of you in the soccer skills room just before you left the centre in December, and I was very impressed. I had a word with some of my friends at Spurs, and they sent some scouts to look at you playing for your club, they were also very impressed. They asked me if I could persuade you to consider training and playing with the apprentices at Spurs next season. As I'm sure you are aware, I'm not the sort of person to try to persuade you, but from what I've seen and heard, you have the potential to become a professional footballer. You've watched him play recently George, what do you think?"

George was bursting with excitement, much more than Scott, who seemed almost to be in shock, which JC had, of course, expected and detected.

"I've already told him that I think he's already got more skill than most of these so called top class players I watch each week. I used to watch you play for Spurs years ago JC, and in my opinion, if you think he's good, then he must be. It is another reason why I think that centre of yours performs miracles, and has some sort of magic in it, I can't believe how brilliant a player he's suddenly become."

This comment obviously had an impact on JC, pleased to have such positive feedback on one of his innovations.

"I'm delighted you said that, George. When I created the soccer skills room, I had a vision as to how skills could be developed more rapidly using Superlearning, and Scott is a great example of how effective it can be. What are your views, Ann?"

Ann had not been quite so shocked by JC's suggestion and was able to respond quite calmly.

"Well I haven't been to see him play, but George and Scott's coach and team mates think he's brilliant. Does this mean he would be sent away again?"

Apart from Ann, they all smiled, as they realised this is a comment from a mother who was worried her 'little boy' would be taken away from her again'.
"No, Ann. The Spurs Lodge is in Chigwell, Scott will be able to get there on public transport. Well, what's your view, Scott?"
JC was aware that Scott should've had enough time to think more calmly about the offer now.
"As I said, it's always a dream of mine, and if there's chance it could happen, yes please. I mean thank you."
JC realised that the initial excitement or shock would mean Scott would struggle to really think clearly, so he spoke to Ann and George.
"Spurs will contact you and make all the arrangements for Scott to start preseason training. It will probably be towards the end of July, after he's completed his exams. They'll probably want one of you to be with him to sign the forms."
JC then shifted his attention to Scott.
"Scott, it is very important you continue with your studies, and please don't get your hopes up too much. There are lots of casualties in professional sport, and a very small proportion reaches the top level for all sorts of reasons, especially injuries, of course."
The new Scott was much more skilled at managing feelings and able to think cognitively about JC's advice.
"I will JC, I developed my cognitive skills in your centre to improve my decision making. Although I'll give it my best shot, I don't expect to succeed. As one of the posters said, 'Expect Nothing, Appreciate Everything'. There are too many potential difficulties over which I have no control, so I'll just keep trying to appreciate the learning opportunities."
"That's someone with a Growth Mindset, talking."
Stacey had been quiet until then, but could not resist making that here.
"Very true, Stace. He has certainly become a good disciple for us, hasn't he? Perhaps that's a good point for us to start making our way back to the centre, Stace."
JCs comment caused Stacey to look at her wrist monitor.
"Oh yes, JC, I'd not realised the time. I'm sorry Uncle George, Auntie Ann and Scott, we're gonna have to leave now."
JC and Stacey sprang up, and said farewell with a series of hugs.
"It's been a real pleasure to have finally met you, Ann and George. Scott, good luck in your exams and your training with Spurs, I'm confident you'll do well in both. All the best to you."
As JC and Stacey drove away, Scott and his parents waved, each feeling their lives would never be the same again.

Chapter 28
"it's like he's just arrived from the planet Krypton."

"Mum, dad, I got picked, I'm in the team for Saturday!"
Scott had just home from a days training with Spurs in August. This was GCSE results day, and his mum and dad were desperate for Scott to get home to open up the envelope containing his exam results. The news from Scott deflected their thoughts for a moment. Dad was first to respond
"Brilliant, son. I thought you would, I thought once they saw how good you are, they'd have to pick you. Who's it against and where is it?"
"West Ham, Dad. It's at home, at Spurs Lodge, 11 o'clock kick off. Are you coming?"
"Definitely."
He replied bristling with both pride and enthusiasm.
"What about you, mum?" Scott asked.
"I'll be there, son!"
She responded positively, but really her emotions and thoughts were more focused on the envelope.
"But can you open your results envelope, now please, I can't wait any longer, I'm fit to burst!"
"Oh yes, sorry mum, I got carried away. I'd completely forgotten about that. I'll do it straightaway."
"Can we go into the lounge first son, please, so I can sit down?"
"Of course, good idea."
They all went into the lounge, mum sat on the sofa, dad in his usual armchair, Scott in the other one. Scott carefully opened the envelope and unfolded the paper inside. He scanned it as quickly as he could and began reading it out loud.
"Business Studies, 'A';
English Language, 'A';
History, 'C';
Mathematics 'A*';
P.E. 'A';
Science, double, both 'A''.
That's it, seven in total."
Scott's mum and dad sat there motionless and speechless, both with their mouths open. Scott had actually read them out and not really reflected on them and reread the paper to check that he'd not made any errors. His face began to change colour and expression as he began to understand the information. There was complete silence for several seconds.
"Are you sure, son?" Dad asked disbelievingly.
"Yes, dad, I've read it three times now, I've got one 'A' star, 5 grade 'A's and a 'C'."

Dad tried to get up, but his limbs were slow to respond and used the arm of the chair to help him. He then grabbed hold of Scott's hand a shook it violently.
"Well done, son, they are incredible, absolutely brilliant, another bloody miracle."
Mum slowly got up, moved over to her son, leant over him, to give him a huge kiss and hug. She was crying quite profusely but managed to comment.
"Last year, I would've said that achieving those grades was impossible, I could never have dreamt that you could do so well. Well done, son."
"Impossible, is about right, mum. Since he's come out of that centre, I've begun to believe almost anything is possible."
Scott had finally had a chance to reflect more deeply on his results and was now able to provide an incisive response.
"I think what this actually shows is how very effective SUPERlearning can be when it is applied to exams."
Mum and dad were gradually becoming used to this new Scott, providing rational analytical responses, instead of the old aggressive grunts, and smiled proudly. But both were keen to provide more praise for their son, and dad summed it up.
"And you are a great role model and disciple for it, son."
All three got into a great hug.

*

The weather for the Saturday morning was hot and sunny, good for watching football perhaps, but probably too warm for playing. Scott's parents were on the sideline with many other friends and relatives of the young Spurs team, on the opposite side of the pitch were the same for the West Ham team. This was an under 18 Premier Academy League match, and virtually all the players were apprentices. Scott was very unusual as he had no representative honours and had played only at a comparatively low level, basically almost nobody knew anything about him. At the start of the match, Scott's parents could overhear a number of parents asking who he was. After a few minutes, an athletic looking man in his early thirties with short hair, wearing a Spurs tracksuit came over to them and introduced himself politely.
"Good morning, I'm Jason, one of the scouts here at Spurs, I believe you are Mr and Mrs Spicer, Scott's parents."
He held out his hand and they both shook it.
"I was one of the scouts who went to see Scott play for his club. I was very impressed, shocked in fact, to be honest, that such a good player should be playing at that level. He's caused a great buzz of excitement since he's been training here with us, we can't understand how nobody has ever heard of him before."
George smiled as he become used to this sort of question and half expected it.
"Until just over a year ago, he was a huge problem, a complete waste of space. He was in trouble with everyone, and I'm afraid I thought there was a good

chance that by now, he would either be locked up or even dead. In football, he was so out of control, he couldn't even stay on the pitch until the end of the game in most matches."

Jason was finding this very difficult to believe and interrupted.

"That's amazing, he's nothing like that now; I think he's the most mature kid we've ever had. So what happened?"

"Last year he spent six months in one of the 'Learning For Success Centres' that JC Learner set up. When he came out at Christmas, he was a completely different person and his soccer skills had improved enormously."

Almost as though it was on cue, they both threw their arms in the air, as Scott kicked a ball on the volley with his left foot, from the left hand corner of the penalty area, into the top right hand corner of the goal.

George, Ann, Jason and all the people along their side of the pitch were joyously jumping up and down. Eventually, Jason managed to calm down to carry on his conversation.

"What great timing! He keeps doing things like that. His first touch and volleying is absolutely incredible. He impresses everyone in training continually. Alex, the under 18 coach, has struggled to believe how he has suddenly appeared, he said it's like he's just arrived from the planet Krypton."

George and Ann laughed, and then George added.

"I can imagine, we think it's as though he's just come back from Hogwarts, they nickname the centre, 'School of Magic', because it performs so many miracles."

"But seriously, how has he suddenly become so good at football?"

"Apparently, while he was in JC's centre, he spent over 800 hours in what's called a soccer skills room."

"Ah, I've heard of them. I think there are going to be some of them in our new place being built in Enfield. If Scott's anything to go by, they must be very effective. I mean look at that, he seems to be able to control the ball at almost any height and speed."

Jason pointed to Scott controlling the football instantly with his right foot, which had been fired at him at about waist height.

George was keen to help Jason understand the effectiveness of these rooms and explained.

"Scott says that he reckons each hour of practice in the soccer skills room was worth about 10 hours of normal practice. He reckons his incredible improvement is simply due to the effective practice he got in that room."

"I suppose if JC Learner's behind it, we shouldn't be surprised. I assume it is through him that we've been given the nod about Scott. I'm bloody glad we did, he's obviously very special. Look at that, it's amazing!"

Jason was referring to another example of Scott's soccer skill, in which he headed the ball from a corner against the crossbar, by jumping to an incredible height at about the penalty spot.

Jason stayed with Scott's parents throughout the game, clearly trying to discover as much as he could about Scott. The match ended with Spurs winning 3-1 and Scott scored two goals. At the end of the game after Scott had thanked the officials, opposition and team-mates, he came over to his parents.
"What did you think mum, dad?"
Scott's mum had not seen him play for many years and spoke first.
"Very impressive, son. I thought you were very good, well done."
"Very good, mum, he was brilliant, his two goals were outstanding!"
Scott's dad added enthusiastically.
"I agree with your dad, Scott. You were excellent."
Scott looked at Jason, who had made this comment, but did not recognise him.
"I'm Jason, one of the scouts who watched you play for your club, but you probably didn't know I was there."
Scott shook his hand firmly as Jason continued.
"I was impressed when I saw you then, and every time I see you, I'm even more amazed. Your ball control and volleying is probably the best I've ever seen, and your two goals today were great, well done."
"Thank you very much Jason, I appreciate that, but I must apologise, I think I've got to go now, Alex, our coach wants to talk to us. I'll meet you in café mum, dad, see you later, Jason."
Scott then rushed off to join the rest of his team making their way to the changing rooms.

*

"What you doing tomorrow evening dad, mum?"
Scott asked simply as he entered the lounge where his parents were sitting watching TV on a dark Tuesday March evening, after another days training at Spurs Lodge.
"Nothing special, son, why?"
Mum was first to ask.
"I just wondered if you wanted to come to White Hart Lane and watch me make my debut for the Spurs first team, that's all."
Scott replied, still trying to avoid showing any expression of emotion on his face.
Mum didn't realise immediately what he meant but his dad did, he leapt out of his chair and hugged his son.
"You're in, you're playing tomorrow! Well done son!"
Now mum realised the significance of what Scott had said.
"You mean you're playing tomorrow night for the first team?"
"Yes, mum, me, I'm actually playing."
She pulled her husband away and smothered her son with hugs and kisses.
"Easy mum, you're gonna drown or crush me, I've got to be fit for tomorrow's match."
Scott was now smiling broadly.
"It's Wolves, ain't it?" Dad asked.

"Yeah, because we've got the sixth round of the FA cup on Sunday, some of the players are being rested tomorrow, so I'm in."
"Well, we'll be there to support you, tomorrow, won't we dad."
"Not arf! Who'd have thought it, my son playing for Spurs first team, eh? Two years ago I thought there was more chance of playing for Wormwood Scrubs."
Scott laughed at this comment but he reflected on how much of a pain he'd been in those early teenage years and responded accordingly.
"I agree, dad, I just hope I can make up for that and get you to be proud of me."
His mum resumed hugging and kissing him again on hearing her son makes this remark.
"We are already very proud of you, son, don't worry about that."
"It's been worth all that hassle to see how you've turned out." His dad added.
"Thanks mum, thanks dad, I really appreciate that. Now what's for tea?"

*

Ann and George took their seats in the stand, excited at the prospect of seeing their son play his first game for the first team of a Premier League team, before he'd even reached 17th birthday. This was actually the first time Ann had been to a football match of this level, and just being in a stadium of this calibre was exciting for her. As the kick off for the match occurred, they could hear a conversation behind them which clearly related to Scott.
"Who's this kid we've got playing up front, I've never even heard of him before."
"Apparently this is his debut for the first team and it says in the programme that he's only 16. It seems he joined the academy side at the beginning of this season, he has had quite few games for the reserves and scored lots of goals."
"Well he's a big lad for 16, he must be well over 6 foot."
Ann and George looked at each other and smiled, feeling a pride for their son that they had not felt in his early teenage years, and they began watching the match. It is probably more accurate to say that Ann just kept watching her son, showing little interest in the rest of the players or match.
"They seem to be kicking and pushing Scott a great deal, George?"
George was very aware that Ann had not taken a great deal of interest in football in the past, so thought he'd try to answer her question as fully as he could.
"He is the main striker and target man, so our defence and midfield try to kick the ball to him a lot. I suspect that the Wolves defenders have realised how young he is and are trying to intimidate and wind him up. If they'd have done that to him a couple of years ago, he'd have been in a fight and sent off by now. But not anymore, nothing seems to upset him, in fact, he seems to thrive on it."
Just then, Scott ran from the right hand corner of the penalty area, to the edge of the penalty circle, as the ball was passed to him, or more accurately, fired at him, from the left wing. By raising his left foot to about waist height, with one touch, he caused the ball to drop instantly to the floor in front of him; he then kicked it very hard towards the bottom left hand corner of the goal.

Understandably, the goalkeeper had not been expecting the ball to be instantly controlled, or such a hard shot immediately afterwards, and his dive was far too late to stop the ball going just inside his right hand post.
"Goal!"
Virtually everyone leapt out of their seats around, including, Ann and George. Scott had scored his first goal for Spurs first team.
"I think we can see why he's scored so many goals in the reserves."
Ann and George again listened to the conversation behind them.
"That was remarkable. This boy's first touch is probably the best I've seen, I think only Berbatov comes anywhere near him. That shot was like a missile, it was with his left foot, I thought he was right footed."
"I think we've found a star here, if this boy is meant to be sixteen, I think they should check his birth certificate."
"To check his age or which planet he comes from?"
All the people around them laughed.
As the match came to a close, Spurs were winning 3-1, and Scott had scored two goals.
"They're bringing him off."
George had spotted Scott's number 55 on the board about to be held up by the fourth official.
"What do you mean?"
Ann asked.
"Scott is going to be substituted."
"Why? I thought he was playing really well, he's scored two goals hasn't he?"
"Managers often do this at the end of the game. He's going to be replaced with a defender, and it is his first game."
The fourth official held up the board as the referee stopped the game for the substitution to be made. The crowd stood up, the clapping was deafening as Scott walked over to the dugout to be replaced.
The manager shook his hand vigorously and patted him on the back very hard, the coaching staff and subs bench greeted him in a similarly enthusiastic manner.
Ann and George smiled and hugged each other as they overheard the comment behind them.
"What a debut! I've been coming here for over forty years and I've never seen anyone have as good a first match for us as that, let alone a sixteen year old kid. That was genius, absolutely remarkable!"

Chapter 29
"maturity comes from learning not ageing"

"I have another video clip here that should help you understand how mature, eloquent and remarkable this boy became in less than a year."
Dave Mackay, the editor of The Sun newspaper, continued his presentation to his four reporters.
"This is an interview with Scott Spicer that was shown yesterday on Sky Sports Soccer Saturday. It is a football programme shown every week during the football season, presented by Jeff Stelling. It is important to note that this boy only made his debut in Spurs first team a few weeks ago, but he's been a sensation in all of his matches, even more than when Wayne Rooney first appeared for Everton and scored an incredible winner against Arsenal. Normally, clubs like Spurs and United are quite protective of their youngsters, but I think you'll quickly see why Spurs made an exception for this lad. Remember he is not seventeen for another 10 weeks, so sit back and be prepared to be astonished."
Dave sat down alongside his four reporters and the video began.
An attractive blond haired Sky Sports News presenter, Charlotte Jackson, appeared first and gave some background information.
"A few weeks ago, Scott Spicer made his debut for Spurs against Wolves at the age of 16 years 270 days, they won 3-1 and he scored two stunning goals. He's now played four times and scored six goals. Although this in itself is quite remarkable, what is even more incredible is that until the start of this season, he was a complete unknown. This was partly because when he turned 15, his behaviour was so bad he was sent to a residential centre in East Anglia to try to 'sort him out'. Fortunately, this centre has JC Learner as its sponsor, and it seems the radical approach there, turned him around completely in only six months and a new star began to shine."
Some clips of Scott's amazing goals were then shown. The video then showed Charlotte and Scott both sitting in armchairs, facing each other at a slight angle. Charlotte began the interview.
"Scott, thank you so much for agreeing to chat with us today, and we'd like to thank Spurs for allowing us this opportunity. We understand that less than two years ago you were in so much trouble that you were sent away to a centre to be helped or reformed, yet tomorrow you will be playing for Spurs in the semi-final of the F.A. cup. This seems too unbelievable to be true, can you believe what's happened to you in the last couple of years?"
"Good morning, Charlotte. Thank you for giving me this chance to share my story. It is indeed very difficult to believe what's happened to me in the last two years. My story does seem miraculous, but I think when people realise how brilliant JC Learner is and how magical his centres are, they will not only accept

that my transformation is possible, but it could occur for many other troubled young people like me."

"Can you explain for us the involvement of JC Learner in your success?"

"First of all, he invited my cousin Stacey to his 'Learning For Success Centre' several years ago, and it helped transform her into a wonderful person, who eventually became a mentor in there. Through her, two years ago, I went to this centre for six months with Stacey as my mentor. Over the six months I changed from a huge problem and waste of space to the person you see today, a small problem and waste of space."

Scott had a huge grin as he said this and Charlotte laughed.

"But how did it happen, what occurred in the six months you were in the centre to transform you into the mature man in front of me."

"That's very kind of you, Charlotte. Describing me as mature is very helpful since maturity comes from learning not from ageing. Unfortunately many people get older but don't mature at all. The quality and quantity of learning that I had from my six months in the centre was probably greater than many people have in their whole lifetime."

"Wow?"

Charlotte's face expressed her complete shock at having such a deep philosophical reply from a 16 year old and a footballer. She managed to regain her composure slightly.

"How did that happen?"

"The centres apply the science of learning as thoroughly as possible to try to ensure all learning is very effective. Everyone and everything focuses on unlocking our huge potential for learning, so that it becomes a pleasure and focused on developing the 8 skills we need to succeed."

Scott studied Charlotte's eyes and face carefully, realising that she was impressed but struggling to understand him.

"Scott, although you are not yet 17 you sound like a university lecturer. Could you explain this a bit more for us, please?"

"Of course, Charlotte. It is not easy to understand as it is so different and such a miraculous place and to paraphrase Albert Einstein, I will try to explain it as simply as I can, but no simpler.. For many years there has been extensive research into how we learn and what we most need to learn. We now know that successful people have invariably learnt 8 key skills that have caused them to succeed. When we are born, we are hopeless and helpless, very reliant on others, but capable of great learning. So the first skill we need is effective learning, and this means we can keep learning and developing throughout our life to overcome the various difficulties we are likely to meet.

The second is cognitive, which are about being able to analyse information and solve problems, this one used to be referred to as intelligence. This is very important in making good decisions, and improving this skill has also been a great help in the numerous situations I meet in matches.

Communication is third, being able to pick up and pass on information effectively is central to all that we do. This includes non-verbal, reading facial expressions, body language and tone, as well as speaking, listening, reading and writing. The other five skills are sometimes called social and emotional, or emotional intelligence.

The first being self-awareness, knowing accurately, who we are, our strengths and weaknesses, and what we need to improve. Poor development in this is central to low self-esteem.

Managing feelings is next, as babies we cannot control our emotions at all, but we can learn to do this, if given opportunities to do so. I used to be very poor at controlling my temper, I got very easily wound up and sent off frequently. I now expect people to try to kick and aggravate me, all very good players should expect that, but I won't react anymore.

Motivation follows this, and I've developed a growth mindset now. This means that I see everything as a learning opportunity, especially set backs, there is no failure for me anymore.

The last two are interpersonal skills, the first being empathy. Good development in empathy means we can understand how others are thinking and feeling, so I'm often able to predict what my team mates and opponents are going to do. The last one, social and relationship skills, means I can now work with all sorts of people easily, fit into teams, and cope comfortably in all sorts of situations, organisations, opposition, authority."

If Charlotte was shocked before, she now seemed almost paralysed in amazement. Was this really a 16 year old footballer speaking? Clearly her script or format had not catered for this sort of response. Scott waited patiently, he was aware his reply had surprised her.

"What you are saying is amazing. It sounds remarkable and if you are anything to go by, it works. It helps to explain why you seem so polite and intelligent. But how did you become so good at football?"

"Thank you, Charlotte, that's very kind of you to say so. JC Learner is an expert in the science of learning, as well as an ex-professional footballer, and he created incredible soccer skills rooms in the centre. In recent years there's been lots of research, Anders Ericsson and John Sloboda for example, with excellent books by Matthew Syed and Malcolm Gladwell that clearly demonstrates that about 10000 hours of deliberate practice is needed to become an expert. The soccer skills rooms in the centre caused the practice to be so effective that this time could be reduced tenfold. I spent over 800 hours in there practising my soccer skills."

Charlotte was now more prepared for such complex answers and able to respond promptly.

"Is that why, until Spurs showed an interest last year, nobody knew anything about you?"

"Yes, I'd only ever played at a relatively low level. It was JC again who helped me with his contacts in Spurs. Some scouts watched me at the end of last season and I joined the Spurs Academy in the summer."

"I understand that you are also studying for your 'A' levels."

"Yes. Before I went into the JC's centre, I was rubbish at studying and exams, but I learnt a completely new approach called SUPERlearning in there, and since then I've not only become good at studying and exams but I actually enjoy both."

Again Charlotte's face expressed her astonishment.

"Professional footballers are not known for their joy of learning and exam success, yet another example of how unusual you are, why is this?"

"That's easy to answer, Success Feelosophy! Two years ago I was a very typical teenager, in trouble all the time, with low self esteem, frequently frustrated and struggling to cope each day. But, I had the opportunity to experience Success Feelosophy and SUPERlearning which helped me learn how to succeed. Until now, very few have had this chance, but if it can help me, it can help anyone."

Charlotte was informed that they needed to wind up the interview.

"I was going to say that I've never met any teenager like you, but I've never met a footballer or even a man like you. If you are anything to go by, this Success Feelosophy and SUPERlearning certainly works."

"That's kind of you, Charlotte. Thank you."

"Sadly we have time for only one more question. Clearly much has happened to you in a very short time, and incredibly you could be playing in an FA cup semi final this weekend. Have you got any particular hopes for the future?"

"My life has been transformed because of the opportunities provided by JC Learner, and he has become a great role model for me. As you can see from this interview, I aim to do as much as I can to support his Success Feelosophy, and I hope anything that I achieve will be used to publicise it."

"Wow! That wasn't the sort of answer that I expected. In fact, this whole interview has been as amazing as your story. You've certainly been an excellent advert for Success Feelosophy, I've very much enjoyed today and I've learnt so much as well. Thank you very much Scott and the best of luck in the future."

"Thank you Charlotte. It's been a pleasure."

The video clip ended and the reporters clapped!

Dave Mackay swivelled around in his chair and smiled broadly at their bizarre response.

"I think clapping a video interview illustrates that like everyone else, you are amazed, and I've proved my point."

The sports reporter was so impressed he felt compelled to comment.

"I have seen many interviews with professional footballers over the years, but nothing like that. I don't think most managers can give as mature or incisive

answers as that. We've seen some surprisingly mature youngsters in sport like Sam Warburton or Jonny Wilkinson, but not from a 16 year old or as remarkable as him!"
"Or politicians!"
The politics reporter added and they all laughed.
Okay, Dave, you've certainly made your point. If that kid is not yet seventeen and two years ago was a complete no hoper, then we could indeed be witnessing a learning revolution."
The business reporter sitting next to Dave responded, as he patted him on the back.
Dave was pleased they were convinced, but suddenly brought them down to Earth.
"I thought you'd agree, but if he dies it will probably be front page news in other papers as well. I don't think too many editors will have seen the Sky Sports interview, but I think we need to be quick, because word will soon spread about him."
They all mumbled agreement, stood up and left the room in a hurry.

Chapter 30
"could help everyone learn to succeed"

"Is this 'déjà vu'? It's about two years since I was last in hospital like this."
Scott was sat up in a hospital bed, his badly cut head bandaged, but this time in a plush single room, looking more like a hotel room than a hospital. He was talking to the other two people in the room his mum and dad. His mum sitting on the edge of the bed, holding his hand, his dad sitting in an armchair to the side of the bed.
"But when you got knocked out before you was because you were being a complete pratt, this time you're a hero." George responded.
"I can't remember anything about it, dad. I can remember the first half but nothing at all after half time."
"Don't worry, son. You'll soon get to see the match and your winning goal over and over again, I suspect. I've never heard such an ovation when they carried you off, I've never known the losing supporters clap off the player who's just put them out of the cup, it was amazing."
Just then a very familiar figure appeared at the doorway.
"Stacey! What a surprise!"
George exclaimed as he lept to his feet. Scott looked across, as usual, she was wearing her black successfeelosophy.com T shirt with black trousers and trainers. She rushed across to him arms wide open ready to hug Scott and they hugged each other tightly.
"I was so worried, Scott. How are you? They kept saying on the car radio you'd been carried off unconscious."

They stopped hugging to have their conversation.
"Yes, apparently I hit my head on the goalpost after I headed the ball, I've had a load of stitches in my head and I got knocked out. I've got a shocking headache. How do you come to be here?"
"I'm so relieved; it sounded so bad listening to what happened on the radio. They told me as soon as possible in the centre what had happened and I left immediately. Oh sorry, Auntie Ann and Uncle George, I've been so preoccupied I've not said hallo."
Stacey, Ann and George hugged and greeted each other.
"It's like a rugby scrum out there. Have you got the paparazzi following you now or something, there's press everywhere? I didn't think they were going to let me see you."
George was first to reply to Stacey's comment.
"Since Scott made his first team debut a few weeks ago, there has been a growing interest in him and he has become a real media celebrity and that was before his wonder goal and injury."
"The way they were talking about him on the radio was fantastic. They kept referring to him as 'Superboy' or something. They actually mentioned 'Success Feelosophy', JC Learner and that he'd been in the centre, I was gob smacked."
Scott smiled but kept quiet and let George explain.
"When he started playing for Spurs first team, the media begun to take an interest in him. He scored some brilliant goals, then they discovered his background, the problems he'd had and how JC Learner got involved. It's was like a juggernaut running downhill as more interest grew and he scored more goals. A couple of days ago he did a TV interview, which everyone thought he was so mature and brilliant. The media have started calling him Superboy or Superkid, I don't know what's going to happen now!"
"They were calling him a 'Superhero' on the radio, they were talking about him risking his life in scoring this winning goal. It was very worrying driving down, not even knowing if he was alive. I just kept thinking that like me, he'd done so well when he got a second chance from Arthur, how could it be taken from him now!"
Stacey hugged Scott again, and all four of them were crying. Eventually Scott managed to speak.
"Stace, I'm sorry I worried you so much. After everything you've done for me, especially. All I've done is score some goals for Spurs and suddenly they've gone mad. Spurs didn't want me to be interviewed on TV but I persuaded them I'd be okay. I thought it would be a great opportunity to publicise Success Feelosophy, Superlearning, JC Learner and the Learning For Success Centre. I'm hoping to use this celebrity status and fame to do as much 'spreading the word' as I can and I'm hoping JC will contact me and help me as much as he can with this."

"He will. That explains why the radio mentioned them, well done. JC contacted me when I was driving here and I'm sure he will be visiting you very soon."
"Brilliant, I was confident he'd be there to help, he always does."
Stacey hugged Scott again. Ann had been quiet until then, weeping and glowing with pride at her son, but now commented.
"He's becoming a great disciple Stacey, just like you. You are both wonderful role models for all those poor struggling kids out there."
George was delighted to add to that comment.
"I agree completely. You both provide hope for your generation and proof that if our society follow the Success Feelosophy approach, we can help everyone learn to succeed."

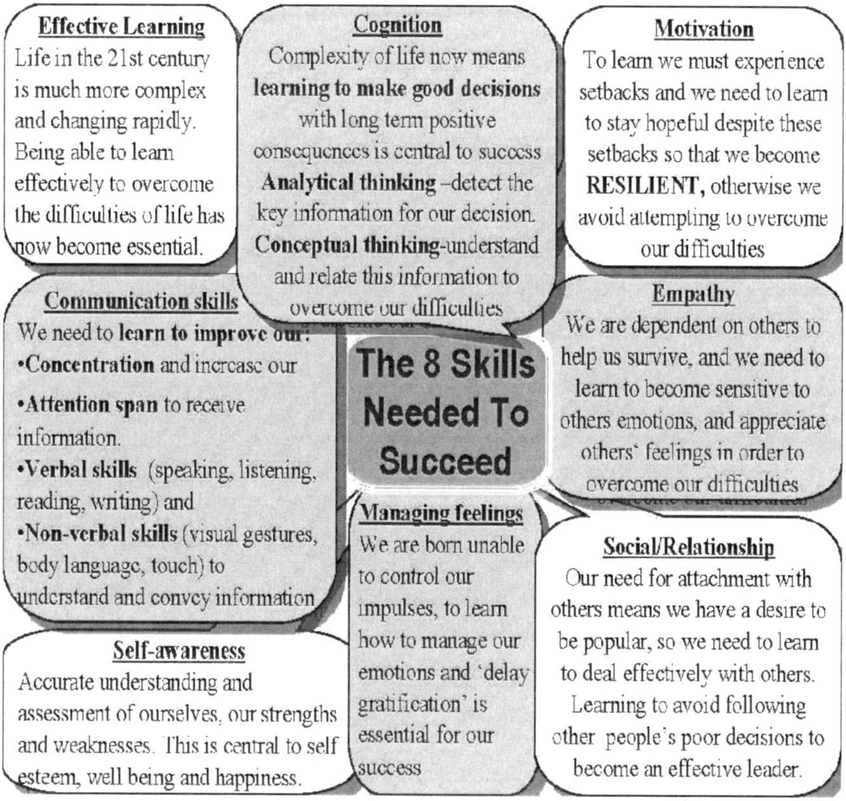

Some key books used in the writing of 'Miraculous!'

TITLE	AUTHOR
Emotional Intelligence: Why it Can Matter More Than IQ	Daniel Goleman
Freedom's Orphan's: Raising Youth in a Changing World	Julia Margo & Mike Dixon
Child Of Our Time	Tessa Livingstone
Seven Habits of Highly Effective People	Stephen Covey
The Fifth Discipline	Peter Senge
Mindset –The New Psychology of Success	Carol Dweck
The Learning Revolution	Gordon Dryden & Jeanette Vos
Outliers: The Story of Success	Malcolm Gladwell
Bounce: The Myth of Talent and the Power of Practice	Matthew Syed
Spiral Dynamics: Mastering Values, Leadership, and Change	Don Beck & Christopher Cowan
Flow: The Psychology of Optimal Experience	Mihaly Csikszentmihalyi
Good To Great: Why Some Companies Make The Leap....	Jim Collins
The Genius In All of Us	David Shenk
Assessment for Learning: Putting it into Practice	Paul Black, Dylan Wiliam et al.
Building Learning Power: Helping Young People Become Better Learners.	Tessa Livingstone
Shackleton's Way: Leadership Lessons from the Great Antarctic Explorer	Morgot Morrell & Stephanie Capparell
Winning!	Clive Woodward
Happiness: Lessons from a New Science	Richard Layard
The Logic of Life	Tim Harford
The Road To Excellence: The Acquisition of Expert Performance in the Arts and Sciences, Sports and Games	K. Anders Ericsson
Teenagers: A Natural History	David Bainbridge
NLP: The New Technology of Achievement	Steve Andreas & Charles Faulkner
The Meme Machine	Susan Blackmore
The Learning Brain: Lessons for Education	Sarah-Jayne Blackmore & Uta Frith
Breaking Night	Liz Murray
The Human Mind and How to Make the Most of it	Robert Winston
Action Inquiry: The secret of Timely and Transforming Leadership	William R Torbert et al.
Sophie's World: A Novel About the History of Philosophy	Jostein Gaarder
Frames of Mind: The Theory Of Multiple Intelligences	Howard Gardner

Printed and Published by:
Connoisseur Crafts Ltd., Hartlepool TS24 8EY
01429 236294 email: concrafts@onebillnet.com,

www.successfeelosophy.com